DVS MINDZ

DVS MINDZ

THE TWENTY-YEAR SAGA OF THE GREATEST RAP GROUP TO ALMOST MAKE IT OUTTA KANSAS

GEOFF HARKNESS

Columbia University Press   *New York*

Columbia University Press
Publishers Since 1893
New York   Chichester, West Sussex
cup.columbia.edu

Copyright © 2023 Geoff Harkness
All rights reserved

Library of Congress Cataloging-in-Publication Data
Names: Harkness, Geoffrey Victor, author.
Title: DVS Mindz : the twenty-year saga of the greatest rap group to
almost make it outta Kansas / Geoff Harkness.
Description: [1.] | New York : Columbia University Press, 2023. |
Includes bibliographical references and index.
Identifiers: LCCN 2022028321 | ISBN 9780231208727 (hardback) |
ISBN 9780231208734 (trade paperback) |
ISBN 9780231557573 (ebook)
Subjects: LCSH: DVS Mindz (Musical group) |
Rap musicians—Kansas—Topeka—Biography.
Classification: LCC ML421.D94 D84 2023 |
DDC 782.421649092/2 [B]—dc23/eng/20220615
LC record available at https://lccn.loc.gov/2022028321

Columbia University Press books are printed on permanent
and durable acid-free paper.
Printed in the United States of America

Cover design: Noah Arlow
Cover images: Band members: courtesy of Barry Rice,
Stuart Tidwell; cassette: iStock

CONTENTS

III 2004-2020

CAST OF CHARACTERS

Barry Rice Killa the Hun, 40 Killa, Killa, Smokey Rob-him-some

Daymond Douglas D.O.P.E, Dangerous On Paper and Etcetera, the Invisible Man, Dope Man, Dopey Loc

De'Juan Knight DL, Dark Thoughts Lovely Lyrics, Dark and Lovely

Stu Tidwell Str8jakkett, Wrexx, Special Agent Wrexx, Stuart

Aunt Tang Daymond and De'Juan's cousin and matron to DVS Mindz

Bobby Tek Denver-based rap musician

Carla Daniels DVS Mindz's first manager

CGz Co-host of student radio program Hip Hop Hype

Keith Loneker Actor and former NFL player who started an independent record label

Ken Wheeler Kansas City area concert promoter

Kevin "The Wolf" Douglas Daymond's brother and De'Juan's cousin and best friend since childhood

Randy Smith A longtime friend who went on to manage DVS Mindz

Scorpeez (Joseph Johnson II) Topeka-based rap musician

Shawn Edwards Kansas City journalist

Steve "S.G." Garcia Producer of some of DVS Mindz's seminal early recordings

Troy "Def DJ" Owens DVS Mindz's first DJ

Vandon "DJV" Pittman Rias Topeka-based DJ and producer

Will Wilson Lawrence-based music producer

PREFACE

Liberty Hall, Lawrence, Kansas, August 7, 2000

As the band prepares to take the stage, 1,050 music lovers stand watching in anticipation. Tonight's headliner, the Wu-Tang Clan, is among the most legendary rap groups of all time. Its eight living members have not performed together in years. This concert has already been postponed once, and rumors circulate that Wu-Tang is not even in town. Regardless, the venue is packed with local celebrities, musicians, DJs, journalists, glitterati, wannabes, and hangers-on. For rap music fans in the Kansas City region, the Wu-Tang show is the hottest ticket in town.

The opening act is DVS Mindz, a four-man rap group from Topeka known for their raucous live shows. DVS Mindz has been together for five years, slowly converting audiences one concert at a time via performances that crackle with energy and high-wire verbal gymnastics. DVS Mindz's debut album dropped a few weeks ago to positive reviews, and the Wu-Tang show is poised to take the quartet to the next level. Backstage, the promoters are already floating ideas to DVS's manager about regional and national tours, as phone numbers, business cards, and CDs trade hands in a flurry.

DVS Mindz knows how to open a show. The band begins their concerts theatrically, sometimes employing props and costumes. The group rarely takes the stage en masse but each member joins the song and the performance one at a time. Every show is unique.

Tonight, I'm standing right there on the side of the stage, just out of view of the audience, video camera in hand, watching and waiting. The floodlights shimmer in shades of red and blue, while dry ice creates an eerie atmosphere. The members of DVS never reveal how they will open a concert, and I am eager to see what they've come up with tonight—their biggest show ever.

I'm surprised when they don't begin with a spectacle. Rather, the group members gather on the side of the stage, where De'Juan, one of the rappers, aims a wireless microphone at his mouth and addresses the crowd. "Is Lawrence, Kansas, in this motherfucker?"

The audience roars its approval. The room is vibrating, bursting with excitement for the Wu-Tang.

De'Juan is unmoved. He implores louder, "Is Lawrence, Kansas, in this motherfucker, *what?*"

More applause.

"That ain't enough noise," the rapper says.

The crowd is amped up and ready to hear some music, but De'Juan continues. "How many of y'all know about the *Pitch*? Who read that shit?"

A few people clap, but the question mostly generates confusion. De'Juan continues anyway, ranting about a local newspaper story that is the focus of his ire.

It is the biggest night of the band's career, and all anyone can wonder is what will happen next.

INTRODUCTION

"U-God Outshined by Topeka Group"

I t is the fall of 1999, and I am beginning graduate studies in sociology at the University of Kansas when I land a part-time job writing for *The Mag*. *The Mag* is an arts-and-entertainment weekly published by the *Lawrence Journal-World*, the local newspaper in Lawrence, Kansas. *The Mag* is included as an insert to the daily paper each Friday and also has standalone distribution in Lawrence and some nearby cities.

The Mag is a small operation staffed by one full-time writer-editor and a handful of freelancers. There is a movie critic, restaurant reviewer, and scribe who covers the theater scene. I am hired to write about music. For $6 per hour, I am assigned to produce three music-related pieces each week, a combination of feature stories, editorials, and reviews. On my first day, I conduct a phone interview with Ahmir "Questlove" Thompson from the Roots. For me, a lifelong musician, music geek, and concertgoer, it is a dream job.

Lawrence is a classic Midwestern college town located about an hour's drive west of Kansas City, Missouri, and renowned for its music scene. In its early-1990s heyday, downtown Lawrence was a bustling entertainment district—home to restaurants, cafés, record stores, head shops, used booksellers, and more than twenty live-music venues. With thirty thousand fun-loving college students just steps away, the streets of downtown Lawrence were flooded each weekend with music lovers who would club hop to catch their favorite local acts. Lawrence rock bands such as Baghdad Jones, the L.A. Ramblers,[1] and the Salty Iguanas were practically stars, selling out shows, signing autographs, and moving stacks of CDs in local stores.

By 1992, with grunge ascending, Lawrence's music scene had become so well-known that *Rolling Stone* predicted it would become one of the country's "next Seattles." Lawrence alt-rock bands that inked major-label record deals during this era included Stick (Arista) and Tenderloin (Warner Brothers). Local heroes Kill Creek landed a contract with feted indie label Mammoth. But no Lawrence band soared higher than Paw, a Pearl Jam soundalike that signed to A&M Records and scored a national hit with its 1993 song, "Jessie."

Grunge peaked in the mid-1990s, followed by the rise of gangsta rap and then boy bands and Britney as the millennium approached. By 1999, the internet, video games, and hundreds of cable TV channels were competing with live entertainment, and guitar-based music scenes like Lawrence's were beginning to dry up.

Still, Lawrence, at the turn of the century, is populated by members of uber-cool emo act the Get Up Kids and successful transplants, such as California psychedelic-rock band the Appleseed Cast. A Lawrence-based alt-rock trio, Frogpond, has an album out with Columbia Records, and the lead singer from alt-rock quintet the Anniversary is dating actress Chloë Sevigny, fresh off an Oscar-nominated performance in *Boys Don't Cry*.

In 1999, downtown Lawrence remains home to about a dozen venues that host a mix of national, regional, and local acts.

"The Lawrence music scene emerged as one of the great college music breeding grounds of the early 1990s," says Jon Niccum, a Lawrence-based writer who has covered film and music in the region for three decades. "By 2000, the luster of live original music had worn off nationally. Yet Lawrence was still going strong, boasting clubs that showcased local and touring artists. It wasn't exactly Seattle of 1991, but for a non-metropolis in the middle of a 'flyover state,' it was undeniably thriving. And the bands were damn good, too."[2]

As the lone music journalist for Lawrence's newspaper, I cover it all. On December 7, 1999, I am assigned to review a concert by U-God, an original member of one of rap's most celebrated groups, the Wu-Tang Clan. U-God is performing at the Bottleneck, a 350-patron stalwart of Lawrence's live music scene known for booking acts like Radiohead and Marilyn Manson long before they were famous.

My review of U-God's performance will be published in the daily newspaper the morning after next, and I have a hard 2:00 a.m. deadline. That means that I have to attend the concert, take notes, go home, write a review, and email it to the paper, all within a few hours. I am on the Bottleneck's guest list plus-one; Greg, a buddy from grad school, tags along. As we arrive, the opening act is already onstage.

Greg and I make our way to the bar, find two empty stools, and sit down. My music-journalism gig has turned me into a semiregular at the Bottleneck, and I am friendly with the staff. As I chat with one of the bartenders, Greg watches the opener, engrossed.

A minute later, he taps me on the shoulder. "These guys are pretty good. Check them out." I am assigned to write a review of U-God, the headliner, but Greg is right. The opening act is something special.

Pressed together on the Bottleneck's small stage, four MCs operate as a cohesive unit. They trade rhymes effortlessly, playing off one another and finishing each other's lines with the familiarity of old married couples. Their performance is as physical as it is verbal. The MCs trade up and tag the next rapper like prizefighters spinning and sparring in the ring. Before one MC's line is finished, the next rapper has already been shoved to the front of the stage, taking over for a few bars before falling back and letting the next MC have a turn. The group members look and sound like stars who have been doing this their entire lives.

Greg and I are not the only ones who appreciate the performance. The audience presses toward the stage, arms swaying in unison, shouting along with every word like something out of a movie. As the song thunders to a close, one of the MCs steps up and introduces the next number. "This is our most controversial joint," he asserts in a gravelly tone as a slow-crawling drum beat kicks in.

The backing tracks to rap songs are sometimes mini works of art, with samples, effects, and instruments chopped up and layered into soundscapes that serve as their own form of musical expression and commentary. By contrast, this group's approach is positively minimalist. A sparse beat pounds like a slap to the face, closely accompanied by a rolling bass line with a couple of airy piano notes floating over the top. Sonically, there is almost as much open space as there is sound.

The MC continues his introduction, speaking in time with the beat. "This is the song that almost got us banned from the radio," he intones. "This is the song that almost got us blacklisted. This is 'Niggaz.'"

In unison, the four MCs shout, "Nigga, who is you?"

Stu "Str8jakkett" Tidwell is lean, muscular, and square-jawed. He wears baggy blue jeans over tan Timberland boots, topped off by a loose white T-shirt and a dark knit cap affixed tightly to his skull. The sparse instrumentation and lack of sonic distractions direct the listener's attention toward the MC, foregrounding his lyrics and delivery almost entirely. Stu rhymes in a staccato patter—short, sharp bursts of machine-gun fire—each word enunciated so precisely that you can make out every syllable, even as the words fly by at light speed.

Stu finishes his verse, takes a step back, and the next MC strides into the spotlight.

"Nigga, who is you?" the group asks in unison.

Daymond "D.O.P.E" Douglas looks more like a movie star than a rapper, even in sweatpants and a plain white T-shirt. He is an energetic, visceral performer, bobbing and weaving like a boxer and waving his hands like he's stranded on a desert island, flagging down an airplane. As Daymond raps his verse, the other three MCs stay engaged, adding backup vocals to certain words or phrases and pantomiming the lyrics with hand signs and gestures. They listen and interject.

Daymond finishes, and the rest of the group cries, "Nigga, who is you?" the audience now joining in the chant.

At twenty-two, De'Juan "DL" Knight is the youngest member of the band; he could have easily passed for eighteen. Like the rest of the group, De'Juan has striking features that draw the eye. He is dark-skinned and physically sculpted, with hair that frays upward in all directions like a firecracker caught mid-explosion. He completes the image with a prison-issue neon orange T-shirt that can be seen from the back of the club. De'Juan opens with a line about being placed on intensive supervised probation, and the knowing look in his eye makes it clear he's writing nonfiction.

In addition to the group's committed performance, I am struck by the lack of musical conventions. The song, "Niggaz (1137)," does not follow a traditional structure. It features no hook or chorus,³ zero variation in the background music, and the MCs do not rap for equal amounts of time. The rhymes are meticulously written, but the format is akin to a cipher—bar upon bar of hard-punching rhymes without timekeeping or distraction. This relentless approach creates an almost hypnotic effect.

"Nigga, who is you?" the entire venue thunders as the last MC glides to the forefront. Barry "Killa the Hun" Rice is dressed in dark gray sweatpants and fresh pair of Nikes. He sports a white tank top that shows off numerous tattoos covering his muscular arms. He wears a diamond earring in each lobe, a thick gold watch, a strawberry-sized pinky ring on his right hand, and a long gold chain with a diamond-encrusted medallion of the Crucifixion that swings from the end. Microphone in his right hand, gesturing with his left, Barry introduces himself with a gravelly twang that splits the difference between the bayou and the Ozarks.

The quartet concludes their set to thunderous applause and departs the stage. I scrawl furiously in my rectangular reporter's notebook. I've already decided to praise the group in my concert review. I also want to know how to get ahold of their recordings. In 1999, instant access to music is limited. Broadband technology has just begun to penetrate the United States, and internet service is not yet widespread. At the time, even cell phones are relatively rare, and smartphones will not appear for nearly a decade. There is no YouTube, no Facebook, no Twitter, no Instagram. Even MySpace and Friendster are years away. Napster, which facilitates MP3 file-sharing, debuted in June but is just beginning to gain traction and features mostly top-selling acts.

Given their level of talent, stage presence, and memorable songs, I assume the band I just saw is a New York act touring the country with U-God. I ask the bartender if he knows their name, and he tells me the group is DVS Mindz, which he pronounces "devious minds." I am surprised when he adds that DVS Mindz is from Topeka, Kansas's maligned capital city, twenty miles west of Lawrence. He points me in the direction of the band's manager, Randy, who is standing with the group in the wings of the stage.

I walk over and introduce myself, but the club is so loud it's difficult to have a conversation. I shout something to Randy about reviewing the concert and ask him to write down his number in my notebook.

By the time U-God makes his way to the stage thirty minutes later, it is too late. The Wu-Tang Clan member's one-man show is no match for the four-way frenzy that just took place. Having exhausted its energy on the opening act, the crowd now stands there, listless as U-God strains to light a spark.

The audience has nothing for him.

It's official. DVS Mindz has blown the headliner off the stage.

I submit a rave review, printed in the newspaper two days later under the headline, "U-God Outshined by Topeka Group." In the piece, I write that the Wu-Tang Clan member was "completely overshadowed by a phenomenal opening act, Topeka's DVS Mindz, who nearly brought down the house with a charismatic, energetic, and smooth-flowing set."[4]

My editor at *The Mag* assigns me to write a feature story about DVS Mindz. I get in touch with Randy, and he sets up a time for me to talk to the band. Our first interview takes place on the afternoon of December 31, 1999, at Randy's apartment in Topeka. I bring along copies of the U-God review, which instantly endears me to everyone. The interview lasts an hour and a half. I only ask three questions.

Afterward, the band insists that I come out to Stu's car, where they blast an instrumental and perform "Niggaz (1137)," spitting furious rhymes into the shoebox-sized Sony cassette recorder that I used to tape our interview.

A couple of weeks later, on January 17, 2000, I am back at Randy's apartment to take pictures for the band's *The Mag* feature. I had assigned the job to one of the newspaper's photographers, but they canceled at the last minute. Wanting to salvage things, I drove to Topeka with my camcorder, hoping that the newspaper could use video still frames instead of traditional photos.

I had recently begun experimenting with video as a research tool for my master's thesis project, a study of pawn shops. Just prior to attending my first DVS Mindz concert, I had used student loans to purchase an entry-level camcorder. My intention was to make a documentary film about pawn shops to accompany my written thesis. I spent the fall and winter of 1999 amassing footage of the stores and conducting on-camera interviews with pawnbrokers and clients in Kansas, Missouri, and Illinois.

At Randy's apartment, I record a few minutes of footage of the guys and their entourage. Barry waxes rhapsodically about the heavyweight bout between Roy Jones Jr. and David Telesco two nights ago. Jones had entered the arena dressed in a tuxedo, with Redman and Method Man alongside him, rapping. "He came out with our boys, Red and Meth, clownin'" Barry says, laughing. "They did 'Da Rockwilder.' He went on stage and got his dance on." Barry demonstrates with a couple of swivel-hipped moves, breaking up the room.

Barry suggests we shoot the photos on the steps of the Kansas State Capitol building. We set out in five cars, a dozen of us in all. We spend twenty minutes walking around the Capitol, combating a brusque January wind, as the band members stop to pose in alleyways and stand on fire escapes.

After the shoot, Daymond invites everyone over to his house, where a massive spread of homemade food is laid out. The entourage is growing now, with wives, girlfriends, cousins, and small children running around. Lenora Douglas, Daymond's mother and De'Juan's aunt, serves up generous plates of chicken, macaroni and cheese, green beans, and cornbread and then comes around to dish out seconds. "This is a every-weekend thing," Daymond tells me, looking around happily.

After gorging ourselves, the band and I go to the backyard, shooting a final round of photos in the "golden hour" light. As I'm getting ready to leave, De'Juan and Barry invite me to the band's show in Lawrence the following week.

Eight days later, on January 25, 2000, I attend my second DVS Mindz concert, this time bringing my video camera and taping the group's four-song set. It is an energetic performance, with the audience in a good mood and Barry rolling onto the stage atop a tricked-out lowrider bicycle.

After the concert, the band members, their entourage, and I reconvene in front of the venue, located on downtown Lawrence's main drag, Massachusetts Street. I hand out a recent edition of *The Mag*. The cover story is a feature I wrote about *Hip Hop Hype*, a rap-themed college radio show hosted by a couple of University of Kansas (KU) students. I also have some news about the upcoming DVS Mindz feature in *The Mag*. "We're putting you on the cover," I tell the band. They can't believe it.

The newspaper was able to use the video still shots we took at the Capitol building and in Daymond's backyard. My feature on DVS Mindz will run as the cover story of the February 10, 2000, issue of *The Mag*. High fives and daps go around.

"Man, you already part of the fam," Barry whispers to me warmly, pulling me in close for a one-armed hug.

As we stand there, a twenty-something guy comes out of the venue's front door and approaches the group. He looks tipsy, swaying woozily from side to side and waving a crumpled dollar bill in his left hand. He asks if anyone has a cigarette to sell.

As Stu reaches into his jacket pocket, the guy claps Barry on the shoulder and mumbles something unintelligible.

Barry draws back and stops. "What did you say?" he asks the man, sharply.

The entire group goes silent.

The drunk guy raises his index finger, about to respond, but before he can get a word out, Barry draws his right fist back and lets loose, punching the man squarely across the jaw with a roundhouse blow. He is knocked back to the sidewalk, out cold. We are standing in front of a crowded nightclub on a busy, well-lit street. There are people everywhere. The band and their entourage instantly set off in all directions. I rush away, too.

I get to my car, unlock the door, and sit down, rattled. I wonder exactly what kind of "fam" I just joined. Thirty minutes earlier, I thought I knew. Now, I have no idea what I am getting myself into. Never could I have imagined that this would be the beginning of a two-decade relationship with DVS Mindz.

DVS MINDZ

This is the story of DVS Mindz, the greatest rap group most people have never heard of. The band formed in Topeka, Kansas, in the early 1990s and developed a reputation for ferocious rhyming and frenetic live performances. Like the best bands, they were greater than the sum of their parts. Each member was distinct and provided an essential ingredient that contributed to the collective chemistry. The group's internal volatility often produced greatness but sometimes resulted in catastrophe.

During their heyday in the late 1990s and early 2000s, DVS Mindz released a critically acclaimed CD, was covered by the local music press, was nominated for prestigious awards, and opened for notables that include Run-D.M.C., Redman, De La Soul, Das EFX, and many more. In doing so, DVS Mindz helped pioneer Topeka rap music, a legacy that has been overshadowed by prominent Kansas City (KC) artists, most notably chart-topping superstar Tech N9ne. This book serves as an amendment to the region's musical history, giving DVS their proper due more than two decades after the fact. But this book is also one that challenges and complicates notions of success.

Our music, movies, TV shows, sports, video games, photos, apps, and social media flood us with an endless stream of success stories, where struggles are overcome, and disappointment begets accomplishment. Even our stories of failure are success stories. "Failing upward" and "failing fast" are status claims in Silicon Valley, where entrepreneurs whose startups flop learn from these setbacks and use those lessons to achieve victory. Failure is glorified as part of a "growth mindset," and *Forbes* publishes articles with titles like "Why Failure is Essential to Success." In academia, Princeton Professor Johannes Haushofer is praised for posting a "CV of Failures" listing declined job applications, paper rejections, and failed submissions for grant funding.

Not everyone who fails, however, goes on to lead another company or profess at Princeton. For many, failure is not a path to career success, wealth, or personal growth. This book is about a band trying to make it in the music industry, an aspiration understood by anyone who has ever had a big dream. It is also about falling short of achieving a big dream and what happens afterward. Failure to achieve big dreams is a common outcome but a story rarely told.

The members of DVS Mindz were talented, charismatic, and hard-working. They deserved to make it. They didn't make it because most bands don't make it. Only three in ten thousand high school athletes go on to play sports professionally—yet rarely do we learn about the other 9,997 players. Their stories are important because they are universal. We all encounter disappointment and find ways to pick ourselves up and continue.

In this book, I focus on the lives and experiences of the band members but offer no theoretical explanations of any kind. I do so deliberately because I believe the life histories of the group members should speak for themselves. The biographies of Jay-Z and Led Zeppelin do not cry out for theoretical analysis, and DVS Mindz's story does not either. As such, this book can serve as a platform for theoretical inquiry, application, and discussion—or not.

THE BOOK'S ORGANIZATION

The book is divided into three parts, spanning about fifty years. Part 1 covers the period from 1970 to 1999. It recounts the early life histories of Stu, Barry, Daymond, and De'Juan. Their Topeka-based families range from middle-class to impoverished, but all of their childhoods are impacted to varying degrees by divorce, absentee fathers, and abandonment. For some, there is considerable domestic violence and substance abuse within the household.

These family dynamics have far-reaching implications for the boys, exacting a toll in their teenage years that includes, to varying degrees, poor educational and occupational outcomes, involvement in gangs, crime, acts of violence toward others, incarceration, and teenage parenthood. Stu and Barry largely avoid trouble during their adolescence and early twenties, but Daymond and De'Juan have considerable contact with various branches of the criminal justice system.

Part 1 also recounts the formation of DVS Mindz and their early history, when the group members live together in a Topeka house, writing songs and rehearsing around the clock. The band places a premium on hard work and skills, founded on a belief that outworking and outperforming their peers is the ticket to the top. They spend four years grinding relentlessly, securing management, networking around the country, launching their own record label, and opening for some of the biggest names in the music industry. There are setbacks and challenges along the way, but as part 1 concludes, DVS Mindz seems poised for bigger things.

Part 2 covers the period from 2000–2003. At the onset of this era, DVS Mindz is in their artistic prime and at the peak of their popularity. We follow the band backstage, onstage, to recording sessions, and hang out with them at home.

Part 2 is based upon fifty-plus hours of video and audio recordings created from 1999–2003. I recorded much of this material myself, but I was sometimes assisted by my friends Greg Douros, Doug Lerner, Kepler Miner, Eliott Reeder, and Jeff Roos. In March 2000, I directed and edited DVS Mindz's first music video, "Tired of Talking." This partnership led to further collaborations, including two more music videos, a short fictional film, and a full-length documentary, *DVStory: The DVS Mindz Documentary*. The latter project entailed interviewing everyone in the band and their manager, Randy, recording fifteen live performances, and following the group as they pursued music stardom. My friends and I videotaped DVS Mindz performing, writing and recording songs, having group meetings, appearing at radio stations, and hanging out at house parties and barbeques. I conducted short, informal interviews on several occasions not only with the band but also with fans, family, and members of the group's entourage, all of which were videotaped.

My interest in working with DVS Mindz was not scholarly or journalistic. I simply loved their music, and the group's musical pursuits paired well with my nascent interest in filmmaking. Through these collaborations, I became close with several members of the band. During this time, it was common for members of DVS to drop by my apartment in Lawrence, often unannounced, usually with several members of their entourage in tow. Similarly, I spent time with them in Topeka, often in a bedroom or basement recording studio. This generally entailed hanging out, but on a few occasions, I brought along a guitar, and we collaborated musically. When the film crew and I accompanied the band to a live performance or recording studio session, we became members of DVS's entourage.

Every interview quote from part 2 of the book comes exclusively from the 1999–2003 recordings. This enabled me to capture who the group members were at the time and demonstrate how they came to reflect on this era in subsequent decades. During this same period, I worked as a music journalist, including coverage of the regional scene. I interviewed hundreds of local musicians and I draw upon some of those interviews in part 2.

Part 3 takes place from 2004 until 2020. The members of DVS Mindz are now in their forties and early fifties. Some of them are grandfathers. The band has long since broken up, and everyone has gone in different directions. With dreams of musical stardom behind them, how do the four men redefine their lives?

An appendix to the book provides an update on its central characters. It also describes the impact of the events of 2020 and 2021 on the members of DVS Mindz, including the COVID-19 pandemic, the 2020 presidential election, and the murder of George Floyd and the protests that followed.

Portions of the book are based on in-person interviews I conducted in 2009, 2014, and 2022 as well as virtual interviews that took place from 2018–2022. In an appendix, I provide more details about my research methods.

This book is not an exposé or an exhaustive historical account of DVS Mindz. Throughout the text, I have changed the names of everyone except for the members of DVS Mindz, their managers, their parents, their current spouses (where applicable), their children, and public figures.

Most of the concerts, music videos, and songs I describe in the book are available to stream online for free and without advertising at https://www.youtube.com/c/DVSMindz1137.

At the end of the book, I have provided a guide to the band's songs, music videos, and live performances. There is also a discography, a first-ever attempt to catalog the group's extensive body of band and solo projects. I hope this is the first step toward chronicling the complete musical and cultural contributions of Daymond, Barry, De'Juan, and Stu. May DVS Mindz live on, long after us all.

DVS MINDZ

I

1970–1999

1

THE GENESIS

Lowman Hill Elementary School, Topeka, Kansas, March 2000

Stu and Barry take me to Lowman Hill, an elementary school located on Garfield Avenue in Elmhurst, a central Topeka neighborhood. Built in 1959, Lowman is a nondescript one-story building with a red brick foundation topped by tall windows that run continuously around the structure. We are there on a Sunday, so the schoolyard is deserted. Almost.

Across the playground, three Black men who appear to be in their late teens or early twenties are horsing around on Lowman's swing set. As we approach, they stop and look over at us.

"DVS Mindz!" one of the men yells.

"You *know*!" Stu bellows back, pleased at the recognition.

"You see, that's the love," Barry tells me.

Stu and Barry brought me to Lowman Hill because this is where they became friends, entering kindergarten together twenty-five years earlier, in 1975. The boys had been introduced the year before when they attended the same Head Start program. "When we met, we were four or five years old," Stu says. "This is where we spent most of our time getting to know each other. We were in Head Start, kindergarten, first grade, all the way 'til it was his freshman year of high school."

As Stu talks, the twenty-nine-year-old rubs his palms together, trying to keep the March chill at bay. Stu's hands are encased in thick black ski gloves that match his jacket, a black windbreaker with a white DVS Mindz logo silkscreened on the front and back. The jacket and gloves are offset by white jeans, a white T-shirt, and a white wool cap pulled low over his right eye. Stu sports a light goatee, gone fuzzy after a couple of days without shaving. His only jewelry is a short necklace composed of small silver beads.

I ask Stu what Barry was like as a kid. The question elicits laughter from both men as they weigh potential responses. "Same cat, just younger," Stu says, looking over at Barry, who recently turned thirty. "Very artistic, loved to draw shit."

"Anybody that knows Stu, he is the exact same person, just taller and the Afro's missing." Barry says, laughing uproariously. "Stuart wouldn't be the smart-ass type [in school]. He'd be sitting there, hands in his pockets. But just the look on Stuart's face made it hilarious."

Barry grins and rocks from his left foot to his right. While Stu is the kind of guy who thinks paying top dollar for a pair of tennis shoes is the height of foolishness, Barry seems to have a new pair every other week. Today, he sports gleaming white Nikes with blue swooshes, coordinated to match the rest of his outfit: baggy blue jeans, a black T-shirt, and a royal blue leather baseball jacket that features insignias and Japanese lettering on the back, sleeves, and chest. Barry has the collar popped high. The jacket is the exact same shade of blue as his Dodgers ball cap, which Barry wears cocked to the right and placed atop a black skull cap. He sports light facial hair and wears small diamond earrings and a long gold chain.

Barry speaks with a distinct Midwestern twang that makes his every utterance sound slightly amused, transforming simple statements into grand proclamations, often exaggerated for comedic effect. He begins spinning yarns about his school-day foibles with Stu, describing some of the pair's legendary pranks, recalling the names of the aggrieved, hard-ass teachers who had it out for them. "I remember times, man, where Stuart and I used to just act a fool so much in school, man, where we used to get in trouble. Sometimes, we'd get in trouble when we weren't even *trying* to cut up on purpose. Just because stuff he'd do or whatever would just be so hilarious. We'd just be uncontrollable with laughter."

Stu listens fondly but is more circumspect. "I can't really tell you that I can take any fond memories of the learning process," he says. "As far as my friends and the situations, the dumb shit we used to pull, the things we got away with, the shit that we didn't get away with, that was cool. All that other shit, no. I can't sit still for that damn long. I'm just hyper. I can't do it."

I ask Stu and Barry if they graduated from high school. Barry nods. "Went through some shit to do it, but yeah. If I had it to do all over again, I sure would do a hell a lot of shit different. If I knew what I know now, and I could go back to high school, I'd be nothing to fuck with. Not at all. I'd be handling shit like I should have been. Believe it. Class, books, all that shit. I'd be hitting them up and still doing shit that I wanted to do. Where I would have did the shit correct. But you gotta learn it on your own to really get the shit to sink in."

Stu shakes his head in response to my question about graduating. "I got a GED. My first child was conceived when I was in high school. She'll be twelve this year."

STU

Stuart Tidwell was born Elvin Anthony Redmon on July 31, 1970, at St. Francis Hospital in Wichita, Kansas. His mother, Janice Redmon, was just eighteen years old and already had a young daughter. His father, William Roberson, was already married with children. Stu's mother decided to put the newborn up for adoption. Stu spent a few months in state care before being taken in by a couple from Topeka, Winfred and Christine Tidwell.

In 1951, when Winfred was eleven years old, a group of parents filed a class-action lawsuit against the Topeka Board of Education, claiming that its system of "separate but equal" schooling was unconstitutional and discriminatory. *Brown v. Board of Education* eventually went to the Supreme Court, which ruled in favor of the plaintiffs in 1954. This victory paved the way for the integration of public schools and the civil rights movement.

Winfred earned a bachelor's degree from Pittsburg State University and a master's degree from Emporia State University. He spent almost ten years employed as a schoolteacher and administrator for three elementary schools. In 1969, he became the principal of Monroe Elementary School, only the third Black principal of a racially integrated Topeka elementary school.[1] Christine worked as a clerk for Kansas Power and Light, the local electric company. In 1970, they adopted a baby and changed his name from Elvin to Stuart. The family lived in a house at 1137 Washburn Avenue, located in a working-class Topeka neighborhood.

Stu's early life as an adoptee was far from idyllic. A year after bringing the boy home from Wichita, Winfred and Christine separated and then later divorced. Stu continued to live with Christine at 1137 Washburn, visiting Winfred on weekends. Before long, Winfred married a woman named Clementine, who had a daughter from a previous marriage. The couple then had two more children, a boy and a girl. Stu remembers, "Five days a week, I'd be an only kid and then when my dad had visitation, I'd come over to his house on the weekend. I'd have a brother and two sisters. It was a contrast."

Stu describes an adolescence filled with sports and video games with the local kids. "I remember playing football one day after school and [the temperature has] got to be in the teens or single digits, close to a foot of snow on the ground. We got one of those little toy footballs and there's about ten or eleven of us out there laughing in a parking lot, playing tackle football outside."

In his early teens, Stu became interested in music, especially rap. Run-D.M.C., LL Cool J, Kurtis Blow, and the Fat Boys were favorites. Stu reminisces, "When I first started listening to hip-hop, there wasn't anybody around here doing it. So, whoever was on the airwaves, that's how we listened. The radio." Stu soaked it in, even trying his hand at graffiti and break dancing before becoming an adept beatboxer during his sophomore year at Topeka High School. "At that time, there was maybe one or two rappers at the school. They would cipher," he recalls. "They would be rapping and needed a beat. And I was there. It was something I used to walk around doing at the house on my own. Listening to the Fat Boys and Doug E. Fresh, just doing the beatboxing. So when these ciphers would happen at lunch or before school or after school, I'm the guy providing the sound. That's how I got into it."

A self-described low-B or C student, Stu did enough to get by at school and stayed out of trouble. In his midteens, he got caught skipping class, and his mom busted him joyriding in her car one time, but he mostly toed the line.

When he was sixteen, Stu landed a job in the kitchen at McDonald's, where his grade-school buddy Barry also worked. Barry went to a different high school than Stu, but they had remained friends over the years. "If we didn't see each other in school, we would see each other at McDonald's," Barry recalls. "If we didn't see each other at McDonald's, we were going to see each other in the neighborhood. Either on the hill or at a friend's house. We had mutual friends, we always hung out."

During the winter holidays of 1986, Stu and his mother flew to California to visit her older brother, Stu's uncle, Joe. Joe worked at McDonnell Douglass, the aerospace manufacturing giant. During the trip, Stu got to spend time with his cousins, a couple of older guys who had an apartment in Long Beach. One was an accomplished DJ and had a pair of turntables set up in his bedroom. He showed Stu some of his moves, scratching and mixing two LPs together in real time. Stu's jaw hit the floor. "First time I'd ever seen that before in my life," Stu remembers. "He started doing that shit, man. I was sitting there [looking] like a four- or five-year-old kid with my mouth wide open. I want to do that shit; I want to do *that!*"

Stu decided then and there that he would be a DJ. "I went home and tore up my mom's turntable all to hell. She had one of them old-school players with the eight-track and the radio. I was cutting and scratching on that, taking little pieces of notebook paper, cutting them out so my records would slide a little better."

Back home in Topeka, the sixteen-year-old began to clash with his mother, Christine—arguments that turned increasingly violent. One morning, during a quarrel, Christine slapped Stu across the face. He was infuriated. "You have no damn call to hit me like that!" Stu shouted, turning to leave. Christine ran to the kitchen, grabbed a butcher knife, and came running at him. "I'm out of there. I stayed gone for five or six hours that day. The next day, she told me, 'You're going to live with your dad.'" By this point, Stu's father, Winfred, had split from his second wife and was living in a one-bedroom apartment on Twilight Avenue. Stu moved in.

In the fall of 1987, at the start of his senior year of high school, Stu decided to form a DJ group. The act would be modeled after popular Topeka turntable troupes such as the

T-Town Rockers and the Gucci Guys, whose dazzling live performances featured dancers, flashing lights, and multiple turntable wizards. "It's crowd reaction. I wanted to move crowds," Stu recalls. He approached Barry, his longtime friend, and a couple of other buddies. "Let's start a DJ group!" Barry shook his head. No way. They had no equipment and no experience. "Don't worry about it, we'll handle that, we're going to do this," Stu told him. A female friend from school headed the Black Student Union and hired Stu and Barry's DJ troupe to perform at a monthly party, held in the cafeteria. They would be paid one hundred dollars. Barry was in. The quartet dubbed itself the 2 Def Crew and used some of the money to rent a professional DJ setup from a friend who worked with Stu and Barry at McDonald's.

The DJ group was a hit at high school, but Stu's life took two dramatic turns that year. The first came when his father, Winfred, was diagnosed with Hodgkin's disease. A lifelong smoker and drinker, Winfred went cold turkey and began chemotherapy. The second major event took place a few months later when Stu's girlfriend, Mary, told him she was pregnant. Stu was seventeen years old. Just six credits shy of graduation, the news rattled him. He lost focus and dropped out. Winfred, the respected schoolteacher and principal, was not pleased.

"Why don't you go back for another year to at least graduate?" he pleaded.

Stu stood his ground. "No. I got a child on the way. I'm gonna take the GED and I'm going to go to work. I can't put a child on you or my mother. I did this. It's my responsibility."

Weary from his battle with Hodgkin's, Winfred relented. Not yet a legal adult himself, Stu was about to become a father.

In the summer of 1988, Stu and Mary found a small apartment in Topeka and moved in together. Their daughter, Britnea, was born that fall, a few months after Stu's eighteenth birthday. "Scary," he recalls of his feelings at the time. "Unknown. Eighteen. You're responsible for another human being, two other human beings. You gotta work together to make that happen. That was scary."

At the time, Stu was making four dollars an hour as a janitor's assistant for the local school district, hardly enough to support a family. Through a connection of Mary's, Stu landed a job at a local manufacturing plant, a wire factory that produced reels of copper cable for large-scale electrical projects. At $8.50 per hour, the job paid more than twice his current wage. "That was a big relief," he recalls. "This job was decent. I was like okay, I can finally bring some decent money in."

Mary took a series of part-time jobs, clerking in an office and running the register at a nearby gas station. Between long working hours and the pressures of a new baby, the teenage couple's relationship became strained. Stu started seeing another woman on the side. He and Mary split in 1989 but eventually got back together. They remained a couple for another year but then fractured again. "We met when we were seventeen," Stu recalls. "The responsibilities of a child, and then the responsibilities of a relationship, the give and the take, the trust, the ins and outs. It didn't work."

Stu moved back to Winfred's house and continued to put in shifts at the wire plant. Mary and Britnea stayed in the apartment. Stu recalls it as a low point. "I felt defeated," he says. "I felt like I lost, like I let my daughter down. It bothered me to put a child through what I went through, having parents and then they're divorced. Mom's here and Dad's over there. I never wanted that. I wanted to be in the house, to raise my child with her mother, together." A couple of years after the split, Mary remarried and moved to Georgia, taking Britnea with her.

Not long after the split with Mary, Stu and another girl-friend, April, became pregnant. Still stinging from his failed relationship with Mary, Stu went all-out and asked April to marry him. She agreed. The pair signed up for a joint banking account and started saving money to rent an apartment. Stu recalls, "We're going to get our own place. We're going to move out of our parents' homes, and we're gonna raise our child together. Well, it didn't work." Stu's second daughter, Tahnae, was born in December 1992. Soon after, April met another man, married, and moved to the southern United States, taking Tahnae with her.

To make matters worse, Winfred's Hodgkin's disease returned with a vengeance. "He tried his best to keep it away, but I lived with him," Stu recalls. "I remember being up some nights, just being in my room watching TV, and he would be in his room, coughing for hours. Just coughing and coughing and coughing. I was twenty-two. I didn't know what was going on. This is my dad, and he's sick right now. They're gonna give him the treatment and he's gonna be all right. The next thing I know . . ."

In mid-June 1993, Stu was driving to work one day when he noticed Winfred's Monte Carlo at a stop sign, motion-less. "He's just sitting there, his head is down," Stu recalls. "He didn't look good. I pulled up behind him, waiting for him to go. And he's not going. I honked my horn, and he lifts his head up and looks around—he doesn't even know it's me. He pulls onto the street, so I get behind him and keep honking my horn, like, 'Hey, Dad.'"

Stu was unable to get Winfred's attention but called two days later, on Father's Day. Winfred had recently remarried for the third time and was staying at his new wife's house. "He could barely talk," Stu recalls of their brief phone conversation.

That night, Stu had just finished watching the last game of the NBA Finals, where Michael Jordan scored thirty-three points for the Chicago Bulls in a 99–98 victory over the Phoenix Suns. The phone rang. It was the hospital; Winfred had passed. "I break down in tears," Stu recalls. "I gotta pull myself together. I go up to the hospital. I went to view my dad's body, laying there. I walk to the bed and I went to hold his hand. It was cold and it was stiff. It broke me down; I didn't know what to think. I'm in shock. Dad's gone."

Winfred had a long and distinguished career as a Topeka educator, including serving as president of the Topeka Principals Association. Every year since 1993, Topeka Parks and Recreation has commemorated him by sponsoring the Winfred Tidwell Memorial Golf Tournament.[2] Winfred's death was complicated by his third marriage, which had taken place only weeks before he passed. With four children from three different wives, there was bickering over insurance money and the division of property. Too numb to consider any of it with a clear head, Stu signed where he was told to sign. "That was a blow," he recalls. "To lose my father, who I felt I let down because of having the kid and not graduating. Just not being more productive, not being some type of a success. I wanted my dad to see me do something good. He told me he was proud of me for stepping up and taking care of my responsibilities and doing everything that I was supposed to do. But for me, I didn't think that was good enough. And then to lose him, and he was gone, that threw me in a tailspin."

Despondent over Winfred's passing and disgusted with squabbling relatives, Stu began drinking heavily. Prior to his father's passing, Stu had been a casual drinker whose intake was modest. Now he was imbibing beer every day. He also had nowhere to live—Winfred's house was being sold in the estate proceedings. Stu's mother, Christine, had recently relocated to Kansas City but still owned her old house in Topeka at 1137 Washburn, where Stu grew up. She let Stu move in and eventually deeded the property to him.

Initially, Stu lived at 1137 alone, tending to the house's maintenance needs and paying the bills from his job at the wire company. Things were shaky at work, where he had been placed on probation for missing too many days. Some of Stu's absences stemmed from on-the-job injuries he sustained, including a popped disc in his back and an elbow that shattered into six pieces, bone damage that was not entirely repairable. "They couldn't fix it," Stu says. "They just had to take the pieces out and just shave off the end of the bone." When his claims were partly denied, Stu filed two workman's compensation lawsuits.

One afternoon, following a particularly trying day at work, Stu returned home, opened his mail, and gasped. There were checks totaling about $50,000, proceeds from his father's estate and a workman's compensation settlement from the wire company.[3] He immediately picked up the phone and called his cousin, Earl. "'I gotta get out of here. I want to go on a vacation to California. Don't worry about the money. Just book the flights, get the rental car and all that stuff straight.' And we went. I was supposed to be back at work on Monday. I couldn't miss another day. Ended up staying in L.A. an extra day. I knew what was gonna happen. I came back on a Tuesday. They called me in and said, 'You're over your limit. You gotta go.'"

Losing his father and his job in the same period was rough. The $50,000 windfall proved to be as much a blessing as a curse for the twenty-three-year-old. "That was a real trying time," Stu recalls. "After he passed, I had to take the rest of that damned year off. I was still in shock. I felt I had to play a role and put on a smile. I drank to bury that pain."

As Stu ruminated alone at 1137 Washburn, he began writing, describing his pain in prose and poems, filling page after page of notebooks. "I started writing," he says. "I don't know where this is gonna take me. It felt good. I fell in love with the process of writing rhymes and making music. It was new. I knew there was room for me to grow and learn and get out and explore."

Stu's high-school DJ group, 2 Def Crew, had dissolved years ago, but he and his cousin Earl continued to perform as DJs at parties, mostly in north Kansas City, where Earl attended night school. It was going well enough that the pair decided to recruit a few rappers and form a band. "I wanted to start a group, but I never wanted to be the front man," Stu says. "I'm gonna be the guy back here, running the music, that's me."

But Stu also had a love for music that was so strong, it kept him awake at night. Nothing made him feel better, more alive, more inspired. "The feeling that I got listening to Run-D.M.C., listening to LL Cool J, listening to KRS-One, listening to Redman, just getting excited. Back then, people would buy albums just to read who produced what. That J-card with the foldouts and everything, those things were like gold. A new record's coming out. 'Redman's on it! I gotta hear it.' That was the feeling I wanted to give to other people through our music. I wanted to return that feeling in some way, shape, or form."

After his new group's lead rapper was sent to prison, Stu decided to assume center stage himself. "I'm trying to move forward," he recalls. "The situation forced my hand. I was going to have to step out front. I didn't think I had enough to offer, that I would be enough. If I have to step out front, I don't want to do it by myself. So, I go look for Barry. We lost contact after high school."

Barry was a longtime friend and had been a member of 2 Def Crew, making him a good fit in Stu's mind. Although Barry had never rapped, Stu believed he could learn the craft in short order. "Growing up with Barry, I watched him pick up things quickly," Stu says, snapping his fingers. "It was effortless with him. I knew if I showed him the basics of MC-ing, he would pick it up and he would be up and running. I needed somebody that would be able to do that, somebody that I knew I could get along with, and we'd be cohesive together in the group. Barry is the guy I'm looking for."

There was a problem. Stu hadn't seen Barry in years and had no idea where to track him down. "I don't know if I'm ever gonna find this dude," Stu thought. "But I want to find him. I need to get him."

2

A PIRATE POET

The Granada, Lawrence, Kansas, April 23, 2001

The Granada is a cavernous, eight-hundred-capacity venue that was built in the 1930s as a silent movie theater. Now it is a nightclub, bringing in DJs for popular weekend dance parties and booking local, regional, and national acts. Like the other downtown Lawrence venues, the Granada's proximity to the University of Kansas's (KU) thirty thousand college students keeps it busy much of the time.

Tonight, a boisterous throng of KU students are on hand to party with the headliners, the rollicking Oakland rap outfit Digital Underground. Everyone is in a good mood. The bartenders are serving beers two at a time, and the opening act, DVS Mindz, can seemingly do no wrong. The quartet begins their set with a pulse-quickening version of "Madness" that transforms the audience—in a single song—into rabid disciples, with hundreds of attendees windshield-wiping their arms in unison. DVS follows with pummeling takes on "Heat" and "Niggaz (1137)" that keep the energy levels high. Showmen to the core and reading the room, the band knows it's time to switch things up.

Daymond is DVS's ringleader during live performances, interacting with the crowd and directing the proceedings. Tonight, he assumes center stage and addresses the audience. "Aye. If y'all didn't know, this is some authentic hip-hop back-to-the-streets battle-style shit. And we gonna do some shit that all the real MCs should do. We gonna do some fuckin' a cappella shit with no fuckin' beats."

Hundreds of concertgoers hoist their beers in the air and cheer.

Daymond continues, warming up. "Some of that battle-style, back in the motherfucking park, under the streetlight, up all motherfuckin' night rhyming type shit."

Daymond exaggeratingly cocks a hand to his left ear. "Who want to hear some of that type shit?"

The audience hollers back, clapping and cheering louder.

Daymond cranks it up another notch, a hip-hop tent-revival preacher, rocking his body back and forth as he speaks. "Y'all didn't hear me. I said under the *street lights*, in the motherfuckin' *park*, rhyming battle-style shit. Who want to hear some of that shit, make some noise!"

The crowd goes berserk.

Stu's official rap moniker is Str8jakkett, but, like the rest of the band, he goes by a series of nicknames, some of them referencing years-old private jokes and known only to insiders. Daymond introduces Stu to the Granada crowd: "The first motherfucker we got up is dragon head number one. My nigga who started this DVS Mindz saga, Str8jakkett. Special Agent Wrexx. Y'all show some love!"

"Asshole number one," Stu replies sarcastically, stepping into the spotlight. "'Cause I *am* an asshole."

Stu's type-A stage demeanor is serious and in-your-face. His rhymes are jittery, all sharp elbows and quick right turns. Stu wants to be the best rapper in the room. He spent years preparing, practicing, and honing his craft to get there. When Stu walks onstage, he looks like a fighter girding for a championship bout. Stu is not here to rap; he is here to destroy you. In concert, Stu is the band's secret weapon. If there is a lull in the show, Stu can spit a sixty-second rapid-fire a cappella that will rouse the crowd back to life. Tonight, Stu slays as usual, ending his flurry of rhymes with a knowing look and a smile.

"Y'all give it up for Str8jakkett," Daymond says to heavy applause. "Next up we got my nigga. Dragon head number two, asshole number two. Forty Killa. Killa the Hun. Smokey Rob-him-some."

If Stu's stage presence is powerful and serious, Barry looks like he's wandering Bourbon Street on a Sunday afternoon, cocktail in hand. Stu is a machine of precision and tightly controlled energy; Barry is a pirate poet, a silver-tongued outlaw, boozed up and blunted. Dean Martin to Stu's Sinatra, Barry is the coolest and cockiest member of a group that has no shortage of either quality.

"What up, what up, what up?" he patters, ambling to the front of the stage without a concern. If this was the 1940s, Barry would be decked out in a high-waisted zoot suit topped off by a wide-brimmed fedora. Tonight, he's adorned in a contemporary variation of the urban cat—a long, black Nike-branded Lakers jersey, sleeveless to better show off a series of tattoos on each arm, with a matching skull cap on top. He sports a crucifix that swings on a silver chain near his navel, dime-sized diamonds that twinkle from each ear, and a perennial wink in his eye.

Barry surveys the scene, taking it all in for a moment. A couple of attendees to his left shout and clap. Barry points over to them and smiles. "You guys like me, don't you?" he says affectionately, adding, "I like you guys, too."

"Smokey!" someone hollers from way in the back.

Barry spins around and grins. "You *know* this! And I'm gonna be lookin' for it. You know what the fuck. I'm mad 'cause I don't smell none yet, so fuck it." The audience snickers at Barry's pot reference as he launches into an a cappella whose lyrics mix ax-murderer movie tropes with wry humor. The crowd eats it up, and Barry finishes to a thunderous ovation, taking his time as he saunters back toward the DJ riser.

BARRY

John "Barry" Rice III was born January 29, 1970, in Holton, Kansas, a tiny town about thirty miles north of Topeka. Like Stu, Barry was adopted as an infant and grew up in Topeka. "They had reasons for putting me up for adoption. I'm not going to hold nothing like that against them," Barry says of his biological parents, without elaboration.

Barry was adopted by John and Barbara Rice, a couple that already had three biological daughters. The youngest, Trisha, was four years older than Barry, and Theresa and Marsha were a year or two older than her. The family lived in Fillmore, a central Topeka neighborhood. "It wasn't like super-project fucked up or nothing," Barry recalls. "It was middle class; it was pretty good. We weren't spoiled—have everything you wanted—but you had the shit you needed."

Barry's childhood interests included drawing, painting, and all variety of sports. This being the mid-1970s, Barry was also a martial arts enthusiast. "I was a fucking Bruce Lee fanatic," he laughs. "Crazy about it. Karate, I used to do all that stuff."

Barry's mother, Barbara, worked for the state and then later for a series of community-oriented nonprofits. Barry's father,

John, worked at the Goodyear factory and was involved in car racing and other hobbies. John was also known around town as an organist, using a truck to haul a massive pipe organ that he would play at hospitals and children's parties. John often brought Barry with him. One weekend, John was slated to play an overnight gig, and Barry begged to go along. His mother forbade it. "I was really upset about it, mad as hell," Barry recalls.

He woke the next morning to the news. A drunk driver had run his father off the road. "As his truck went into a ditch, his organ came unsnapped from the back, rolled forward, and crushed him to death. How fucking crazy is that? The thing that he loved doing ended up being your demise. I thought about how mad I was I couldn't go, how upset my mom would have been to lose both of us at the same time. Losing him was bad enough. That made me start to pay more attention to music and then eventually starting to want to do it."

It was now Barry and four females at home. "I learned a lot from growing up with my sisters and my mom," he says. "The stereotypical things people talk about—there wasn't a man in the house and that's why I'm fucked up. I don't buy that shit because I grew up with all women and I'm not fucked up."

Friends since kindergarten, Barry usually hung out at Stu's house after school, where the pair would watch serialized movies that played at the time. Each week, a local TV station would broadcast a series of five films, one per day, centered around a single theme: Godzilla, Planet of the Apes, Elvis Presley musicals. Barry and Stu devoured it all.

Barry's interest in movies shifted to music in 1979, when he first heard Sugar Hill Gang's seminal hit, "Rapper's Delight." Three years later, a twelve-year-old Barry was riding in his aunt's car when Afrika Bambaataa's "Planet Rock" came on the car radio. "I bugged out," Barry recalls. "I made my aunt buy it for me.

We went straight to Mother Earth [record store] and got it. Man, I was losing it all the way home. I couldn't wait to get home to play it."

This led to an LP-buying obsession, with Barry picking up stacks of rap titles and taking them to Stu's house for review. Popular artists included MC Shan, Ice T, and Egyptian Lover, and then later Erik B. and Rakim, Boogie Down Productions, King Tee, N.W.A., Mixmaster Spade, Rodney-O and Joe Cooley, and Sir Mix-A-Lot. Stu and Barry bonded over their love for all things hip-hop. "I used to buy records all the time," Barry says. "Stuart and I started DJ-ing, messing around at home, when we came from school. We used to scratch on one those big-ass console TVs with the record player. That's some *real* shit right there. We used to scratch the shit out of that mug. His mom used to be *pissed*. Once we started doing that, we just bought records all the time. I used to DJ, breakdance, and do graffiti."

If Barry wasn't doing something music-related he was playing sports, including football, wrestling, and his favorite, basketball. "Basketball was my first love," Barry recalls. "After school everybody would go to certain parks: Central Park, Cushinberry, Jefferson Square, Crestview. That's where all the so-called real ballers would play. You'd have to be able to play good enough to even get on the court in certain parks. It would get ridiculous. That's the only thing I wanted to do."

Barry and Stu began their freshman year together at Topeka High School. Barry did not miss a single day of classes all semester. He also did not pass any of his courses. "It was terrible!" he says, laughing. "Perfect attendance, didn't pass one class. Didn't pass *gym*. That's how bad I fucked up. Didn't do shit. Just fucking around. Didn't give a fuck. Fools back then."

During this time, Barry became affiliated with a local faction of the Crips street gang, the Brittany Mafia Crip Gangstas

(BMCG). A few of the BMCG members were from Barry's neighborhood, but most lived on Topeka's east side. "Growing up, everybody I hung around with were Crips," he says. "I was always around the motherfuckers, so if I was going to join anything, that's what it would be. I got really into the Crip shit. I'd wear blue all the time and would be always talking about it."

Displeased with her increasingly wayward son, Barbara enrolled Barry in Knollwood, a small, strict Baptist school in south Topeka. The school ran from kindergarten through twelfth grade and only had about a hundred students. Barry was the sole Black student. At an orientation, the school principal laid out the ground rules: uniforms were required, no secular music, no cursing, and males and females were expected to remain at least six inches apart at all times. "Right after he said stay away from the girls and no rap music, I'm like, 'You lost me,'" Barry recalls, laughing. "I'm already thinking of how I can get kicked out of here real quick and get sent back to Topeka High." Barbara threatened to send Barry to a military boarding academy if he got in trouble at Knollwood.

At his new school, Barry was almost instantly in hot water for his wardrobe and demeanor. The teachers continually admonished him to pull up his pants, tuck in his shirt, and stand up straight. Barry found his way by joining the Knollwood basketball team, the Patriots. Barry was already an experienced player, with years spent honing his skills in Topeka's ultra-competitive park pick-up games. Just shy of six feet tall, Barry could dunk. "When I got to Knollwood, I'm like the first Black dude, so it's already motherfuckers looking at me like I'm an exotic animal," Barry recalls. "There's only a hundred students and you pay to go to school. So you can imagine what the basketball team looks like, a mess. The basketball they played was totally different from the basketball I played. They wasn't ready for nobody like me." Barry became an instant basketball star. He was fitting in, finding his stride.

After school, Barry was right back to his neighborhood, where he comingled with the BMCGs and his buddies from Topeka High. Between time spent with the "churched out" white kids at school and gang members on the East Side, Barry learned to code switch, to alternate between the worlds of the white middle class and the Black working class. "I started learning alternative words to cussing," he recalls. "At that school, you can't be doing all that. I'd be hanging out with the homies and I'd say some shit and they just start cracking up. I'd be coming up with other words instead of cussing. They used to bust my balls about it. I'm still the same dude, but it was fucking funny to see me changing from being a total knucklehead to being like okay I can walk into a room and get my white-boy voice on, [snaps fingers] get a fuckin' job, walk right out of there and just cuss and argue with motherfuckers."

Barry says that some of this came from his mother, who insisted that her son understand how to move flexibly between worlds.

"If you don't know how to act around white people, you're not going to get very far at all," Barbara told Barry. "Because they're not going to fuck with you. Period. You got to learn how they think and how to act around certain people so you can achieve things. 'Cause if you're with some other people acting like a fucking fool, they're just going to rope you into that too."

Barry listened, watched, and learned. "I really toned it down," he says. "Even though I didn't want to be there, I was slowly changing into a better person. I really started concentrating on school."

This transformation was influenced by a new friend Barry made in the fall of 1986 at the beginning of his junior year. Randy Smith was a churchgoing straight-A athlete who transferred to

Knollwood because his strict single mother thought the public schools were too easy. Randy remembers that he and Barry connected the instant they saw one another. "I walked in there and looked and around and there was only one Black guy in the whole school. It was B. When he saw me, he just gave me the biggest smile, like, 'Finally, we got another one.' We've been down ever since. We clicked and became best friends."

"Oh my god, they got *two* Black guys?" Barry says, laughing in mock horror at the memory. "He had the same culture shock I did. Like, 'What the fuck is going on around here?'"

Randy excelled at sports, and he and Barry became a formidable unit, playing together on the high school football and basketball teams. Barry's favorite basketball player was Michael Jordan, and he did his best to emulate the Bulls great with acrobatic plays that delighted spectators and his teammates. "He was very good," Randy recalls. "Best player on the team. The different tournaments that we would sign up for, he was the one that stood out. He was that guy. He had the moves; he had the drive. Plus, he was the class clown. He'd make everybody laugh. You didn't even have to know him. You'd just listen to him talk and everybody laughs and loves him. Funny guy."

Being exposed to new friends and new possibilities made Barry increasingly disenchanted with the risks of gang life. "I still hung out with all of them, but I wasn't shooting at motherfuckers and all that extra shit, going to house parties and turning them out. I would kick it with my people and I'm thinking these motherfuckers are full-blown acting a fool. All I have to do is be around them one time and my ass'll get shot just the same as them. 'How many of y'all's motherfucking peoples is dead or in jail? What the fuck you think is going to happen to us eventually?' So, I start deciphering and picking and choosing the shit I do, and where I be, and the type of motherfuckers I be around.

It changed me in that sense, thinking smarter. There's bigger shit going on out here than the fucking block."

Barry got a job at McDonald's, stayed focused, and graduated from high school in 1988. He had no plans to go to college and few career ambitions. "After high school, the first year I didn't do shit. I was just glad to be the hell out of school. I started working a little bit, and just hanging the fuck out." Barry got a part-time job at Falley's, a local grocery store, and spent weekends carousing with Randy, his friend from high school. The two would drive to St. Joseph, Missouri, a city of about seventy thousand located fifty miles north of Kansas City, where Randy was getting serious with a new girlfriend. The relationship did not pan out, but Randy stayed in St. Joe after landing a good-paying job in a pork slaughterhouse.

Barry went back and forth from Topeka to St. Joe, crashing on Randy's couch. His visits were sporadic at first, but then he started coming by more frequently, and before long, Barry had moved into Randy's altogether. It was a transitory cycle that would recur for much of Barry's adult life. "After we graduated, he was just the guy who just wanted to be taken care of," Randy says. "He didn't want to work so he was always staying on somebody's couch and eventually having a pile of clothes in somebody's corner of the house and officially moving in."

In the fall of 1990, twenty-year-old Barry relocated to Lawrence, Kansas, where he enrolled as a freshman at KU. He intended to study architecture but spent virtually every waking hour shooting hoops in the student gymnasium with his dormmates. "I swear, that's all we used to do, play ball all day," Barry says, savoring the memory. "Play ball for four hours, come back to my room, take a shower, eat a whole fucking big-ass pizza, a twenty box of KFC hot wings, go back to the gym and ball for another six hours."

Barry's girlfriend at the time was a basketball player for the KU women's team who encouraged him to sign up for walk-on tryouts, which were open to all full-time students. KU has one of the most prestigious and storied college basketball teams in the nation, and it recruits the top players in the country each year. Earning a spot on the team as a walk-on was unlikely, but Barry signed up anyway. The initial tryout lasted two days. "I was a nervous wreck," he recalls. "I made the first cut. Then the second practice, it was terrible. I don't know what the hell was wrong with me. But I still ended up making the team."

Barry never saw a minute of game time. For the past couple of years, his mother, Barbara, had endured a series of medical ailments: a cut on her foot that became badly infected, a hysterectomy that was fraught with postsurgical complications. "Her health just kept deteriorating," recalls Barry, who took a leave of absence from college and moved back home to Topeka. "She was in and out of the hospital constantly. Home for a week and then back in the hospital. It was rough on my sisters. I wanted to be closer to her. Let me go back to Topeka, be with Mom, chill out for a while until she gets better."

Barbara's health improved marginally, but Barry did not make it back to KU. When he was twenty years old, Barry was dating a woman named Anna. She got pregnant, and Barry asked her to marry him. Anna hesitated, telling Barry she did not want to interfere with his basketball career. "None of that shit means anything," Barry told her. "We about to have a kid. *That's* more important to me." Anna told Barry she would think about it. "And then she left," Barry says. "She just up and moved to Atlanta. Never seen her again."

Four years later, having had no contact, Anna stopped in town so that Barry could meet his son, Jeffrey. She left the next day, and Barry has not heard from her or Jeffrey since. "That shit just fucks me up from the get-go, just thinking about it," Barry says. "I don't know what he's doing, how he's doing, where he is, or just a means of how to track him down. I think about when I was adopted. A lot of the decisions I make, I think back to that."

Barry never returned to college. An athletic teetotaler throughout his adolescence, he acquired a taste for alcohol, weed, and Newport cigarettes in his twenties. "All my friends that were knuckleheads, I used to harass them about that shit. 'Really? Y'all motherfuckers are smoking?' Four years later, [I was] smoking and drinking like the rest of them." Barry's hoop dreams evaporated, too. "I pretty much just left basketball alone," he says wistfully. "I used to play at the rec center, just for fun. I wish I could have stayed in school. I would have really loved to play ball there."

When Barry first returned to Topeka, he stayed with Chris, an old friend who lived in the Oakland section of town. At a shopping mall one day, Chris ran into Stu and mentioned their mutual friend Barry. Stu had been searching for Barry for months. "We lost contact after high school," Stu recalls. "After he graduated and I went on to work, he went to college. So, it was a good two or three years in there where I hadn't talked to him or seen him. I caught back up with him in '91. I had been looking for Barry because I wanted to get this group thing off the ground. I was pursuing him, and I finally found him."

"I don't know how he found me," Barry says. "One day this dude pulls up at the house and he's like, 'Hey man, you want to take a ride with me real quick?' He got injured at work, so he wasn't supposed to be driving. He wanted me to drive him around so he could take care of some stuff."

As they drove, Stu told Barry about his plans to form a rap group.

"The first person I thought of was you," Stu enthused.

Barry demurred. "You know I don't *rap*," he told Stu. "I do graffiti shit and DJ and shit, everything *but* rapping."

Stu would not be deterred. "I'm telling you, we can do this. It's not going to be that hard. I can teach you."

Barry finally relented. "Okay, if you want to, fuck it, I'm down."

From that moment on, Stu continually urged Barry to freestyle, turning on the radio or even beatboxing to provide background music. "He'd harass me to death," Barry recalls. "He used to just have me on a regimen like that, whenever we get in the car. Now mind you, I've never rapped, so I don't even know what the hell it is basically, let alone thinking of words fast enough to make sense."

Always a quick learner, Barry's rhyme skills improved swiftly. His private-school background, sardonic sense of humor, and love for action movies and horror flicks provided an ample foundation for lyrical creativity. Barry and Stu's initial efforts were party anthems modeled on then-popular groups like Cypress Hill. "Me and Stuart started working on some music, just fucking around," Barry says. "When we first started rapping, most of our music was just having fun, all the shit our homies did. Stuart had a song called 'Straight Out the Bottle,' it was just about drinking and joking around."

Friends since childhood, Stu and Barry's mutual interest in creating music forged a deeper bond. Barry was couch surfing with buddies, and Stu had a three-bedroom house all to himself. It only made sense for Barry to move into 1137 Washburn and really try to make the band happen. "It was me and Barry for a year, at least," Stu recalls. "Barry came up with the name. We weren't called DVS Mindz until Barry joined the group. And I can't even really call it a group. This was still in the stages me trying to put it together."

Stu mostly kept his plan to himself, recalling that his father, Winfred, disapproved of his son's musical ambitions. "I told my dad, and he was like, 'I don't like it.' He didn't like my name, Str8jakkett. I didn't really tell people that I was pursuing music, that I was trying to start a group and actually pursue this thing seriously."

At its inception, DVS Mindz consisted of Stu, Barry, Stu's cousin Earl, who rapped under the name Sandman, and an MC from Lawrence named Will-E. A buddy named Antoine helped set up equipment and also picked up a mic from time to time. Members came and went. Will-E moved to St. Louis, Earl stepped aside, and Antoine drifted away. Barry and Stu continued to write lyrics and develop their vocal skills, and their resolve to make it grew stronger. The pair scoured Topeka for talent that could help DVS Mindz expand. Barry kept bringing up a guy he knew, an MC who many said was the best in all of Topeka. "If you really want to make this motherfucker jump off, I know this cat that just got out of jail."

3

DAYMOND PULLING CHAINS

The Granada, Lawrence, Kansas, April 23, 2001

Digital Underground got the dressing room, but at least DVS Mindz is backstage. Behind the stage, actually. Having been given no separate space to prepare for their opening set, DVS and a small army of Crew members jam into a narrow rectangular strip that stretches the width of the Granada stage. We are flanked by a brick wall on the exterior side and wood stairs and rafters on the other, crowded in among a jumble of timber planks, orange fiberglass ladders, busted cabinets, discarded stage lights, and dusty stacks of chairs.

Stu and Barry stand off to one side, conferring quietly with each other. De'Juan stands on the other end of the space, alone. He hunches over a wobbly old table, hands to temples, silent and speaking to no one.

By contrast, Daymond is in a buoyant mood, perched on the wooden stairs, smiling and looking content. He wears a baby blue and white T-shirt with "Enyce" written across the front in cursive letters. "It's about to catch wreck, nigga," Daymond beams, performing for the camera. "I'm 'bout to hit these motherfuckers with the same motherfuckin' a cappella

I kicked at the Hurricane, but I'm about to do the whole shit tonight. Bitches ain't ready. I'm cyber pimping! Catch you on the internet."

Daymond stands and strips off his sweatshirt to reveal a white tank top, over which he sports a shiny rectangular pendant on a silver chain. "It's war time!" he says, looking towards the stage.

"They call me Dope. D-O-P-E, dangerous on paper and etcetera," Daymond says on stage later that night, introducing himself to the audience. "A.K.A. the Hitman, a.k.a. Dope Man, a.k.a. the Invisible Man, a.k.a. Bruce Illiss."

The last nickname, a play on the actor Bruce Willis, delights the crowd.

"Wait a minute," Daymond says playfully. "I added a new one this weekend. Old school shit."

He pauses for a beat, drawing out the punchline before delivering: "Douglas Fresh."

This generates an even bigger laugh. Daymond steps to the back of the stage and takes a sip of water. He's got the crowd right where he wants them. It's war time.

DAYMOND

Daymond Douglas was born November 16, 1973, in Seminole, Oklahoma. His sister, Katina, had arrived eleven months earlier when Daymond's parents, Charles and Lenora Douglas, were still students at Topeka High School. Charles was a talented basketball player who earned an athletic scholarship to what is now Seminole State College in Seminole, Oklahoma. The young family spent a year there before moving to Muncie, Indiana, where Charles had been recruited to play for Ball State University.

In Muncie, Charles and Lenora had a third child, a boy they named Kevin. In his first year at Ball State, Charles played nearly twenty-three minutes per game but only averaged a little more than two points. Charles was out most of the 1975–1976 season due to ankle injuries; the 6′5″ forward played fewer than seven minutes per game and averaged less than a point.[1] Charles went on to play for two seasons with the Northwest Wreckers, a semi-pro team.

The Douglas family returned to Topeka in 1978. Topeka is home to several large manufacturers, including Hill's Pet Nutrition, best known for its Science Diet pet food brand, snack-food titan Frito-Lay, and Goodyear Tire and Rubber Company. Through family connections, Charles landed a good-paying position at the Goodyear plant, and Lenora got a job packing boxes at Frito-Lay. The family lived in a large house on the west side of Topeka. "We was the only Black family in this neighborhood," Daymond recalls. "It was mostly white kids."

Daymond and his siblings attended Maude Bishop Elementary School; Daymond was heavily into sports. "I was always kind of athletic," he says. "I would try anything. Whether it was riding bikes or playing kickball, tetherball, basketball, baseball."

Some of Daymond's most enduring memories of this time are the material comforts of his family's home. They lived in a large four-bedroom house with a two-car garage and a finished basement. "We had the newest Atari," Daymond recalls. "My dad was the kind of dad who would buy that type of shit. We had a pool table. Even my white friends that would come over, I remember them freaking out. 'You got an Atari *and* a pool table!' Everybody can't just go in their house and play pool. I remember big Christmas trees, dope-ass presents. Anything I seen on TV, that shit was under the tree. We had dogs, a swing set in the backyard. Life was good."

Everything changed dramatically when Daymond's parents divorced when he was in second grade. Lenora took custody of the children, and the four moved to a cramped apartment. "We go from this four-bedroom house, having everything, to the complete opposite," Daymond remembers. "Ain't no pool table, ain't no Atari. We didn't have a dog anymore, wasn't no swing set. My dad wasn't coming around."

The transition was difficult for the entire family, including Lenora, who instantly became a working single mother of three. "It was tough for my mom," Daymond says, adding that, prior to the divorce, "my dad took care of everything. I remember my mom crying so hard. She was just really just fucked up over everything."

The family's stay in the apartment was short-lived. When Daymond was in fourth grade, they relocated to a house on the south side of Topeka. Daymond changed schools. "I had to grow up fast because my dad wasn't around," he recalls. "That's when I came into figuring out who I was as a young man. I had a whole different set of friends, and the south side of Topeka was a little rougher."

The South Side's toughness was reflected in pick-up basketball games, which were more combative than the matches he had played on the West Side. "It was different. It was, 'Nigga, fuck you! I bet y'all ass can't dunk. I'm about to get me thirty this quarter. What's up? Check up.' It was a lot more aggressive."

Daymond attended Highland Park South, now known as Ross Elementary, a racially mixed, low-performing school where almost 90 percent of students are considered low-income.[2] Daymond was athletic and excelled at baseball, football, wrestling, boxing, and karate. He didn't fare as well in his classes. "I had behavioral problems. I wasn't great in school. My dad not coming around and that type of shit."

CARS

Daymond's father, Charles, eventually remarried and had two children, Mychal when Daymond was eleven and Mykesha when he was fourteen. Charles's passion was cars, particularly his 1977 Datsun 280Z. "It was his pride and joy," Daymond remembers. "We used to say he was going to get buried in that car. That was his baby. He didn't keep it stock. My dad was a grease monkey. He changed the cams on it, got the special fuel to race it, the fat-ass tires in back, he painted it. He was just really into cars."

Daymond's memories of his father's car are powerful. "He would come and get us. He wasn't around as much as I would have liked him to be around," Daymond says. "I remember the times he would come and pick me up when I was little. I remember sitting in my dad's car, sitting on my dad's lap, and he would put my hands on the steering wheel. I'm acting like I'm driving. I remember times that my dad would have me in his lap and he would work the pedals and I would steer. When I got a little older, I remember holding on to that steering wheel. I remember feeling the vibration and the power of this car."

Lenora embraced a tough-love parenting style that was intended to make a strong man out of her son. Daymond came home one afternoon crying because he had just lost a fight. His mother ordered him to go back and fight again until he won. "I'm not raising no losers. You're not going to be somebody that runs or tucks they tail," Lenora told her son. "It was that kind of love," Daymond says. "She was a tough mom."

Lenora had issues of her own. She had been involved in a long string of physically abusive relationships. Daymond remembers only one boyfriend who did *not* beat his mother. "I grew up seeing that type of shit," he says. "My mom was dating this Spanish guy. I remember him beating up my mom. I remember seeing my mom with busted lips, black eyes, him just being very violent. I was too young to do anything. I was just so scared."

The treatment was the same with Lenora's other boyfriends. Daymond resented his father's absence during these years. "I felt like my dad could have got us out of that situation or came and got us. If I had a kid and he told me, 'I don't want to go home, my mom's getting beat up,' I would come to the rescue. At the very minimum, I'd be like, 'My kid is coming with me. He's not going to be around this environment. If y'all want to be stupid and beat up on each other, that's your business. But my business is my kid. My kid is not going to be around this. And if you got a problem with that, hey, we can go to court or whatever.'"

Daymond says that his parents' divorce had a huge impact on him growing up, something he did not fully appreciate until later. "Not being able to see my dad, I was fucked up. I took that into my adult life where I would hit my girlfriends. It was a learned behavior. This is what I seen; I seen my dad do it, too. I went to therapy a few times with that because I didn't want to be that type."

To escape his home life, Daymond spent his summers playing sports at the local Boys Club—official matches, pick-up games, basketball, kickball, anything. "When I was on the South Side maze, families didn't have a lot of extra money to put kids into organized sports. I spent a lot of time at the Boys Club, man. That's how we ate lunch. Snacks. Learning how to play basketball and getting into fights damn near every game. I was a sponge back then. I always kind of moved around. I have different sets of friends or whatever, so I would just try to soak up everything I could."

In addition to sports, Daymond also started messing around with music. He played trumpet in the school band, but his real love was hip-hop. Daymond was obsessed with the preeminent rappers and DJs of the day—Big Daddy Kane, LL Cool J, the Juice Crew, and DJ Marley Marl. In the fourth grade, Daymond started rapping with his buddy Raul. "His parents had money," Daymond recalls. "He had a drum machine, he had DJ equipment. We had this little rap group called the DND Crushing Crew, like we're going to be something."

When he was in the seventh grade, Daymond began attending Eisenhower Middle School, a racially mixed institution where 94 percent of students are considered low-income.[3] Daymond's grades bottomed out. He failed so many classes the first year that he had to repeat the entire grade. "I started fucking up early," Daymond recalls. "I flunked because just being mad about my dad, just trying to get some pussy and just doing dumb shit, not really thinking about my education."

Furious, his mother used a friend's address so Daymond could repeat seventh grade at Jardine, a public school located in a wealthy, white enclave on Topeka's west side. Daymond remembers Eisenhower as a mostly Black school, reflecting neighborhood demographics at the time. At predominantly white Jardine, Daymond was one of three Black students in the entire school.

"Where Jardine was at, you can walk in any direction and be like, 'Damn, this motherfucker is *nice*,'" recalls Daymond, who was reluctant to attend. "All I knew at the time was, man, I'm fitting to be around all these white kids. None of my friends was there. Nobody I felt like I could relate to was there."

Daymond got his first job at fifteen, putting in late-night shifts as a busboy at a local Shoney's restaurant. The venue became particularly busy on weekends after midnight as clubgoers departed the local venues in search of late-night fare. Daymond was in awe of the flashy young players whose wealth and power were the envy of the neighborhood. "I remember all them hustlers coming into Shoney's after the club. Jewels, cars, come in stunting. They was loud and shit. They ballers. They have the attitude of like, 'I'll *buy* this Shoney's' and they probably could. They would leave me huge tips."

The hustlers recognized Daymond from the neighborhood. Their approbation felt good to the teenage busboy. "People knew who I was just from being on the block or whatever," Daymond says. "I always hung around somebody that was connected, who knew somebody. 'Nah, man, leave that little nigga alone. That's little D.'"

The biggest impression, however, was the hustlers' access to the high life. Daymond saw it and wanted it for himself. "I wanted Jordans, I wanted jewels, I wanted cars, I wanted women, I wanted all that cool shit that I seen from these cats."

GUCCI GUYS

In the mid-1980s, breakdancing was a prominent element of hip-hop culture, reflected in popular dance-themed movies of the era, such as *Beat Street* and *Breakin'*. One of the hottest acts in Topeka at the time was the Gucci Guys, an outfit that combined DJ-ing, rapping, and breakdancing into a complete show that was a hit with local audiences. Barry recalls being blown away the first time he saw the Gucci Guys performing at a community festival. "They had the DJs, the rapper, the dancer, all the shit. They were doing the damn thing. To us, they were hip-hop icons in Topeka."

Gucci Guys was cofounded by Troy Owens, who began DJ-ing in 1983 after he saw Herbie Hancock perform "Rockit" on television. Troy purchased two turntables from a local pawn shop for thirty dollars and started to experiment with the hand-ful of LPs he owned.

One afternoon, Troy got home from school, where his father was napping on the couch, having just worked a double shift. Troy, who had recently landed a job at the Topeka record store, Mother Earth, started mixing LPs together. "At that time, I didn't know what it was called," he says. "I just knew that I can mix, say, Janet Jackson with Colonel Abrams, and they would be on beat and they would sound good together. That's what I was doing. My dad woke up and looked around and said, 'Well hell, we could rent out a place, throw some parties, you guys can make some money.'"

Troy's father rented out the Jayhawk Theatre, a historic down-town Topeka venue that originally opened in 1926. Troy assumed the stage name Def DJ and recruited some hip-hop-obsessed buddies from Topeka High School, Vandon "DJV" Pittman Rias, Carlos Steele, and Cornell Ross. (Jack Davis, Ricky Steele, Jason Williams, and Bobby Thomas joined later.) The Gucci Guys' debut was a success. "That was our first gig," Troy says. "We didn't have any idea what we were doing but people liked us. We got a following from that."

At the time, Topeka was home to popular outfits such as DJs United, which performed at parties and community centers, playing one song after another like a radio station. The Gucci Guys had something else in mind, dazzling crowds with its two-DJ, four-turntable setup and merging records from Zapp, Joeski Love, and Doug E. Fresh in ear-bending ways. Audi-ences ate it up.

"Initially we were just DJs, and Vandon and Cornell would dance," Troy recalls. "We were doing parties at KU, K-State, Emporia, Atchison. Then Carlos and some of the guys decided they wanted to be rappers, so it ended up being a rap group."

Daymond attended as many Gucci Guys gigs as possible, taking in every sight and sound. In his mind, they were legends. "The Gucci Guys was famous," Daymond recalls. "They had parties on the Jayhawk roof, on the East Lawn, Cushinberry Park. Gucci Guys was the thing to be."

Daymond was inspired and quickly became immersed in hip-hop dance. Topeka is a small city, and by 1986, the thirteen-year-old had become so skilled that Gucci Guys' rapper Carlos Steele recruited him as a backup dancer. "He was young at the time," Troy recalls, "I think he was in high school. But he came around, like one of the last guys to come into the group."

Daymond was recruited strictly as a dancer, but he had other aspirations. "This was back in the day, where hip-hop was dancing, where all the rappers would have dancers," Daymond says. "That's all I did was just dance. Secretly I rapped, but nobody knew. I was determined to be the illest motherfucker that anybody ever heard. I honed my craft every day. If I didn't write a song that day, I didn't feel right. Sixteen bars. I understood a hook, a chorus, a bridge, music."

Daymond soaked up the varied sounds and styles coming from new rap artists of the era, including Eric B. & Rakim, DJ Jazzy Jeff and the Fresh Prince, Salt-N-Pepa, N.W.A., and Naughty by Nature. Taking his stage name from an action movie he watched on late-night television, Daymond dubbed himself MC Hitman. In the ninth grade, MC Hitman performed for the first time at a Highland Park High School talent show, where Daymond combined his rhyme skills with hip-hop-inspired dancing. This was at the height of the New Jack Swing craze, dominated by rap-influenced R&B artists such as Bobby Brown and Guy. Daymond had the looks and moves to pull off a credible version.

Daymond's talent-show set caught the eye of Trinice Thompson, a female rapper who went by the name MC Tae. Daymond invited her onstage to rap a few bars at his next performance, and the audience went nuts. The two became overnight neighborhood celebrities. A local promoter named Curtis Pitts saw the performance and secured the pair a couple of small gigs in Topeka and later at Worlds of Fun, a Kansas City amusement park. After that show, some audience members stopped the fifteen-year-old Daymond and asked for his autograph, the first time it had ever happened. The dopamine rush was immediate. "My autograph? This could be something. This is when I was like, 'I want to do this as a real job.'" Pitts took Hitman and MC Tae on the road, where they performed at community centers and amusement parks across Florida and Texas. The duo eventually went their separate ways, but Daymond left the experience with a thirst for rap music stardom.

Daymond's travels through the southern U.S. caused no issues at home. At fifteen, Daymond was one of three siblings living at Lenora's house, and his mother gave him considerable autonomy. Lenora also had her own problems to contend with. "My mom was real big into letting me be a man at a early age," Daymond says. "My mom never hid drugs from us. She was on drugs for quite some time, smoking weed and then she started doing heavier drugs. She never really shielded me from certain things. She wanted me to get those experiences."

Increasingly, those experiences included more direct knowledge of street life. One of Daymond's high-school buddies, Luke, was a football player with NFL dreams; he and Daymond had bonded over a mutual love of sports. When Luke invited Daymond to spend a summer with his family in his hometown, Tulsa, Oklahoma, Lenora gave her consent. "She let me go for a whole summer," Daymond marvels. "That was a trip. That's when hood-ass Daymond kicked in."

TULSA

In Topeka, Luke was just another high-school football player, but in Tulsa, he was a member of the 107 Hoover faction of the Crips street gang. As soon as he and Daymond got to town, everything changed.

"We Crips," Luke told Daymond.

Daymond was incredulous. "In Oklahoma? Y'all ain't got any Crips out here."

"No, for real," Luke told him.

Having his buddy in the gang made the entire endeavor seem relatively harmless. Before long, Daymond joined too, getting jumped in by half a dozen gang members. "One dude pulled out a knife. I caught it with my hand but he still got me in the side. I was screaming, 'Somebody stabbed me!' After that, I was 107 Hoover Crip."

As a Crip, Daymond was exposed to an entirely new way of life. He spent the summer learning the ins and outs of the criminal trades: "How to bag up weed, how to cut up crack. Learning how to hustle, man. How to make money. We start buying cocaine, rocking it up, learning how to count money, rolling dice. People shooting heroin, crack. That's the first time I ever seen wet. They called it dips—joints dipped in embalming fluid. I've seen bombs, grenades, AR-15s. I learned about guns, how to shoot guns. Knives, how to fight. This was Warrior School. 107 Hoover Crips. They taught me how to throw up the Crip sign, the Hoover sign, 107."

By the time Daymond returned to Topeka for his senior year of high school that fall, he was hustling full time. He and Luke started stealing cars in front of Topeka convenience stores and gas stations. "Back then, people would pull in to a store and run in and grab a pack of cigarettes or something to drink. They would just park and leave the car running. We would jump in their car and take off." The pair would drive the stolen car to Tulsa, where the 107 Hoovers had amassed ties within the local Crip network.

On December 30, 1991, Daymond and Luke were at a Tulsa convenience store, standing outside, debating their next move. They had driven there from Topeka in a stolen car. They were supposed to sell it to some guy, but he never showed up. Now, they wanted to get the hot car off their hands, quick.

They decided to abandon the car at the convenience store. As they talked, a twenty-something white guy pulled into the parking lot in a late-model Cutlass Supreme. Rap music blared from the car's stereo system. The guy seemed alright, so Daymond and Luke asked him for a ride. The guy was easygoing and told them to hop in. Relieved to be rid of the stolen car, they took off.

As they drove, the guy casually mentioned that he sold weed and asked if they needed any. Daymond wasn't a big pot smoker, but Luke was. They drove to the guy's apartment building, and the three went inside. Luke and the dealer went into the bedroom. They came out moments later. "I remember seeing the dude's face," Daymond recalls. "This dude look like he seen a ghost. He looked really shook. He walked past us and I seen my partner. Oh shit, he had a gun on him. He walked him outside."

Dazed at the unexpected turn of events, Daymond heard a commotion coming from the parking lot. He followed the sound. Luke held the dealer at gunpoint and ordered him into the trunk of the car.

"Man, you tripping," Daymond told him.

Luke tried to hand the gun to Daymond. "Pop this motherfucker!" he ordered.

Daymond shook his head. "Hell no!"

As Daymond and Luke bickered, the dealer took off, screaming at the top of his lungs. Lights flickered on throughout the apartment building. Daymond and Luke hopped in the guy's car and raced away, Luke at the wheel. They sped past a police car, which instantly did a U-turn and pursued. Luke took a hard right and stopped. He and Daymond jumped out of the car and ran. Only Luke escaped.

"I was running for a long time," Daymond remembers. "I jumped over this fence and the fence caught my finger and tore it. I'm bleeding. My hand is hurt. When he arrested me, they threw me on the ground, couple of jabs and elbows and shit."

The officer put Daymond in the back of a squad car, pressing him to identify the driver from the chase. "I didn't tell," Daymond recalls. "I didn't say who I was with, I didn't say what happened. They knew I wasn't by myself 'cause they seen two of us jump out the car."

The police told Daymond that if he refused to give them the driver's name, they would charge him with a long list of crimes. He sank lower in his seat. "I ain't never getting out of here," Daymond thought to himself. But he refused to give any names or other information.

According to Daymond, the interrogation took an ominous turn. The police had shut off the streetlights to provide a better view for a helicopter that was circling overhead, scanning the streets for Luke with a spotlight. "I'm by myself. We on this fucking dark-ass street."

"Where's your friend?" the cop asked menacingly.

"I told you, I by myself," Daymond pleaded.

The officer took out his gun, cocked it, and put it to Daymond's temple. "Just give me one reason, just try to run. I'll blow your motherfucking brains out. I'm going to ask you one more time, where is your friend?"

"This motherfucker is going to kill me," Daymond thought to himself. Still, he refused to waver, and the officer eventually holstered his weapon. Daymond was taken to the hospital, where he received stitches for his hand before being brought to jail.

"They had me in this holding cell that smelled like shit and piss," he recalls. "I remember sitting there, crying like a baby thinking I can't believe this shit just happened. I tried to go to sleep. I used a roll of toilet paper as my pillow. Then they moved me to this other cell where it was so overly populated, there was nowhere to sleep. It was a cell that was for maybe four people and there were twenty of us."

The next day, Daymond went through classification, where the jail assigns new inmates to certain wings of the institution. According to Daymond, the jail was segregated by group: whites, Latinos, sex offenders, Bloods, and Crips. "I remember this dude explaining to me like a narrator of a movie, saying, 'You don't want to go to T-Tank. That's where all the Crips is at. People get beat up, they drag people from out of there.'" Daymond decided to keep his gang affiliation to himself, but he was classified a Crip anyway and placed into T-Tank. "This is probably the first time when I was in jail that I was scared. For real."

T-TANK

Daymond was charged with armed robbery, kidnapping, and possession of a stolen vehicle. He was assigned a public defender who encouraged him to accept a plea bargain that included a fifteen-year prison sentence: "You're a young man," the attorney told Daymond. "You'll still be a young man when you get out." The judge assigned to Daymond's case was notorious for the long sentences he handed down to defendants who refused to accept plea bargains. But Daymond had not robbed or kidnapped anyone, so he rejected the deal, opting for a full-blown jury trial instead. This resulted in a long delay. Ultimately, Daymond spent seven months in county jail awaiting trial. "Seven months was hell. I seen people get beat up, attempted murder cases, getting into it with the Bloods. The county jail, man, that shit ain't for nobody."

Although Daymond was classified a Crip and housed within a Crip division of the prison, he had never taken gang membership all that seriously. During Daymond's summer in Tulsa, Luke and some of the other 107 Hoovers got Crip tattoos, but Daymond demurred. In prison, he played down the affiliation. Instead, Daymond turned to his most prized resource, rapping. At the time, there were few rappers in the county jail, and Daymond's skills kept him out of trouble. "Music calms the savage beast. I never got in a fight with anybody. I just rapped. Every day, people would be like, 'Hey Dayme, let me hear something.' I would write something about what was happening at the time in the jail, writing about the guards or about certain situations."

At Daymond's trial, the victim testified favorably for Daymond. "He told the truth," Daymond says. "He said that I didn't do anything, that I was part of the reason why he *didn't* get shot." There were also conflicting accounts from the two arresting officers. One testified that Daymond jumped out of the driver's side of the car, but the other swore that he jumped from the passenger side. The distinction can have legal implications because it can be easier to convict drivers rather than passengers for possession of a stolen vehicle.

Besides his presence during the commission of a crime, there was little evidence of Daymond's guilt. His public defender delivered at a crucial juncture. "He was a badass," Daymond says. "He did what he was supposed to do. He did everything right.

He got up there and cross-examined the detective. [The detective] was saying some crazy shit, just making up shit. My lawyer knew that he didn't have proof of anything. So, my lawyer tore up his ass, for real."

"Do you have any kind of recording?"

"No."

"Do you have any kind of statement?"

"No."

"Do you got any kind of witnesses?"

"No."

"How long have you been a detective?"

Daymond was certain his lawyer had beaten the case. "He really made the officer look incompetent. I felt I was going to go home."

The jury rendered its decision the following day. It acquitted Daymond on the two most serious charges, armed robbery and kidnapping, but found him guilty of possession of a stolen vehicle. Daymond's lawyer argued that because Daymond was the passenger, he was guilty of misdemeanor joyriding, not felony possession. The judge was unmoved. The public defender argued that as a first-time offender who was still in high school, Daymond should be sentenced to time served, seven months. Instead, the judge gave Daymond the maximum sentence, two years in the state penitentiary.

PULLING CHAINS

"When you go from the county jail to prison, they call it pulling chains," Daymond explains. "I pulled chains in July." He was sentenced to spend the next thirteen months in Stringtown, Oklahoma, at Mack Alford Correctional Center (MACC).

MACC is a minimum-security prison that was built in the 1930s. Housing about eight hundred inmates, it is intended to separate first-time prisoners like Daymond from those with histories of incarceration. At MACC, there are no cells, bars, or fences. Inmates sleep in dormitory-style rooms. Thus, in nearly all regards, this state penal institution had better accommodations and was safer than the county jail. Daymond enjoyed spending long stretches outside, working as part of a highway-cleaning crew. There were some Crip-Blood tensions, but they were minor. Daymond was involved in two fights during his time at MACC, both with fellow Crips.

In 1984, Oklahoma passed the Prison Overcrowding Emergency Powers Act, which offered time credits, known as "cap" credits, during periods of overcrowding. Whenever the inmate population exceeded 95 percent of authorized capacity, the state authorized each facility to grant sixty days of credit to nonviolent offenders. These credits were to be given out every sixty days until the capacity was below 95 percent.[4]

Due to cap credits, Daymond was scheduled to be released in spring 1993, about eight months early. On Christmas Eve 1992, however, he was selected for the prison's annual "Christmas kick out," where convicts are released, handed bus tickets, and sent home for the holidays. Thrilled, Daymond gave away all his belongings and joined a celebratory group of fellow inmates. "They're processing everybody. We're high fiving. Everybody's happy because one, we're leaving, and two, it's Christmas. I'm about to see my family at Christmas. Boom. Let's go."

As Daymond stood in line, he heard the phone ring. A few minutes later, the warden pulled him aside and told him the news. Years earlier, a gang-member acquaintance from Topeka robbed a restaurant and gave the police Daymond's name instead of his own. Now the authorities in Kansas wanted to talk to Daymond and had filed an interstate warrant to have him detained. He would be held in Oklahoma for another thirty days before being extradited to Kansas. Daymond stood watching as the other inmates were loaded into passenger vans, headed to the Greyhound bus station.

Technically, Daymond had already been processed out of MACC. Prison bureaucracy made it impossible for him to simply check back in, as one might at a hotel. The state of Oklahoma would have to find another place to keep Daymond for a month until Kansas came to pick him up. That night, there was only one state facility with a spare bed, the Oklahoma State Penitentiary.

OSP is a maximum-security prison located in McAlester, Oklahoma. Built in 1908, OSP has the highest level of security of any prison in the state and includes a death row.[5] It is Oklahoma's oldest prison, far removed from the dorm rooms at MACC. Daymond was housed in a twenty-man unit in the general population, with inmates being processed in and out at all hours of the day and night. "It looked like a dungeon," Daymond recalls. "There was no windows. You just had to assume what time it was based on what you was eating. When the marshals came and got me, I walked outside for the first time in thirty days seeing the sun, my eyes just hurt so bad."

Daymond was extradited to Topeka, where the robbery case against him quickly fell apart. He spent a few days in the county lockup before his lawyer got him off. He stepped out of jail, free for the first time in fifteen months. "I didn't call a ride," he says. "I didn't call nothing. I walked. All the way home."

Daymond wasn't back long before he caught up with Luke and his other gang-member buddies. As soon as Luke heard Daymond was in Topeka, he drove over and picked him up.

"He took me to this house, showed me how to cook crack. He gave me some money, a pistol, and a beeper and said it's on."

Luke had partnered with a local crack addict, whose house had been turned into an open drug market. In exchange for the use of his house, the addict got round-the-clock access to crack and a small cut of the profits. "I made some real quick money," Daymond says. "All we did was drink gin and juice and listen to Dr. Dre's *Chronic* album. Played spades and dominoes and sold crack. All day, every day. I made enough money to buy a car, get some clothes, get on my feet." Daymond even started dating a young woman. Things were looking up.

But Daymond knew he no longer had the heart for the criminal trade. One night, arguing with Luke over their latest drug deal, Daymond decided he'd had enough.

"You know what man, I don't think this is for me, after all the shit I been through."

Luke blamed it on jail. "Jail made you soft. You ain't down no more," he told Daymond.

"No, it ain't that," Daymond countered. "I just got to be smart. I ain't trying to go back to jail."

Luke was partly right—jail had changed Daymond. While incarcerated, Daymond carved a niche for himself, not through his gang affiliation or criminal knowledge but through rapping. And now that he was free, Daymond knew that it was through rapping that he would climb his way to the top.

4

1137 WASHBURN AVENUE

1137 Washburn Avenue, Topeka, Kansas, March 2000

We stand on the front lawn of 1137 Washburn Avenue, Stu's childhood home. This is the house where Stu and Barry spent boyhood afternoons watching TV in the living room, giving way to hip-hop pursuits during their teenage years. It's a small place with an aging roof of gray shingles and white paint peeling from the wooden siding. There's a single step up to the small front porch, which wraps around the side of the dwelling. From the front, two small windows overlook a busy street. A dog chained to a tether-ball pole barks from a nearby yard as traffic whizzes by.

"This is where it began," Stu tells me. "This was my block. I grew up in this house. I lived here for sixteen years." As he talks, Stu pulls on a Newport. An unlit second cigarette is tucked behind his left ear.

Barry steps up beside Stu. "It's got a lot of memories, too much to name," he says, nodding towards the house. "We used to come here every day after school for monster week and shit like that. So much stuff we used to do, man, good, bad, everything. We grew up here. When we moved back, it seemed like something that had to be."

After Stu's father passed away in 1993, his mother gave him the place. Barry moved in not long after. "We were the same age, twenty-three," Stu recalls. "Barry didn't want to go live with his mother; my house was open. I was like, 'Fuck it. Come on, man. You can stay with me.'"

"We ended up all living here," says Barry, who has "1137" tattooed in an arch that spans his abdomen. "It was like family. A lot of us was going through shit where our *family* families, we couldn't contact them, or we were going through shit where they didn't want to be bothered or they wouldn't understand. So we made our own family. We did everything together. One person eating, we all eating. One person starving, we all starving. One person having a problem, we all having a problem. So it was like a *unit*, like a *fist*, all the time."

Stu and Barry's earliest songs were booze-and-weed-drenched party anthems styled after then-popular acts such as Cypress Hill and House of Pain. Stu wanted to recruit a ringer, a skilled MC who could take the group to the next level. Barry continued to float Daymond's name. "Stuart didn't know him, but I knew of him," Barry remembers. "We weren't the best of friends, but we knew each other. I'm like, 'The boy's no punk. He's been handling the business for a while. We should holler at him and see if he want to get down.'"

In 1993, Carlos Steele, a member of the Gucci Guys, introduced Stu to Daymond, hosting a sit-down between the two at his apartment. "I had been hearing about a cat named Dopey Loc or Hitman," Stu recalls. "So when I meet him, I already know who Daymond is. I've heard of him before."

"They already knew of me," Daymond says. "When Carlos is telling Stuart about me, I don't think he told him who he was about to come and meet. Stu was like, 'Oh shit. That's *Hitman*. Everybody knows who he is. If we get Daymond, with his name, they going to take us serious.'"

Stu and Daymond traded verses back and forth, and then Stu invited him to come to the house at 1137 Washburn. "We had a party, kicking it, throwing rhymes back and forth," Stu says. "Everything clicked. From there, the nucleus started."

Stu and Barry were eager to bring Daymond on board, but Daymond had reservations about getting involved with a group. Having served as a backup dancer for the Gucci Guys, he was eager to take center stage. "I always knew it was Stu's group," Daymond says. "At first, I was like, 'I really don't want to be in a group, I want to be a solo artist.' DVS Mindz was already established when I got in the crew. I only had one thing to say: If it ain't real, I ain't fucking with it. That's bottom line." Daymond was in.

Daymond's presence in DVS Mindz changed everything. An experienced MC, he urged Stu and Barry to be attentive to the technical elements of songwriting and to be thoughtful about their lyrics. "Daymond is responsible for more of the structure," Barry says. "Our songs was fun and lighthearted— just fucking around. He got us more into metaphors, to actually talking about some shit and saying it doper than just, 'I did this and that.' Daymond recalls, "I wasn't trying to change anything, I was just trying to enhance it. I listened to some of the stuff they was doing, I was like, 'Y'all can rap, but the timing is off.'"

Daymond had only been in DVS for a few weeks when, on November 4, 1993, they signed up for a rap talent contest held at Washburn University. The show's featured performer was Aaron Yates, an up-and-coming artist from Kansas City who went by the name Tech N9ne. Tech had pioneered a hyperkinetic rap style that involved packing as many syllables as possible into each line, overwhelming listeners with cascades of intricate wordplay. Tech N9ne's jaw-dropping double-time rhymes had earned him high praise and a growing base of devoted fans. He was currently under contract with Perspective Records, a boutique label run by megaproducers Jimmy Jam and Terry Lewis.

The Washburn University talent show was co-organized by Carla Daniels, a mass media major who helped put together events for the student activities board. Carla was not a traditional undergraduate student. She was a twenty-eight-year-old single mother raising two children she gave birth to as a teenager. A welfare recipient when she entered college, Carla worked full-time as a secretary for the Kansas Neurological Institute and went to school at night.

When DVS Mindz arrived at Washburn's campus for the talent show sound check, the somewhat reserved Carla was drawn to the band's energy and charisma, to their natural star power. "Just connecting with them and interacting with them, it put me into that world, that rap world," Carla recalls. "Even before the show, during rehearsals, I was like, 'These guys got something.' And then when I saw them perform, when they got into their performance mode, it was *ridiculous*. I was like 'Okay, okay, they've *definitely* got something.'"

DVS Mindz took the stage at Washburn in front of a 10' × 10' banner that featured the group's name, then spelled Devious Mindz. Stu entered from stage left, rapping over a thunderous beat provided by Gucci Guys turntablist Troy Owens, who was DJ-ing for DVS that night. Wireless mic in his right hand, fist-pumping rhythmically with his left, Stu hollered, "DVS is in the house!" Barry arrived half a minute later, rhyming over an instrumental of A Tribe Called Quest's "Scenario." Daymond came last, sporting a striped T-shirt, baggy pants, tennis shoes, and a White Sox cap. He strode to center stage, flowing rapidly and then freezing into an exaggerated b-boy stance as he hit the last line of his verse.

DVS Mindz would develop into a potent live act, but even at their first concert, the band tore the place up. "Hometown Topeka, coming through your speaker," the three MCs chanted, bobbing and weaving rhythmically. The crowd was totally into it, waving their hands from side to side as the group matched exuberance with verbal skills. "They were electric," Carla Daniels recalls. "We're talking about Das EFX, Sticky Fingas, Onyx, that was their influence. Then here come Method Man, and Redman, so that was their influence. It was a lot of East Coast, New York type, there was some Southern, like Scarface and the Geto Boys. They were just all over the stage killing it. Everyone was like, 'They about to do something, they about to go somewhere.'"

The VIP of the show was Daymond, who bounced off his bandmates and hammed it up for the crowd, doing crab-walking knee dips in time with the music. "Daymond had been rapping long before he had gotten into our group," Stu recalls. "He knew how to get up and control the crowd."

"I learned early on that you could control the crowd," Daymond affirms. "This is where MC came from, right? If you hype, they going to be hype. If you kinda walk around, say nothing, do nothing, slow your energy, you're going to attract what you reflect. So we're hype, jumping around, jumping into the crowd, coming in from the back. We ain't up there flashy, with gold chains, talking about all the shit we got. We're up there rhyming. Period, point blank. Give me the mic, watch what the fuck I do."

DVS concluded their first concert with an embryonic version of "Niggaz (1137)," which would later morph into one of the group's most popular songs. But even at the Washburn talent show, the crowd loved it. "November fourth, 1993, we bombed the set, we blew the spot," Stu recalls proudly. "We went in and killed it."

DVS took second place in the contest that night. They also impressed the attendees, including Tech N9ne, who freestyled with the group after the show. Stu remembers, "That was our first time meeting Tech N9ne. We got to cipher with Tech N9ne, so it was a big deal." Barry recalls that Tech assumed they were signed to a major label. "They sat down and watched our set. He was like, 'I don't understand why y'all ain't signed.' We don't either."

Carla Daniels stopped by after the show and invited the trio to perform at another Washburn event in a few weeks. "We clicked, we just kind of hit it off," she recalls. "I was always interested in the industry. Because I worked in student activities, I got to do contracts, and go to concerts, and bring [musical acts] to campus. So they are listening to me talking about some of the things that I'm doing and they were like, 'Can you manage us?' I had never managed anybody, but I was like, 'Yeah.' That's how it happened. It wasn't even a signed contract; it was word of mouth and a handshake."

DVS Mindz couldn't believe their luck. They had just played their first live concert and rocked the house. They ciphered and networked with Tech N9ne. And to top it off, they had secured a manager who was eager to take them to the next level.

CARLA

What Carla Daniels lacked in music industry experience, she made up for with courage and ambition. "One of my strengths is input," she says. "So with what little knowledge I had, I went and found the information and started working it. 'This group is coming here. Let's go talk to them and see if we can get a show.' I started putting [the band] in front of folks. It was all about going and getting in front of people."

Using the few connections she had in the regional music industry, Carla started bringing DVS Mindz along with her to concerts. The idea was simply to introduce the trio to regional promoters and other industry types in hopes that it might open some doors. In early 1994, she invited the band to an E-40 gig in Kansas City and then to a Das EFX performance in Omaha. The guys were awestruck. "We're backstage for that one," Stu recalls. "They're taking us around like we're a part of the show. Carla was the one that got us in all that."

"It was crazy," Carla recalls. "The reason I really wanted to get them to that show was because, for Stu, Das EFX, that was it. They got to go to the room. When they got to meet Das EFX, I thought Stuart was going to *explode.* He was like, 'I could have died and gone to heaven that day.' It was just amazing."

A couple of weeks after that, in February 1994, Carla and the group were in Lincoln, Nebraska, hanging out backstage at a Boss and Onyx concert. There was inclement weather, and the promoter received word that the headliners would be delayed. The audience had started filing into the venue an hour ago. Frantic, the promoter approached Daniels and the group. "Hey, do you guys rap? Could you go out and do a thirty or forty-five-minute set?"

The three MCs looked at each other. No one said a word. Finally, Barry broke the silence, telling the guys, "Let's just do what the fuck we do, we ain't got shit to lose."

Moments later, DVS Mindz was ushered onstage. The venue held a thousand patrons and was nearly sold out. "I remember just how big the stage was and how many people were there," Barry recalls. "To be able to be on a stage that big, out of town, being local rappers out of state, nobody's heard of us or our music, to see that many people. You could just feel the energy from all three of us."

If this was a movie, DVS would have brought the house down. Instead, the band was heckled. "There were people out there booing us when we first started," Stu recalls. "But by the time we ended, we got the *okay*." Stu imitates the audience, clapping halfheartedly.

Indifferent concertgoers aside, performing their first show at a major venue and opening for nationally known headliners offered a glimpse of the big time. The promoter was impressed enough to book DVS for another performance, this time opening for Oakland rap legend Too Short. The second attempt went better.

Carla recalls that, even in the early days, the group had a natural charisma that drew attention. Hanging out backstage, the members of DVS Mindz may have been nobodies, but they *seemed* like somebodies. They were cool looking and carried themselves like stars. "You have these [famous rappers] with name recognition and then you had DVS just out there doing their thing. They was always on a professional level, they were always on their business. But they started getting fans and groupies just like that [snaps fingers]. 'We saw you all onstage, who are you?' The mental was just like, it was electric. The guys in the band were feeling it. Because they really started seeing, 'Oh we really got something. We really can do this.'"

A new song called "Gett 'Em Up" reflected the group's growing self-assurance. Inspired by Run-D.M.C.'s back-and-forth rhyming, Stu, Barry, and Daymond concocted an intricate three-way rap that was a step up from anything they'd previously written.

The trio captured the song on a borrowed four-track recorder, huddled around a single microphone in the living room of 1137 Washburn, clutching over-ear headphones and passing a pint of Hennessey between takes.

By the end of the session, everyone agreed that "Gett 'Em Up" was on another level. "'This is it,'" Daymond thought to himself. "Before that point, didn't nobody really know each other. We were still feeling each other out. That song was built, then we recorded it, it was over."

Daymond moved into 1137 a few days later. It was time to put everything else aside and go all-in on music.

HIP-HOP 360

Stu had his $50,000 windfall to keep everyone afloat for a while, so he, Daymond, and Barry focused on DVS Mindz full time. They cleared everything out of 1137 Washburn's living room, and two DJs from the Gucci Guys, Troy Owens and Vandon Pittman Rias, set up their turntables. Stu sprung for a twenty-four-channel mixing board and a pair of massive speakers. At first, DVS did not have original beats or any way to record songs. Everyone usually rapped a cappella or rhymed over the instrumental versions of popular rap numbers. Undeterred, the group focused almost exclusively on writing lyrics and developing their delivery and vocal technique. "It was hip-hop 360," Stu recalls.

Because the trio lived together, DVS Mindz instituted a collaborative songwriting process. One member would suggest a topic or concept, and everyone would go off and write individually. The band would come back together later and share their ideas. Living room and front porch ciphers could go on for hours, sometimes until dawn. "We'd be up all night, watching the sun come up, creating music," Daymond recalls. "Vandon had all of his equipment in Stuart's house. Troy had his turntable setup in Stuart's house. There was always somebody there. It was just family."

Round-the-clock creativity characterized life at 1137 Washburn during this period. "We were always at the house," Barry remembers. "We didn't really go anywhere. Everything used to pretty much come to us. They come over, bring all their shit. Turntables and all that shit set up in the house where you think it was a house party, but no. Motherfuckers would get a wild hair. 'I got an idea for a song!' And we go right over and start fucking around. We were really tight back then."

Through this process, through endless hours of writing and rapping together, DVS forged a sound grounded in ciphering, where lyrical prowess took precedence over everything else. The trio's standout quality was the way they rhymed as a unit, verbally weaving in and out of one another. "Something everybody said about us was, 'Y'all really feed off each other, y'all really understand each other's styles. Y'all can rap each other's verse like you wrote it.'" Daymond says. "Part of that is because we lived together. We knew each other's strengths and weaknesses. We would help each other. Everybody wrote their own raps, but it always was, 'That's dope, but say it like this.' We would study each other. So it was more than just a rap group. We gelled together just naturally. But it took some time to get like that."

The band cooked up "Check the Kids from Kansas," a new song that showcased their growing rhyme skills. Influenced by Das EFX and Native Tongue hip-hop of the era, the track offers a glimpse of DVS in their formative stages. The group members were still developing their signature delivery styles, but the trio's dynamic interplay reflected the vibe DVS was creating at 1137 Washburn every night. The song's lyrics embraced Kansas, inviting listeners to "follow the yellow brick road back to the land of Oz," and making it sound like this unheralded region was the center of the universe.[1]

1137 Washburn was ground zero for DVS Mindz, an artist's studio and party pad where weed, alcohol, and rap music flowed at all hours. A constant stream of friends and associates came through to hang out, party, and rap, and the house became known to all as simply 1137. "It was a party every day," Barry says, laughing. "From eleven in the morning until whenever the hell everybody left, it was just crazy. It was wild. There was no less than thirty motherfuckers in our house, always. Just hangin' the fuck out. Man, we loved every minute of it."

DJ Troy Owens, who worked the turntables for many a late-night session at 1137, recalls, "It was a bunch of young males having free rein to do whatever they wanted. Refrigerator full of beer, weed everywhere. Typical young adults having fun. I remember a lot of partying over there. They wanted to do the music full time. For the most part, that was all we did."

Barry, Stu, and Daymond each had one of the three bedrooms at the house. The living room served as a hangout for a handful of regulars, including a pair of sixteen-year-old high-schoolers who loved rap music—Daymond's younger brother Kevin and his best friend and cousin De'Juan. "They used to come by after school to hang out and listen to us practice," Barry recalls. "They used to rap, too, fucking around. They would battle us when they would come over and vice versa, just to keep everybody sharp. From there it just started to grow, like wherever we go, they'd be with us. Then it just turned into some family shit."

This group of friends, girlfriends, musicians, and partygoers formed the inaugural version of the Crew, a fluid collective of inner-circle DVS Mindz fans that performed key services for the band, including transportation, promotion, counseling, financial support, and security. Female members of the Crew, including wives, relatives, girlfriends, and short-term hookups, provided additional emotional and monetary support. Everyone helped affirm the group's appeal during live performances.

The Crew hung out with DVS at 1137 and attended all their shows, cheering and rapping along to each song. Members of the Crew came and went, but their involvement was always related to their appreciation for DVS Mindz as a band. The Crew's personal connection to the group only amplified their fandom.

With so many people hanging out at 1137, there was essentially a concert slash jam session every night. Rather than merely rehearsing, DVS and friends performed for the Crew and anyone else who showed up. These early audiences provided a critical sounding board for new ideas, and the band spent countless hours perfecting a live act that became second to none. "They developed it," says Troy Owens about the group's live show. "That came from practice. Early on, they were just kind of on stage being themselves. But the more shows they did, the more they interacted with the crowd, it fueled them to do a better performance. They all loved it. They had a passion for it."

DVS Mindz was willing to appear anywhere that would have them. Troy says that one of his favorite DVS concerts of all time took place at a Hastings bookstore. "It was more like kind of a ad-libs session. We hadn't practiced or anything, and I hadn't let them hear any of the instrumentals I was going to use. It was just kind of all off the top of our heads. There was no cussing, just them rapping about whatever. It was one of the best shows I ever heard them do. Ever. To this day. They were phenomenal."

As DVS began to perform more frequently, word circulated among promoters that this was a hot act that could hype up a crowd. Carla began to secure bookings at bigger venues, sometimes in Lawrence, Kansas City, or even Omaha, with DVS opening for nationally known acts such as Das EFX, DRS, and Black Moon. "I was calling, trying to get on shows," Carla recalls. "Whatever I could do to get them out there, performing, which is what they loved."

These experiences were thrilling, but they yielded little or no revenue. The promoters would pay huge amounts of money to hire a famous headliner and get locals like DVS to open for free. The band rarely got a check at the end of the night, but they gained exposure, the opportunity to perform in front of large audiences at prestigious venues, and—most importantly—personal contact with the headliners. "It was really getting you in front of the artist that they're bringing," Carla explains. "Because now you're in the green room. You're backstage, you get this access that you don't have if you're just in the audience. That's where the crazy stuff happened, in the green room. Because people are just walking around back there, chilling and getting ready. They're having rap offs and little low-key battles with artists. It really gave them a first-hand look on what it's like when someone sends you on tour—how it is when people bring you out, and what to expect, and how to act. So, they may not be able to pay you, but they kind of treated you like they were paying you. You had food and stuff to drink, and green room status."

Of course, a band cannot pay for airfare or hotels with green room status. Traveling to out-of-town shows was costly, and everyone was expected to pay their own way. "We were all coming out of pocket for the stuff," Carla recalls. "So if we was going out of town, ante up the money. We'd spend all the money we had renting a car and getting where we needed to go or buying airfare. Sometimes we all had to room up together. We were all sleeping in one hotel room because that was all the money we had. We had to do what we had to do."

The traveling and late nights began to take their toll on Carla, who continued to work full time, attend college, and raise two young children. As DVS's ambitions grew, managing the band required more and more work. Carla found assistance from Randy Smith, Barry's best friend from high school and a recent member of the Crew.

RANDY

Randy and Barry had spent two years playing sports and hanging out in high school. After graduating in 1988, Randy moved to St. Joseph, Missouri, where he stayed after finding work in a pork slaughterhouse. Randy was also a full-time single father to his son, Randy Jr., who was born in 1991.

Randy returned to Topeka in 1994, quitting his job at the slaughterhouse and taking a position as a maintenance man at Blue Cross Blue Shield. Within months, Randy had worked his way up to the payroll office. "You know how they say, 'Get a job in the mailroom?' That's basically what I did," he explains. "I was able to get in there with a small position doing maintenance. Once I got my foot in the door, I just worked myself up the ladder. The next four jobs, I got 'em, and ended up working in payroll. Payroll was my thing. To me it was basically math. Making pretty good money, working with numbers on the regular."

As soon as Randy moved back to Topeka, he rekindled his friendship with Barry and became a Crew member at 1137. "That was the hangout spot," Randy recalls. "It became a daily thing. I was always there, but I ended up going back home at the end of the day."

Randy was busy working at Blue Cross Blue Shield and taking care of his son, but he was intrigued by the business of music.

From a distance, he watched the dealings of DVS Mindz and Carla. "I was just a fly on the wall," Randy recalls. "I was at Eleven-Third and I would see Carla around. I'd be in the cut, just listening to what they were talking about, what their plans were, and how they were moving. I found it interesting, what her role was with DVS—more like a business role. I've always liked the business side of things. I don't rap. The man behind the scenes has always been my thing. So, I'm learning. I'm soaking up as much as I can."

Randy was the same age as Barry and Stu, but with his white-collar job and businesslike demeanor, he seemed older, more grown-up. He acted the part, too, assuming the role of the band's big brother and keeping an eye on everyone. "Randy was probably the most mature out of all of them," Troy Owens recalls. "He was the one that was focused on keeping them on track to do things."

According to Troy, everyone in the band carved out a niche for themselves within the DVS stratosphere. "Stuart was the unofficial leader of the group. Barry was always the life of the party. He was the most charismatic one of the group. Daymond was a little more reserved. He didn't really open up to people he didn't know. There were a lot of heads butting. They have strong personalities and they kind of clash at times."

With the band focused on music, Stu's dwindling $50,000 windfall was the primary source of money. He doled it out generously. "Stuart took care of us," Daymond says. "He's the one who had all the money, because his mom gave him the house and his dad left him some money. Early on, Stuart paid for everything. I'm talking about nights where if it wasn't for Stuart, we would not have ate. Stuart has one of the biggest hearts ever. He didn't have to do that because we were grown men. The only thing that matter to Stu was he just wanted to be there with his brothers creating memories, being creative with music. Because it wasn't the same if all of us were somewhere else. We all needed to be there."

Stu was so bighearted that his cash was eventually gone. "I blew through it in a year," he admits. "Friends moved in. I'm buying cars, I'm buying rims, I'm buying stereos, I'm buying drinks, I'm eating out. I'm buying clothes. I'm doing everything that I'm not supposed to do."

With Stu's savings depleted, the group started to let things slide at 1137. They stopped paying the gas bill. Then the phone got shut off. Someone sold the lawnmower, so the yard became overgrown and weedy. After the house's lone toilet broke, everyone started peeing in the sink.

Stu went back to work in September 1994, landing a job with the Youth Project, which refurbished homes and organized community service projects in conjunction with AmeriCorps. At night, he put in shifts as a janitor. He was still broke. In part, this was due to his covering the bills at 1137 but also from dual child-support payments. "It was a depressing time," Stu recalls. "Working two jobs and having no car, no water in the house, no money. I gotta ask for rides. I gotta ask people to use their bathroom, to take showers and baths. Begging for money for liquor. Stealing from the grocery store just to get food. I felt like I would never get out of this rut of just working and having no money."

The one utility Stu paid faithfully was the electric bill, enough to keep the beer cold, the PlayStation humming, and the music flowing. With the gas shut off, everyone used portable heaters in their bedrooms during winter, causing the electric bill to soar. "Everything was ran off of electricity," Stu recalls. "The bills were so high throughout the winter, you're trying to catch up in the summertime. Barely get close and then [claps hands together], another six or seven-hundred-dollar electricity bill. The water got cut off. We got behind on that bill. It did get turned back on, but we didn't have any hot water. If all you have in the house is electricity, you're only going to be able to do so many things. We had electricity to run the turntables and the music, so that's what we did. Just dive straight into music."

THE MIDBEST

DVS Mindz's earliest recordings were created in the living room of 1137, using whatever equipment could be borrowed from Crew members, who would typically double as producers. Vandon Pittman Rias had a Tascam four-track cassette recorder, and used it to capture a few of the band's initial songs. But Rias was not an experienced record maker and had only limited time to hang out at 1137. DVS did not have any recording equipment or an in-house producer who could record the band at all hours.

"We learned how to perform before we learned how to record," Daymond recalls. " 'Cause we didn't have a studio. We didn't really record like that. We was writing a lot of music but we wasn't recording it." Nascent living room demos such as "Gett 'Em Up" and "Katchin Wreck" are lost, possibly forever.

From the moment DVS began writing songs, the group situated itself within Topeka, Kansas, and the Midwest. Regional specificity is inherent in early DVS tracks such as "Check the Kids from Kansas" and "Central Time Zone," where the lyrics index specific locations, neighborhoods, schools, and local landmarks. Kansas was immortalized in the 1939 movie *The Wizard of Oz*, which began and ended on a farm. Considered by some to be the most-watched film of all time, *Oz* helped cement a still-prevailing image of Kansas as wholesome and dreary. One of the movie's signature lines, "We're not in Kansas anymore," has become a universal metaphor for departing the mundane.

DVS Mindz sometimes drew upon these images in their lyrics, but they believed Kansas was misunderstood, typecast as rural and backward. In their songs, the trio describes Topeka— sometimes called Top City, Cop City, T-Town—as being on par with large coastal cities in terms of violence, drugs, and gangs. Kansas is depicted as the opposite of mainstream, white, middle-class America. They sometimes rename it "Klansas," a reference to the state's history of racial turmoil.[2] In other songs, "Skanlass" combines the words scandalous and Kansas, insinuating that the Free State is not all corn fields and tractors.

DVS situated Topeka and Kansas within a larger Midwestern framework that it defined along the lines of rap's three major geographical areas: the East Coast, the West Coast, and the South. DVS describes "midbest" rap as a blend of rap subgenres from other parts of the country, which intersect in the Midwest to create a distinct sonic bouillabaisse. "There's so many people here, so many different cultures and religions," Daymond says. "The Midwest is right in the middle, and everybody kind of migrate to the Midwest and it brings the sound. We don't speak just for DVS Mindz, we speak for Topeka. We speak for our Midwest region. Midwest, bottom line, off the top, for real. And we're going to keep holding that down for life. DVS Mindz for life. It ain't a motherfucking name, it's a way of life."

DVS insisted that the entire region had been ignored by the rap music industry. "We're just the unseen. Zero visibility," Stu says. Daymond adds, "We all feel like we're in the lost civilization, being from the Midwest. West Coast, down South, East Coast done already blown up. The Midwest is getting overlooked. We about to wake everybody up though."

HOW CAN I BE DOWN?

With Carla at the helm, DVS Mindz spent nearly two years pursuing a major-label record deal. "Back then, the only way in was through the A&R [artists and repertoire] people," Carla explains. "They were gods of the industry. You had to go through these gatekeepers. That's how you got in. You had to do whatever you had to do to make it. There was no YouTube, there was no Facebook. You couldn't just sit and post videos all day and get millions of likes and then be Instagram famous. No. You had to get likes the hard way—in person."

DVS Mindz was developing a positive reputation within the Kansas City metropolitan region; Carla's goal was to take them national. She and the band began traveling to cities like Atlanta, Dallas, San Francisco, and Chicago, networking with industry insiders, hanging out backstage at concerts, and trying to make connections. "Listen, them are some hard-working brothers," Carla recalls. "They would go to their jobs, and then come back and perform. Go to shows, go to the studio, do whatever they had to do, take care of their families. Especially when you're talking about they got kids."

Randy, who had always been interested in the music business, began helping Carla here and there, doing odd jobs, making flight arrangements, and booking rental cars. "Nobody else was really taking on that," Randy recalls. "That's where I fit in. 'I need your information; I need to book this.' And that is where the beginning of the seed started as far as my involvement with them. Because I was just watching Carla. She asked me to do some very minor things. I was pretty much under her wing, just wanting to know what I could do to help out."

In 1994, Carla and DVS Mindz flew to Miami to attend How Can I Be Down?—a multiday rap-music industry conference.

At a series of workshops, panels, clinics, and concerts, the band rubbed elbows with rappers, producers, record company employees, and promoters. Daymond got into a cipher with Method Man and Inspectah Deck of the Wu-Tang Clan. The group played their demo to a pair of executives from Def Jam.

The reaction was always the same: no one could believe DVS Mindz was from Kansas. "That's all we got all the time," Daymond says. "Nobody believed us. They thought it was a gimmick. Because of the way we rapped. That was our gift and our curse. When they would find out where we were from, we would get shit like, 'There's Black people in Kansas? They got hip-hop in Kansas?'"

But all doubts were erased when DVS performed in concert, showcasing their frenetic stage spectacle for fans and industry figures. As always, the live act impressed everyone who saw it. Carla recalls, "When you perform locally, you're like, 'Okay this is a hometown show. These folks are going to tell us we're hype because we live here.' But when we went out of state and they got that vibe and fire, they was like, 'Oh no. this is legit. We legit.'"

DVS Mindz appeared to be on the verge of striking gold, landing a major label deal that would serve as entree into the music industry. At the time, anything seemed possible, everything within reach.

The band's star was rising. There were fans and groupies, but also industry sharks seeking easy prey. "There was a lot of outside influence," DJ Troy Owens says. "That's part of the music industry. Somebody's always telling somebody, 'You're better without them.' You hear a lot of that. They may or may not listen to it, but that's broken up many a group."

After an especially dynamic performance in Miami, a brawny thirty-something guy approached Daymond and introduced himself. His name was Leon, and he was from the Bronx, where he was starting an independent label called Peerless Records. Leon claimed to have financial backing and a growing roster of artists under development deals.

"I like your performance," Leon told Daymond. "I got a question. Where are you from?"

"I'm from Kansas." Daymond replied.

"Man, you lying. Where are you from for real?"

Daymond rolled his eyes and showed Leon his driver's license.

"Oh shit, you really *are* from Kansas," Leon said. "Listen, I'm starting a label and I want you to be part of it, but I just want *you*. There's something about you. I want you."

Daymond demurred. He was part of a group, a member of DVS Mindz.

"Yeah, I understand that," Leon told him. "But there's some money in this and I see a whole vision for you. It will be just like Method Man did with Wu-Tang Clan. He's a member of the group, but he branched out and did his own thing. It was still love. He's still in the Wu-Tang and they do they music, but he can also look out for himself."

Leon took down Daymond's number and handed him a business card. "Give me a call when you get back to Kansas and let's talk."

Daymond didn't say a word to Carla or the guys in DVS about Leon and Peerless Records, but he phoned when he returned to Topeka. The two talked more over the next several weeks, and Leon offered Daymond a contract with Peerless.

Daymond was ecstatic, but he was unsure how the group would react. He called Stu and told him everything. "I met this dude in Miami, we've been in contact. He just wants me as a solo artist."

Stu was on board with the plan to launch Daymond as a solo act, who would also record as a member of DVS Mindz. "Let's do it," Stu told Daymond without hesitation. "Whatever is going to put us on to do whatever we need to do. This is just another avenue for us to get into the industry. But you gotta tell everybody else."

Daymond called a meeting with the band, Carla, and Randy. He told them the plan. Everyone but Stu hated the idea of Daymond releasing a solo album. Method Man became a solo artist *after* Wu-Tang blew up, not before. They told Daymond he was being selfish and operating behind their backs. They accused him of abandoning DVS right as the group was about to be offered their own major-label recording contract.

Daymond was furious that DVS would stand in the way of his deal with Peerless. "I could have just signed a contract and just did whatever I wanted to do and not tell y'all *shit*," he fumed. "But I respect you all enough to sit down like men and say, 'This is the situation, this is how I want to spin it.' I'm not trying to be slick. I could have just did it but I didn't."

In the end, Daymond never took the deal with Peerless. The experience left him embittered, feeling like he had surrendered his goals for the good of the group. Now, if DVS Mindz failed to make it, Daymond's sacrifice would have been for nothing.

5

UNSIGNED HYPE

The Granada, Lawrence, Kansas, October 29, 1998

"Can I have everyone's attention please?" the official's voice intones brusquely. "I need *everybody's* attention. People, quiet down. This is Special Agent Detainya with some more information. We are tracking a group of psychotic hip-hoppers known as DVS Mindz. They may be among us. So we need you to carefully and quickly exit the building."

It is two days before Halloween, and DVS Mindz has been tapped at the last minute to open for M.O.P. and Hieroglyphics, two respected nationally known acts. Being a Thursday night in a college town, the Granada is abuzz with hip-hop devotees, mostly KU students.

From the intercom, a devilish baritone drones, "You ain't goin' nowhere, bitch. Ahahahhahaha! DVS Mindz is in the house, and we about to set this place on fire, Halloween style. Coming straight from the old school, the underground, the original hip-hoppers, the psychotic axe murderers on the microphone, DVS Mindz!"

The group members stand just off the stage, dressed as iconic characters from famous horror movies. Daymond enters first with both hands raised into fists. He is the Invisible Man, sporting a trench coat and Fedora hat, his face and head wrapped in bandages. Stu is next, appearing as Hannibal Lecter from *Silence of the Lambs*. He is outfitted in a makeshift straitjacket and strapped to a refrigerator dolly. He is wheeled to center stage by Barry, who is outfitted like Jason Vorhees, the maniacal killer from *Friday the 13th*. Barry untethers Stu's bindings. Stu breaks free from the straitjacket, extending his arms like wings. Behind the group, Troy and Vandon, the two DJs, are done up as skeletons. De'Juan, the teenage Crew member, is Leatherface, the serial killer from *The Texas Chainsaw Massacre*. De'Juan is clad in a yellow butcher coat, his face covered with a ghoulish mask. He looks out over the audience, waving a full-sized chainsaw as strobe lights flash.[1]

The introductory music fades, and a nimble beat kicks in. Onstage, the movie monsters spring to life. Daymond peels off his trench coat and throws it into the audience. He sports sweatpants, boots, and a sleeveless white T-shirt with "DVS Mindz" scrawled on the front in black magic marker. "Where y'all at?" he yells to the audience, pumping his fist as the band launches into their opening number.

"We're really known for our live show," Daymond told me the first time I interviewed him, about a year after the Granada concert.

If you just get up there and rap, you might as well just put your box up there and play the tape. Especially when people are paying their money to see a show, you got to give 'em a show.

We taking it back to the roots. Afrika Bambaataa, Soulsonic Force, when they have the feathers in the big hats and the synthesizers. That was a live-ass show. That's why I like them rock 'n' roll motherfuckers. They just go out. That's why we get the respect that we do—because when we get on stage, we're going to give you a show. We're looking at it from the viewer's perspective. If I'm going to pay my money to see a show, I don't want to see a motherfucker get up there and walk back and forth rhyming. I want to see some LL Cool J shit, jump out the box. Big Daddy Kane come up in a jacuzzi and some hoes. That's some real shit. That's a motherfucking show. Let's do some shit like that. We ain't financially stable to jump out a big ass dragon or nothing like that, but if we did have it like that, we'd fly in on a dragon.

By 1998, DVS had spent four years performing in Topeka, Lawrence, and Kansas City and had developed a reputation as a reliable act that arrived on time and delivered a professional-grade show. Promoters such as Jeremy McConnell, who organized concerts from 1992 to 1997 for a hip-hop-themed periodical called *Flavorpak*, put DVS in front of hip-hop heads in KC and Lawrence. Bill Pile at Avalanche Productions scored the trio choice opening slots where they performed for the hordes of KU college students who filled downtown Lawrence venues.

For the Granada Halloween show, the group opens with a boisterous "Rowdy Hip Hoppers," where the MCs playfully portray themselves as action-movie special agents, raiders of lost lyrical arks. As Stu, Daymond, and Barry trade bars back and forth, they name-check everything from Monster X, a three-headed dragon from Godzilla comic books, to actor John Cusack and his 1985 teen comedy, *Better Off Dead*. "Rowdy Hip Hoppers" features little musical variation and no hook, but there is a chanted refrain that doubles as a declaration: "Mad truth to the rumor we the shit."

All those ciphers, those thousands of hours spent rhyming together at 1137, combined with hundreds of gigs in front of every imaginable audience, have sharpened DVS Mindz into a supremely skilled live act. Working as a unit, the trio passes around the "lead" to one MC, who raps his verse. The other two rappers back the lead by punctuating and accenting certain words, interlacing the main lyric. The lead is continually passed around, with the other two verbally ducking and diving about as backup before someone else takes over. Put all together, with the three MCs weaving in and around each other at topflight, it is a dazzling display of musicianship. DVS's frenzied verbal melding is so renowned that the trio gave it a name—the three-headed dragon.

On stage, the trio pair lyrical firepower with perpetual motion. Whichever MC has the lead positions himself up front, near the center, rhyming as hard as possible and punctuating the words with synchronized hand gestures and arm flings. The lead rapper is flanked by the other two MCs, who crouch, dodge, spin, and whirl from one side of the stage to the other. All the while, the MCs continually acknowledge and interact with the audience members.

"There's a lot of people whose music is great but whose live show sucks," says Barry, who devises the band's elaborate concert entrances. He describes a process where the group scrutinizes each element of their live performances for areas of improvement. "We think of things like, 'Why this side of the room wasn't moving? What do we need to do to make that side do this? What was going on that made all them get to tripping that it got everybody doing this?' So our show is much better each time. That's what we do. We don't just rap. We see what we can do next to make it better."

Randy, who watched DVS develop through endless rehearsals at 1137, says that the group's growing fan base stems almost entirely from their live act. "If you see them live, they'll make a believer out of you," he tells me around the time I meet the group. "Them niggas got mad skills. The live performance is tight, the words that they sayin' is tight, the way they interact with the crowd, from the beginning to the end. And even when they do their skits before the shows, all of them has been tight. There ain't too many groups out there that are trying to put it out like them. These niggas got live shows for your ass."

DVS's killer concerts are their primary calling card, a point of differentiation that helps them to stand out in a crowded marketplace. But as the band's star continued to rise, they encountered increasingly stiff competition.

STREET BUZZ

In the pre-social-media era, before artists were able to stream and promote their music online, concert venues were essential sites of interaction for local musicians. Performance spaces were also crucial for promotion and networking, a way to get an act's name out to audiences as well as booking agents, producers, DJs, fellow musicians, and other industry workers. Topeka had few venues dedicated specifically to live music and even fewer that booked rap acts. This, along with Topeka's geographical isolation from Kansas City and Lawrence, led to insular rap microscenes that were small and fragmented.[2]

Lamenting the lack of resources for musicians in the regional scene, music critic J. J. Hensley wrote, "In rap, club appearances are few and far between, limited to low-profile sets at dance halls, such as Tremors in Lawrence, or opening slots when national hip-hop tours roll through town. Radio support is all but nonexistent, meaning street buzz and spins from friends at clubs provide the only means for getting music out to listeners."[3]

Another way to get music to listeners during this time was through record stores, which was where many people purchased CDs. Kansas City, Lawrence, and Topeka were home to numerous new and used record shops. Corporate music chains such as Streetside Records were popular, as were national retailers that sold music, such as Best Buy. These outlets trafficked largely in mainstream, popular fare and devoted little or no shelf space to local bands. Hastings, an entertainment retailer with stores in Lawrence and Topeka, carried some regional releases, and there were a handful of record stores that were active promoters: Mother Earth in Topeka, Love Garden Sounds in Lawrence, and Seventh Heaven, Love Records, Groove Farm, Spiny Normans, Recycled Sounds, and the Music Exchange in KC featured extensive local-music selections, based on consigned deals with regional acts, including rap artists.

The best-known rapper from Topeka at the time was Evil-Loc, whose 1995 self-released cassette, *The 10th Book*, received regional accolades. Loc's calling card was horrorcore, a rap subgenre that takes violent topics, sounds, and images from Hollywood slasher flicks and spins them into cinematic yarns of carnage and murder. On the cover of *The 10th Book*, Loc poses in a graveyard holding a scythe à la the grim reaper. His 1998 follow-up, *2-Deep-N-The-Game*, reportedly sold seventeen thousand copies.[4] Although DVS was friendly with Evil Loc, and the two acts performed together on occasion, Loc's horrorcore was distinct from DVS's lyrical approach.

The biggest name in regional rap was easily Tech N9ne, the Kansas City–based MC who DVS had ciphered with after their first show. For years, Tech had worked to make a name for himself in a music scene dominated by alternative rock and metal bands. He recorded an album for Perspective, the label run by Jimmy Jam and Terry Lewis, but it was never released.

Tech then signed with Qwest Records, which was owned by Warner Bros. Again, he completed an album that was shelved, but his collaboration with QD3, son of Quincy Jones, brought him to the attention of the major recording labels. In 1997, his song "Questions" appeared on the soundtrack to Tupac Shakur's film, *Gang Related*. The collection, which was released by Death Row Records, also featured tracks by Ice Cube, Snoop Dogg, and Shakur. For a relatively unknown artist from the Midwest, these feats were astonishing.

Another rising star in KC were the 57th Street Rogue Dog Villians, a hardcore rap outfit that intermittently featured Tech N9ne as a member. Tech N9ne and the RDVs, as they were known, scored a local underground hit in 1998 with a song titled "Let's Get Fucked Up." Buoyed by an earworm refrain, the track was an unapologetic ode to gangsta-rap hedonism, a vividly described subterrane where crews of men hung together, smoking honey-cognac blunts, swilling hard liquor, and getting backstage blowjobs from star-struck "hoes." The song's slow-crawling, head-knocking beat intensified the sonic experience by underscoring every syllable of its bawdy lyrics. Despite receiving no airplay on mainstream radio, "Let's Get Fucked Up" was a sensation, big enough to make local celebrities out of the RDVs, who paraded around KC in a tricked-out Chevy van plastered bumper to bumper with the band's logo and images. The van's bass heavy stereo system pulsated RDV tunes that could be heard a block away. The RDVs' independent record label, Hogstyle, moved thousands of copies of the group's CD, *It's On Now*, through local and regional music outlets.[5]

The attention generated by these acts helped put the spotlight on Kansas City rap like never before. At the time, rap music was known for broad geographic divisions—East Coast, West Coast, and the South—that yielded further distinctions. As the twenty-first century drew near, there was a sense that the Midwest was unclaimed territory; there was a once-in-a-lifetime opportunity for a Midwestern artist to break through and elevate the entire region to the national level. Tech N9ne and the RDVs seemed poised for larger things, but new aspirants cropped up continually, elbowing to become the Jay-Z or Tupac of the Midwest.

"This has to be our time," Randy insisted. "The East did they thing, West did they thing, and the South ran with it. The industry is going to start looking more in the Midwest. Surely it's got to be our time."

A CAPPELLA

DVS is two songs into their Halloween set at the Granada when Daymond yells for DJs Troy and Vandon to stop the music. "Wait a minute! Cut the beat," he says. The backing track halts abruptly, and Daymond continues. "Yo, I don't think they felt you," he says to Stu, who shakes his head, agreeing. Daymond shouts to the crowd, "Y'all want to hear my man Str8jakkett go a cappella so y'all know it's real?" The audience roars in approval. Daymond looks at Stu. "Go a cappella, nigga. So they won't forget DVS Mindz runs this motherfucker."

Stu strides to center stage and waves his hand to the people up front. "Y'all gotta feel me one time," he says. Barry taps Stu on the shoulder, gesturing toward the drum riser behind them, and says, "Sit down over here and talk to me about it. I'll listen to you." The pair take a seat gazing out at the audience like two old buddies reminiscing on a back porch. A moment later, Daymond hunkers down beside them.

For the next two and a half minutes, Stu raps directly to the audience, beginning in a conversational tone and then rising—physically and tonally—until he is standing at the lip of the stage, barking like a drill sergeant. With no music to back him up, the words and Stu's delivery become the focus of the room. Barry and Daymond remain seated on the drum riser behind him, enthralled.

For hip-hop purists, performing a cappella is the ultimate display of skills. With an a cappella, an MC's victory or defeat—gauged by audience response—is entirely based on their ability to pull off a successful performance. Each member of the group will take a turn doing an a cappella tonight, a regular feature of the band's concerts.

For DVS Mindz, spitting bars until they are blue in the face is a direct carryover from 1137, where the focus was on verbal dexterity and lyrical one-upmanship. The group's recorded output from the late 1990s often lacks songwriting conventions such as hooks. This anticommercial, almost punk-rock approach dominated DVS's music.

DVS's underground ethos is further illustrated by the group's dressed-down look, a visual reprimand of the flashy rappers such as Puff Daddy and the Hot Boys who were topping the charts in 1998. DVS sport the same clothes on and off stage: jeans, sweatpants, T-shirts, hoodies, baseball caps, and sneakers. If anyone exhibits jewelry, it barely stands out. Stu occasionally dons a wool knit cap and a pair of leather gloves for concerts, but that is as close to costuming as it gets.

"We don't get together before the show and be like, 'What you gonna wear, dog?'" Daymond says. "I'm wearing what I got *on*. We come to rock mics and blow motherfuckers out the water. A lot of people don't understand. 'I gotta get my chain on, I gotta get my Timbs.' Man, I ain't even with that shit."

Even Barry, the group's flashiest dresser, insists, "It ain't a fashion show."

For DVS, rap's materialism detracts from hip-hop's pure essence. "The industry's too flooded with bullshit, with motherfuckers that's iced out and got big bank accounts," Daymond says. "Jay-Z got platinum bracelets and expensive cars, but a lot of people can't feel that. Make way for a broke nigga. I got a beat-up Honda. If you ain't riding with me then walk, bitch. This is hip-hop. Hip-hop didn't come from Beverly Hills with motherfuckers in Benzes. It came from the streets, so we gonna keep it street no matter what. DVS Mindz is real. We stand for something. We don't just stand for some mediocre, okay shit."

DVS believes their purist approach will pay dividends in the long run. And money is meaningless if you don't have respect. Stu explains, "That commercial shit, it doesn't get you respect. It'll get you a check, but we want respect. Period. Because we love this music, and we love what we're doing, and we love writing, and we love making it, and we love performing it. If you don't get your respect, it seems like you're doing it for nothing."

SURGEON GENERAL

On stage at the Granada, Stu concludes his a cappella with a flourish, and Daymond immediately introduces the next song, telling the audience, "I get on this fuckin' stage, and every time my shit's realer. Word up. 'Cause DVS Mindz, we represent *real* MCs."

The band launches into "Real MCs," a confident number that finds the trio spitting rhymes as if they cannot get the lyrics out quickly enough. On "Real MCs," the personalities of each member are fully realized—distinct in their rhyme styles, cadences, dictions, deliveries, and choice of words. The track employs a somewhat conventional structure, with the trio trading equally timed verses in a circular rotation. "Real MCs" lacks a traditional hook, but the song sounds massive and features a catchy refrain that doubles as a challenge to all contenders: "Any fool can rap, but can you represent?"

"Real MCs" was one of several new songs produced by Kansas City–based beatmaker Steve Garcia, who worked under the name Surgeon General or S.G. for short. S.G. had created a collection of beats using his newly purchased Ensoniq EPS-16 PLUS, an early keyboard and sampler. DVS agreed to purchase half a dozen beats and hired S.G. to produce the tracks in a Topeka studio.

The studio occupied the basement of a record store that was located in a shopping mall. S.G. and the group walked downstairs to get set up. "They had a team behind them, paying for the studio, investing in them," S.G. recalls. The session ended up going all night. "I was young. I didn't have any kids. I had nothing to lose. Let's make it, let's go, let's do it."

S.G. placed Stu, Barry, and Daymond in separate isolation booths. The three MCs could not see one another, but they could communicate through headphones and record their vocals at the same time. "What made them special was going back and forth and knowing each other's words," S.G. says of the recordings. "It was like they all wrote each other's raps. They were like one. That's why it sounds so organic. It's unlike anything I've ever done."

The record store's basement studio featured the first Pro Tools software S.G. had ever worked with. The software was relatively new at the time and transformed S.G.'s work with DVS Mindz. Rather than being locked into a preexisting track, the MCs could stretch out and rap as long as they wanted, with S.G. copying and pasting instrumental backing tracks to fit. "It blew my mind because I grew up recording on ADATS. I grew up recording on reel-to-reel," the producer recalls. "You had to come to the studio with your shit together and record the song. Pro Tools allowed you to edit and function around the artist."

DVS Mindz's collaboration with S.G. resulted in some of the least commercial, most lyrically potent songs of the band's career. S.G.'s productions sounded amazing and provided a major sonic upgrade for the group. But the producer's backdrops were stripped to the bone, often just a single, unchanging beat accompanied by a recurring bass line. This, combined with DVS's rejection of songwriting conventions, resulted in material that hip-hop heads adored but had no chance of appealing to mainstream audiences or garnering significant radio play. "DVS Mindbender" features no hook, just Daymond, Barry, and Stu passing the mic, relentlessly rhyming without coming up for air. On "Misrepresenters," Stu raps for two straight minutes, followed by Daymond, who goes for more than eighty bars before handing things off to Barry.

"They knew music," the producer says. "They knew how to count bars. They knew when their verse's up. They knew when their verse is done. They knew when a hook comes. Back then it was traditional to do a sixteen-bar verse. This is where the screwball comes. They recognized sixteen bars but it doesn't mean that they would spit sixteen bars. The beauty of Pro Tools is that it allowed you to let the rapper rap. It wasn't sixteen. It could have been twenty, it could have been twenty-four."

"We do what the fuck we want to do," Stu insists. "I'm not thinking about writing a forty-eight-bar song—three sixteens and three eight-bar hooks. I write bars, and if [commercial rappers] stop at twenty-four, then they stop at twenty-four. If I have twenty-eight, then I'm going to rap twenty-eight bars. They gotta sample and make people dance, but I'm not concerned with making people dance. I'm gonna do what's real to me. And that's the reason that we click together and the songs come out they way they do."

Two of the standout S.G.-produced numbers—"Real MCs" and "No Coast"—were featured on a 1998 compilation CD, *ICU: The Revival*. ICU stood for Ill Crew Universal, a California-based online collective whose website was a popular place for DJs to post mixtapes. Troy Owens, who still manned the turntables for DVS Mindz on occasion, was an ICU member. He submitted the two tracks, and the group was tapped for inclusion. *The Revival* CD features mostly unknown acts, but it includes a song from the Coup, a socially progressive Oakland trio with immense credibility in underground hip-hop circles. In a few weeks, DVS will fly to San Francisco and join the Coup, Dilated Peoples, and others for a *Revival* release concert. The three-headed dragon is taking flight.

At the Granada, "Real MCs" is followed by an a cappella from Daymond, who finishes and then launches into a rant about one of his favorite preoccupations, the music industry. "Yo, where all my starving MCs at, trying to make it in the industry, make some noise," Daymond yells to the Granada crowd. It gets big applause. He continues, "Where all my unsigned hype niggas at, that's trying to make it in this fuckin' industry, make some motherfuckin' noise, where y'all at? We about to set it. DVS Mindz first single, dropping in December. 'Unsigned Hype.'"

For years, DVS pursued a major label record deal, but they came up short. The S. G.–produced "Unsigned Hype" chronicles these frustrations, how the band spent a fortune to cipher with celebrities at conferences such as Jack the Rapper's Family Affair in Orlando and the B-Boy Summit in San Diego but had nothing to show for it but memories. "How can I be down for two years and couldn't come up?" Daymond asks in the song.[6]

"We sent a lot of tapes and a lot of CDs around the country to different people," Stu tells me in 1999. "We talked to different record execs. We met people. A lot of people seen us on TV. That shit don't move nothing. When they scared of you, they scared of you. When they don't want to take a chance, they don't want to take a damn chance. That's the reason why 'Unsigned Hype' was made. Put it out there. This is the shit we go through. Unsigned, nice, and still can't manage to get on—even though we've done our homework."

"Unsigned Hype" documents shady record company practices, from one-man operations that front like giant corporations to major label contracts that take everything, from royalties and publishing to an act's name. The concern that they are going to be exploited by the music industry runs rampant within DVS Mindz.

DVS has not generated interest from any of the major record companies, but the group has fielded numerous offers from small-time labels. They are wary. DVS's paranoia about the recording industry makes them suspicious of every business proposition that comes their way. "Signing a deal sounds scary," Stu says. "That sounds like the thing to *not* do. Signing a deal with any record company means you are going to get screwed. We are afraid of signing our creativity away and publishing or possibly being shelved."

THE JOHNNY COCHRAN OF ENTERTAINMENT LAWYERS

For the past four years, Randy had helped DVS in his spare time, booking their travel arrangements and serving as general assistant to the band. In 1996, Carla Daniels stepped down as manager, handing things over to Kim Drivers, also a student at Washburn. "I could only take them so far with the knowledge that I had," Carla explains. "We could have kept going, but at the same time, I still had kids to raise. I really needed to finish this college thing. So when they went with Kim, I was like, 'Great, because I can continue on with my college and go wherever that takes me.'"

Kim managed DVS Mindz from 1996 to 1998, with Randy increasing his involvement each year. When DVS went on the road, Randy made all the transportation and lodging arrangements. At out-of-town gigs, he would meet with the promoter, oversee the stage setup, and even run the sound-board if necessary.

When Kim stepped aside in 1998, Randy became DVS Mindz's manager. Stu recalls, "Randy was always there. He was already doing a lot of managerial stuff. Once Kim took over, Randy stepped in. He was working under her. Then Kim left, and Randy was manager."

"It was like a steppingstone," Randy says. "I went from homeboy to assistant to road manager to VP. Then after Kim left, it was pretty much taking over and being the CEO. That's when I picked up the ball and then everything was on my shoulders."

Bringing Randy forward as manager seemed natural. He, Stu, and Barry had known each other since high school. Randy was a devoted Crew member and an 1137 regular. He had an office job, working with numbers. Over many years, he had proven to be smart, hardworking, and trustworthy. "He started like how we started, so we learned all this shit together at the same time," Barry says of Randy. "That's what makes it extra phat. 'Cause he learned just like how we are, and he's handling the shit. That's a motherfucker we all been cool with, not just somebody we hired 'cause they're the Johnny Cochran of entertainment lawyers. Fuck that. I know if shit goes down, this motherfucker's gonna handle it, fuck me havin' to call him. He'll show up and whup somebody's ass, it come down to it. Fuck the lawsuit. Sometimes it has to be like that. We're not stupid. We got a smart-ass man working for us, handling the business."

Randy agrees that his history with DVS brings a degree of assurance to the enterprise, one that is necessary in the cutthroat music industry. "In this business, you need someone you can deal with and trust who will always have your back," he tells me. "I try to bring organization to the group. The industry alone is a madhouse, and the people that's out there is just so shady. You don't know who to trust, and who's out to get you, who's trying to help you. I feel I'm the backbone to DVS Mindz as far as keeping shit organized and making sure everything is straight for these niggas when they do they thing."

NO COAST

"We represent No Coast," Daymond tells the Granada crowd, which hollers and cheers its approval. "Yo, this ain't the East Coast, this ain't the West Coast. This is No Coast. And if y'all want to put No Coast on the motherfuckin' map, make some noise." He draws out the last word and gets huge applause.

"All y'all motherfuckers that screamed better buy my shit, goddammit," Daymond jokes. The audience cracks up. "I know I been telling you our shit's coming out. It be taking mad time because we started our own record label, No Coast Records."

Chasing a major label deal had not advanced DVS's career. The experience convinced everyone that the best path forward was to start their own company, No Coast Records. "No Coast belongs to all of us, but I'm the one structuring it and keeping everything organized and trying to hold it down," Randy explains.

No Coast was the brainchild of Kim Drivers, who conceived the company as a combination management firm, record label, production company, and publishing house. Randy was less ambitious but saw No Coast as a way to keep the profits in-house and the industry snakes at bay. "The plan originally was to get signed to a major label," Randy explains. "But over the years, and learning the industry, independent was the go-to move. We see the Rap-a-Lots and Def Jams and Death Row and all that. That would be fabulous. But we also see the No Limit, Cash Money. The difference between the two is keeping control. So that was when the focus became more on No Coast."

Starting their own independent label, rather than signing with one, made perfect sense. From rap's inception, MCs founded or signed with independent labels rather than getting tied to major-label deals. Rap's expansion was "facilitated by the emergent trend in the development of artist-owned independent labels and management companies which entered into direct competition with non-artist-owned companies."[7] Pioneers such as N.W.A. and the Geto Boys famously started out on self-launched independent labels. In 1998, moguls such as Puff Daddy and Jay-Z were at the top of their game, running boutique imprints that promoted their brands. Additionally, southerners such as Master P and Cash Money Records founders Bryan and Ronald Williams achieved phenomenal success in the late 1990s by founding independent labels. Closer to home, entrepreneurs such as Evil Loc, Tech N9ne, and the 57th Street Rogue Dogg Villians looked like geniuses for launching startup record companies.

In rap, like many genres, there is a strong conviction that major-label recording contracts are structured to direct revenues to the company rather than the artist. Successful rappers who sign with a major can mitigate this by demanding higher royalty rates or support for a personal, in-house label. Others can pressure record companies to return all or part of their publishing rights and royalties. The most enterprising rappers, however, are thought to be those who take it upon themselves to form independent labels and direct profits inward.

Around this time, I ask Randy if it would make sense for the band to sign with a major. "With all the shady people out there in the industry, I don't see no reason why they'd want to," he replies. "We don't want nobody telling us when we can come out or what we can say or what we got to rap about. We ain't got time for that. We've been held back too long. We got a lot to say. Fuck it, if we coming out with an album every year, then that's what we going to do."

DARK POETRY

"We represent No Coast," Daymond says to the audience at the Granada as a beat kicks in. "DVS Mindz. Next show, Kansas City, November the fourth, Club Mardi Gras. Check for it."

"Tell 'em where we from," Barry says, and the band launches into the opening hook of "No Coast." In the song, DVS positions the Midwest as "neutral," a geographical, ideological, and musical blend of the two major rap regions, "from Dr. Dre to KRS," as Barry puts it in one line.

Midway through the song, Daymond gestures to some Crew members who are standing in the wings, calling them to the stage. They bound single file into the spotlight, bobbing in time with the music. They are followed by the opening act, Qui-Lo, a Kansas City trio that features three young rappers, Godemis,

Joe Good, and Masta Chi. Godemis will go on to form a band, Ces Cru, that later signs a deal with Tech N9ne's Strange Music label. Joe Good will later perform with KC rapper Mac Lethal, as well as SoundsGood, on a collaboration with Lawrence musician Miles Bonny. Masta Chi will change his name to Titanium Frame and become a well-known rapper and producer.[8]

A dozen MCs strong, DVS and company turn "No Coast" into a jubilant posse cut with Crew members and Qui-Lo trading verses with DVS. As the energy peaks, Stu hops into the audience and headbangs along with a group of spirited concertgoers while Daymond leads the room in a loud call-and-response: "Somebody say No Coast."

"No Coast," the audience shouts back.

"Say Midwest!"

"Midwest!"

Daymond hands his microphone to a Crew member, who raps for about a minute before the next MC steps in. Third up is De'Juan, Daymond's little cousin, who spent his high-school years hanging out at 1137, watching the guys write, revise, rehearse, and record. Now, he has become a formidable MC in his own right. Wearing a cherry-red DVS Mindz T-shirt with the sleeves cut off and bobbing up and down like a prizefighter, De'Juan ferociously spits bar after bar of dark poetry.

6

DARK THOUGHTS, LOVELY LYRICS

The Granada, Lawrence, Kansas, April 23, 2001

De'Juan's bandmates introduce him to the audience by using some of his many nicknames.

Barry: The fourth head. Asshole number four. A.K.A. Jesus Crisis.

Daymond: DL.

Stu: Dark and Lovely.

De'Juan steps forward into the spotlight. He wears a white tank top and baggy jeans cinched with a thick tan leather belt. A gold medallion dangles from a thin chain around his neck, and a white hand towel hangs from his back pocket. His hair is parted in the middle and juts out like a bird's nest in all directions.

"Hey, my name's DL, Dark and Lovely," he tells the audience. "But see, dudes be getting on some old punk-ass shit, so I gotta say something. That's Dark thoughts, Lovely lyrics. That's for what I think of. It's Dark and Lovely for the chicks."

De'Juan smiles at his own joke, and the audience giggles along with him.

"Anyway, it's like this. Real MC shit. Let me get down one time."

De'Juan launches into his verse from a new song called "Flamethrower," spitting a series of "made you think" lines, one after the next. De'Juan enunciates every word of his lyrics as clearly as possible. He wants listeners to hear the artistry, to witness the craft, to understand the hours of thought that went into every syllable. Tonight, the Granada audience is with him, locked in and hanging on every turn of phrase.

De'Juan crouches forward, leaning into the words, microphone in his left hand, pointing with his right. A female attendee, sporting a low-cut sleeveless dress and planted front row center with a group of girlfriends, watches, rapt. De'Juan inches closer, low to the stage and looking her directly in the eye, gesturing. "My right hand writes rhymes so fertile and ill, I could touch your shoulder and you'd end up pregnant with a record deal." The woman and her friends giggle, and the audience goes ballistic.

De'Juan is only thirty seconds into his a cappella, but he knows he just scored the knockout punch. "I'm gonna leave it at that," he says, standing. De'Juan turns and walks back to the guys, who congratulate their bandmate with fist bumps, daps, and back slaps.

DE'JUAN

De'Juan "DL" Knight was born November 15, 1977, in Topeka. His mother, Charmaine, had just turned nineteen years old and was already estranged from De'Juan's biological father, Marcus Knight Sr. Marcus relocated from Topeka to Kansas City, where he remarried and had several children. "My dad, he's got kids by different women," De'Juan explains. "So I have half brothers and sisters. I've got a brother, two years older than me. I've got probably five half brothers and sisters. They have brothers and sisters from their households. All their brothers and sisters are my brothers and sisters too."

Charmaine was employed by the state and sang in the church choir. "She cooked, cleaned for people, take care of people," De'Juan says. "She always had a good heart. That was something she loved to do." Charmaine eventually remarried a man named Anthony Everett, who worked at the Goodyear factory. "He wanted her to quit her job and stay home, have some kids. She did." When De'Juan was two, Anthony and Charmaine had a daughter, Bianca, and a son, Anthony Jr., who was born five years later.

The growing family lived in a townhouse in Shawnee Heights, a middle-class neighborhood on the east side of Topeka. De'Juan and his siblings attended Tecumseh North Elementary school, where the student body was almost entirely white. "We had nice lifestyle," De'Juan recalls. "It's a fairly nice neighborhood. I'd go to the park, play football. Come home, dinner's cooked. My house smells good. Living in a nice place. It just felt like what it was supposed to be."

A number of De'Juan's schoolmates lived further east, in outer ring suburbs near Shawnee Lake. "They were neighborhoods that I had never even seen," De'Juan says. When De'Juan was about ten years old, he attended a friend's birthday party, which was held in a massive, opulent home that overlooked a lake. "I remember walking into his house and being like, 'God damn! No shit? People really *do* have houses like this.' His sister was sixteen and had a bright cherry red Camaro. Pretty motherfucker. We got my grandpa's car. We only got a car because he gave it to us, and she was spinning out in the gravel in her Camaro and shit. 'OK, it makes sense. We're not the same.'"

The disparities in material goods were also apparent elsewhere. Around this time, De'Juan was at the mall with a friend who was sporting a new pair of Nikes. Their friends at the mall raved about the shoes and ignored De'Juan completely. He never forgot that feeling of being unseen. De'Juan explains, "The amount of pride that you get from wearing certain things, when you're used to seeing other people with them and you can't get them, they're not even an option for you. It's not even the amount they cost, but the way that people treat you because of it, the respect. That was a very visible thing, right then. Everybody's a fan of him all the sudden and I'm the tagalong. The invisibility."

Larger troubles also began to loom on the home front. Anthony and Charmaine became dependent upon crack cocaine and spiraled into an abyss of drug abuse and domestic violence. "This is where shit took a turn," De'Juan recalls. "They get into the life of addiction, then the household starts to take the hit and shit goes downhill—arguing and breaking shit in the house."

De'Juan began to get into fights at school and developed a reputation among his classmates for violence. "My way of handling issues was to push and punch," he recalls. "'Cause where I was from and what I was seeing at home, that follows you to school. I went to a predominantly white school and fighting in itself was fuckin' outrageous to the other kids. They was like, 'Oh shit, I just ran into a psychopath. He's nuts.'"

When De'Juan was fourteen, Anthony and Charmaine split permanently. Things went from bad to worse. "They divorce, he leaves, she's an unemployed mother of three. We moved from where we were at to the heart of the hood, where the rent was $300."

De'Juan began attending Robinson Middle School, whose students were mostly Black and where he found it hard to fit in. "I was an awkward kid," he recalls. "I was used to being out there, not just with white kids but with rich kids. In middle school, the way I dressed, motherfuckers looked at me like I was ridiculous. I went from being kind of decent to being the laughingstock. I was still tight-rolling my jeans; I thought I was sharp. But nobody tight-roll their jeans where I moved to. It was the hood. Everybody was sagging."

Life at home descended into chaos. Charmaine invited a boyfriend to move in, also an addict. "My mom drank real heavy," De'Juan recalls. "Fighting at the house. I'm over here trying to stop Mom from jumping on him, 'cause she's going off and hitting him with shit. He's going to get fed up and beat her ass up."

The teenage De'Juan was caught between the violent, drunken fights of the adults and the panicked screams of his younger siblings. Over time, the weight of these experiences hardened him. "This is where life started to change for me, as far as being in the streets and the temperament and having that kind of snap mode and the fighting and shit, tearing shit up. By the time I got to sophomore year, I was like 'fuck school.' I ain't slept all night, they at the house fighting."

Not wanting to follow in the footsteps of his substance-abusing mother, De'Juan was an avowed teetotaler. Instead of drinking or doing drugs, he found solace in pen and paper. At first, De'Juan wrote poems, sharing them with a trusted female confidante, who encouraged him to keep writing. Eventually, some of these poems turned into songs. At school, De'Juan began hopping into ciphers here and there, trying out some of his rhymes. It was the process of writing itself, however, that he found most appealing. "We didn't have therapists," he tells me.

"I didn't go to school and say, 'My mom and them are smoking dope at home, and I need help.' That's not the life we live. An old-school upbringing forces you to bottle it and still smile out in public. Writing was, from the beginning, the outlet, therapeutic. All the turmoil that's going on makes it into the lyrics. It's actually the *reason* for the lyrics. You start to organize thoughts through writing and documenting things. You shed light on the situations by being able to process it. That's what it became."

Despite finding an expressive outlet for his feelings, the problems at home were only getting worse. By age sixteen, De'Juan was leaving the house for days at a time, crashing on friends' couches and interacting as little as possible with his mother, Charmaine. De'Juan felt remorse for abandoning his younger siblings but also believed that his own sanity was at stake. "It reached a point inside me that I had to go," he says.

A longtime friend of De'Juan's resided in a foster home run by an elderly religious couple, Nana and Reverend Moore. De'Juan started staying at the Moore's house from time to time, and the couple eventually invited him to move in. De'Juan accepted and became one of seven foster children living in the Moore home.

One afternoon around this time, De'Juan was playing basketball at Central Park, across the street from school. Diving for a ball, he crashed into the bleachers and cut his ankle to the point where he required medical attention. De'Juan went to the nearest emergency room, but the hospital refused to treat him without parental consent. He had no way to get it. De'Juan sat waiting in the emergency room for more than ninety minutes with a deep, bleeding cut on his ankle. De'Juan eventually got his paternal grandfather on the phone, who gave the hospital verbal permission to treat the injury.

This incident proved to be a turning point. Nana Moore offered to help De'Juan file paperwork that would officially appoint the Moores his legal guardians. "I had to take my mom to court, go through the proper channels," De'Juan says, recalling that Charmaine felt blindsided by a legal document that revealed the family's substance abuse and domestic violence to the state. "My mom felt like I shit on her," De'Juan says. "In order for you to be found as a child in need by the state, you have to list what's going on at home. The paperwork says they're getting high, they're drinking, there's violence in the home. Kind of a slap in the face, but it was what I had to do." The judge approved De'Juan's petition. "I walked out of there a foster child," he says, still smiling at the memory. "After I left at sixteen, I never stayed another night at my mom's house."

De'Juan's report led to a state investigation that resulted in Charmaine losing custody of her children, De'Juan's siblings, Anthony Jr. and Bianca, who went to live with their aunt. "My mom went from single mother of three to not having any of her kids at home," De'Juan says. "That pushed her further into her addictions. There was times in there where she was sober for a while, but she always went back to it."

Life in the Moore's foster home provided De'Juan with stability for the first time in years. Nana Moore had a longstanding relationship with Topeka High School, where all her foster children attended. Living under the watchful eye of the Moores, De'Juan could no longer get away with skipping class, but he recalls doing as little as possible while he was there. "I never did a lick of work in high school," he says. "Freshman year, I was still kind of square. Sophomore year, I kind of got more into the chicks. My junior year, school was out the window."

De'Juan's best friend in high school was his cousin, Kevin Douglas, Daymond's younger brother. The two were born just eleven days apart and, because their mothers were sisters, had known each other since childhood. De'Juan and Kevin both had trouble at home. "Kevin was kind of going through some of the same shit at a different address," De'Juan recalls. "His mom worked at Frito-Lay, had a great job, nice house and all that. Addiction started to take place. Daymond went to prison. That's when me and Kevin started kicking it more, 'cause Daymond was gone."

After Daymond returned from prison in Oklahoma and joined DVS Mindz, De'Juan and Kevin would go over to 1137 to hang out and watch the band rap. "I learned everything from DVS," De'Juan says. "I listened to it all day. Them niggas was ill, bringing it, you know, and they were right around the corner." De'Juan would occasionally try out one of his poems on the guys, but he mostly kept rapping to himself.

"Daymond kept telling us that his cousin could rhyme," Stu recalls. "I heard about that I don't know how many times. Cats come through Eleven-Third talking about they could rhyme, or my cousin can rhyme, or my boy can bust and all that bullshit. I was like whatever. But they had him over one day and I was like, 'Okay I'm tired of hearing about it.' I tapped him like, 'Bust something, man. Let me hear you do something.' And he was kind of reserved about it. I don't know if he was nervous or whatever, but then he spit a verse that was so cold that it made me go back and write."

"It was a flophouse," De'Juan recalls of 1137, where the Crew originally formed. "Bronz lived there; he didn't have a room but he lived there. Early Ray was there 90 percent of the time. I was there, Kevin was there. Pontiak. We were staples in that scene and the group activity, all the concerts and shows." DVS would perform at a club, and De'Juan, Kevin, and the rest of the Crew would join them, standing in the front rows and shouting along to the same songs they heard each night in the living room. After the performance, everyone would then return to 1137 for the afterparty, half the audience tagging along.

Now seventeen and emancipated from his family home, De'Juan also started running with a new set of peers, friends whose older brothers were associated with the Gangster Disciples (GD) street gang. Over time, by continuing to mingle and be seen with the Disciples, De'Juan began to be taken for a member of the gang. "Motherfuckers jump me because I'm affiliated with them. If I don't take the steps to be one of them, I'm out here by myself. If I get jumped, I ain't got nobody to call if I don't get put on for real. You run with [a gang] or you get ran over by all."

De'Juan became an official member of a local Black Disciples chapter of the GDs. Unlike Daymond, who was beaten into the Crips, De'Juan said that the GDs "bless you in. That's what they call it. It's almost, if you will, a ceremony. I went through that whole scenario, and got put on BDs, Black Disciples. I got put on and ended up getting further into the lifestyle."

Members were required to attend meetings. "They got all this knowledge you're supposed to learn," De'Juan recalls. It just seemed like boring homework, and De'Juan didn't take any of it very seriously. But his interactions with the gang led to deeper networks. De'Juan was being introduced to GDs from Chicago. What was once a handful of street-corner pals was now a gang that rolled twenty-five deep everywhere it went.

Through his membership in the GDs, De'Juan was given the opportunity to start selling drugs, putting in regular shifts as part of small teams that turned over half the profits to the gang leadership. De'Juan says that no one in the gang was forced to enter the drug trade. Members could choose to be involved or opt-out without penalty. Most of the new recruits were eager to get involved. "We don't have nobody to buy us shoes," De'Juan says. "Who's going go buy us school clothes? I was still going to high school. I can't keep wearing the same shit. It wasn't like I wanted a watch. It was literally for school clothes. Of course, I don't just go to Dollar General and buy shirts. I want some nice shit, too."

De'Juan tried his hand at drug dealing, but there wasn't much income in it. Instead, along with a few GD buddies, De'Juan opted for overt measures of bringing in cash. "We was into the street shit, jacking and shit. It was a crew of four, five, six of us. We just beating motherfuckers up, walking down the street, taking their wallets and disappearing into the alleys. Busting windows on stores and snatching shit. Just terrorizing the city. The police knew who it was, but they couldn't catch us because by the time everything goes off, we're already into thin air."

De'Juan stopped going to classes at some point during his senior year, but he was still planning to attend the end-of-year prom with his girlfriend. On April 27, 1996, De'Juan and some GD associates entered a local mom-and-pop grocery store. "We beat the dude up, held him down, and hit the register. The sole purpose for that robbery was to get money for a tuxedo to go to the prom."

Within hours, the police rounded up De'Juan and his accomplices, and the shopkeeper identified them as the assailants. The police arrested De'Juan and took him to Shawnee County Adult Detention Center, the county jail. De'Juan had just turned eighteen.

A judge set his bond at five thousand dollars. De'Juan would have to come up with 10 percent—five hundred dollars—to bond out of jail while awaiting trial. "Five hundred dollars was like five million," he recalls. "I had no ties other than Nana for anyone to come get me, to bond me out." With no money to make bail, De'Juan spent the next forty-one days in jail, awaiting trial. On August 2, 1996, his court date finally arrived. The judge placed De'Juan on parole and released him that day.

De'Juan returned to the Moore's house, but Reverend Moore stopped him at the front porch. "You know you can't stay here," the reverend told De'Juan. Not only was De'Juan's crime a liability, but the state also did not provide any foster benefits for individuals eighteen and over. "I'm like, okay I don't know where I'm gonna go. I'll pack my shit and go."

There was only one place De'Juan could think of to go, 1137 Washburn. His life of abstinence ended that day. "'Fuck it man, give me a beer.' Life is weighing me down. I started smoking weed and drinking." One morning, De'Juan's parole officer showed up at 1137 for an unannounced visit. A fifteen-year-old answered the door with a lit blunt in his hand. De'Juan's parole officer pulled him aside and tore into him. "You're not gonna do shit staying over here. All those beer bottles everywhere, liquor bottles, all that fucking weed. Sitting around getting high and drunk, that don't lead to nothing. You have *no* goals."

This was not entirely true. De'Juan wanted to make it as a rapper. He was one of several DVS Mindz associates who crashed at 1137, wrote lyrics all day, and tried them out in ciphers at the nightly house parties. Already a prolific writer, De'Juan immersed himself in the artistic environment. "We all wrote together," he recalls. "The atmosphere was exploding with creativity, and it drew everybody else in. There was always motherfuckers at the house. Constantly. You'd write in the midst of chaos. You're in the corner writing and there's a full-fledged house party going on."

Everyone was impressed with De'Juan's progress as a lyricist. De'Juan says that when he first started hanging out at 1137, he was listening almost exclusively to gangsta rap from artists like Tupac Shakur, Mobb Deep, C-Bo, and Brotha Lynch Hung. "That's what we was writing, that's what we were hearing, that's what we were living, for real," De'Juan says. "It was that street shit. Guns, drugs, robbing, stealing, fighting, gangs, that was the lyrical content. That wasn't what DVS was rapping about. They was metaphoric, it was linguistics, it was rhyme scheme, it was vocabulary. I took it on as a challenge. I started stepping up lyrically to where they was at. What I was listening to started to change. Now I'm listening to *It Was Written* by Nas. We get deeper into it, and we got more detailed and intricate. You fine-tune, you spending hours word playing."

All the rappers hanging out at 1137 aspired to join DVS Mindz. Stu, Barry, and Daymond were not interested in adding more MCs to the band; no one wanted to cut into their share of the mic time. Instead, Barry hatched a plan to start a subsidiary act, Mind Kontrol Mafia, composed of the premier bench players from 1137: Pontiak, Bronz, Paww Paww, and De'Juan. "These motherfuckers are putting in just as much work as us," Barry told Stu and Daymond. "We need to have our own team of motherfuckers that we'll bring in when our shit pops off. So, they'll already be groomed and ready to go."

With De'Juan taking the lead, a set of Mind Kontrol Mafia songs was developed, with significant input from Barry, but the act never solidified into a standalone entity. Among the scraps of evidence of Mind Kontrol Mafia's existence is "Inferred Connection," an S.G.-produced track featuring De'Juan, Paww Paww, and Bronz rapping alongside Stu, Barry, and Daymond. Pontiak featured on a different DVS track, "Yellow Brick Road."

"It was the junior DVS," De'Juan recalls of Mind Kontrol Mafia. "There was a lot of guys that fucked with DVS that rapped. Mind Kontrol was more a clique than a group. We never even talked about putting out a CD. We was just riding out at all the shows, rapping and partying."

The constant carousing at 1137 eventually caught up with De'Juan. He blew a urinalysis, and his parole officer gave him thirty days to produce a clean result. De'Juan smoked pot every single day for a month and tested positive again. His parole officer gave him a break, telling him to come back in a few days and get tested a third time. "I'm just buying time," he says. "I ain't stopped smoking a day. She's like, 'You should be clean by now.' She knows I'm lying." Eventually, De'Juan stopped showing up at his parole meetings altogether. A bench warrant was issued for his arrest. Soon after, he was pulled over for a traffic infraction and was arrested. De'Juan was sentenced to six months at Labette Correctional Conservation Camp, a bootcamp-style prison in Oswego, a tiny town in southeast Kansas. He was nineteen years old.

The bootcamp focused on rehabilitating nonviolent offenders through a military-style program of work, education, and physical exercise. Days began at 4:50 a.m., and inmates had a morning-to-night schedule that included only one hour of personal time. "When you first get there, they scare the shit out of you," De'Juan recalls. "They get you in line. They got drill sergeants. He's right here in your face. You can feel him breathing on you and he's at full blast. 'Who you looking at? Who you eyeballing?' The point of this is so when you're back in the streets and somebody has something to say to you, it doesn't bother you like it used to." De'Juan was assigned to a maintenance crew, moving to an outdoor unit as a perk for successfully earning a GED.

After five months in the bootcamp, De'Juan was released. He returned to 1137 and was placed on probation. For several months he complied with the terms, but he eventually returned to drinking and smoking weed with the guys. He failed a series of drug tests and then stopped attending probation meetings. Again, a warrant was issued for De'Juan's arrest, which eventually caught up with him. This time, he only spent one night in jail before being released, but he was placed under intensive supervised probation for an additional twenty-four months. This effectively added two years to De'Juan's original sentence, but with more stringent conditions, such as having to meet with a parole officer three times per week.

As fortune would have it, De'Juan knew his assigned parole officer, who had coached a YMCA basketball team De'Juan played on years before. The officer told De'Juan that he did not have to get drug tested so long as he stayed out of trouble. "I was still smoking weed," De'Juan recalls. "But I didn't have one problem. I never went to jail for that whole twenty-four months, didn't catch no cases or get pulled over. Walked parole down easy, smooth sailing."

As 1999 approached, Barry started talking to Stu and Daymond about taking DVS Mindz to the next level. "It wasn't that DVS Mindz was getting old or stale," Barry explains. "It's about to be a whole new year and we're about to do this shit seriously and bust our ass. We need to let people know who we are."

De'Juan had continued to hang out at 1137 and write with DVS Mindz. "I stayed down with the team and I was still here," De'Juan says. "It seemed like everybody else fell by the wayside." Stu recalls, "De'Juan was just standing over there, a lone guy. Why have him over there alone? Just bring him into the group and keep moving."

De'Juan's integration into DVS was inevitable. He fit in seamlessly and brought something new to the original three-headed dragon lineup, a distinct personality that augmented the collective in new ways. "He's been around since day one," Barry says. "Seeing what we've been through, wanting to do the same thing, and still staying hungry when everybody else disappeared. Through the things he went through, he grew up as a person, as a man and in his rhymes and taking it seriously. Instead of just having him hang around and be on a song or two, he's there for everything. He was always there so it's like he's part of the group. He'd be an asset. He doesn't sound like any of us. He has a whole different type of flow and a whole different perspective."

De'Juan recalls, "They sat down and put it out there for me, just kind of solidified it. 'In case you didn't know, you're DVS. You've been DVS.' There wasn't a ceremony for it, nobody sent you an email, but the songs started being my songs, too." Things were moving forward for the group. DVS was playing more prominent venues in front of larger audiences and opening for more prestigious acts: Redman, Keith Murray, Xhibit, Montell Jordan, Phife Dawg of A Tribe Called Quest, Del the Funky Homosapien, and Mixmaster Mike. "Shit was getting kind of major at the time, the shows that was starting to come up," De'Juan recalls.

"And from there," Stu says, "the rest is history."

II

2000-2003

7

REAL MCs

Area 51 is a shopworn nightclub located in an L-shaped strip mall in Southwest Topeka. The three-hundred-capacity venue is a blend of leftovers from its various incarnations as an entertainment establishment. Area 51 was a disco back in the 1970s and never got rid of the fading silver glitter ball that twinkles above the dancefloor. There are vintage-era wood-paneled walls awash in baseball and football memorabilia, relics from the venue's years as a sports bar. At one point, Area 51 was a strip club, and it retained a jungle gym's worth of horizontal brass guardrails and vertical dancers' poles that run floor to ceiling. There is no stage, but a raised platform overlooks the dancefloor, flanked by two large metal stripper "cages" on either side. These days, Area 51 hosts DJs on Friday and Saturday nights and books metal and rap acts on Sundays. To service live music, the owners upgraded the sound system and installed a rack of stage lights.

Despite these enhancements, Area 51 is known to be sketchy. Topeka nightclub proprietor Joey Pintozzi describes the venue as "an old dance club with a really bad reputation."[1] Fights are common, and a few years from now, a gunman will open fire inside the room, wounding two patrons and killing the club's DJ in the middle of the dancefloor.[2]

Tonight, Area 51 is dark and throbbing. "Major Haters," a pummeling track by DVS collaborators the Zou, blares at top volume, making conversation difficult. It's warm for April, and there is a good turnout of about a hundred and fifty. Patrons stand shouting beer orders at the bartender and sit munching burgers and curly fries at a series of high tables that form a half-circle surrounding the dancefloor. The dancefloor is dominated by the Crew, the band's twenty-deep entourage of assistants, family members, girlfriends, and hangers-on. The Crew is joined by local Topeka musicians, new fans, old friends, and ex-flames, all on hand to check out DVS's hometown performance.

In a short stairwell that leads to the stage area, Barry sits alone, hunched over, deep into some sort of preshow meditative trance. He sports baggy blue jeans and a navy T-shirt worn over a white one. He leans forward, eyes closed, a black skull cap encasing his head. A long gold chain supports a bulky crucifix that dangles between his splayed knees. Barry presses his palms together, holding a wireless microphone between them as if in prayer.

Moments pass, and then Daymond strides over, confident and clutching a bottle of Gatorade. He sits down next to Barry on the stairs. Daymond is wearing a dark blue denim jacket with FUBU embroidered on each sleeve in light blue threading. This is draped over a blue T-shirt, layered over a white T. Around his neck is a thin chain to which Daymond has affixed two rectangular DVS Mindz stickers back-to-back, resembling a backstage pass. As Daymond sits down, Barry awakens from his spell and nods to him. Seated shoulder-to-shoulder on the stairs, the two bandmates chat amiably, looking like a couple of old friends hanging out on a front stoop.

A few minutes later, Randy walks by and signals to Daymond and Barry, who rise and accompany him to a utility closet that doubles as a dressing room. Stu and De'Juan follow them inside. There, the members of DVS Mindz and Randy form a tight huddle, arms locked around one another's shoulders, heads touching, bodies swaying lightly in unison. After a few moments, everyone stands tall, arms to the center, palms on top of one another. They push their hands down in unison, shouting "DVS," and then move toward the exit. Stu smiles as he passes, saying, "On and on. We about to do it on and on."

The four MCs cluster together in the short stairwell, waiting to go onstage. A forty-something woman decked out in her best Sunday dress bustles up, toting a gallon jug of orange juice in one hand and a grocery bag full of empty plastic water bottles in the other. She hands a bottle to Barry and fills it with juice, giving him a big hug and wishing him luck. The woman is Daymond and De'Juan's cousin, matron of the band, and known to all as Aunt Tang. Tang fills juice bottles for everyone and distributes them to each member of the group, brushing the lint off their clothing like they were kids heading to school. De'Juan playfully shoos Tang away.

Shrouded in darkness, De'Juan raises a microphone and addresses the audience, "Make some noise! This is DL, baby." De'Juan wears a plain white T-shirt over baggy blue jeans and sneakers. His hair is blown up into an explosive hi-top fade, with a black pick jutting out of the right side and a Newport tucked behind his left ear. As the crowd cheers, De'Juan grins, pleased at the reception. "For all the haters and noncongratulators that wish they could be participators. And these major haters layers player. Top Town representatives. Nigga, who is you?" A handful of concertgoers recognize the refrain from "Niggaz (1137)" and holler in appreciation. It's showtime.

A series of ominous bass notes reverberate through the club, followed by a sparse piano line, then hi-hats and a staccato snare. Barry enters the stage from the left, head and arms whipping in time with the music, rapping as he goes. The song is "Headhunters," an older number the band recently updated with a fresh instrumental. The original version was built around a funky bass line, but the rebooted track is jittery and tense, creating a sonic dissonance that compliments the MC's double-time rhymes.

Barry raps four bars, followed by Stu, whose DVS Mindz jacket billows as he enters the stage, arms spinning and windmilling. De'Juan follows immediately after, spitting his verse from inside the stage-right stripper cage. Daymond then swoops in from the left, rapping as he hops over the brass guardrail and onto the dancefloor. As Daymond completes his verse, face-to-face with the crowd, De'Juan leaps onto the railing behind him to add backup vocals. "Headhunters" features no hook, so the instant Daymond finishes his lines, it's right back to Barry at the top of the batting order.

Area 51 might not be much to look at, but DVS treats it like Madison Square Garden, turning in a committed set that crackles with self-assurance and energy. The Crew and everyone else on the dancefloor eat it up, rapping along with the songs at top volume. DVS closes with a strident take on "Niggaz (1137)," leading the audience in a back-and-forth chant. As the song resounds to a close, the place goes crazy, cheering and submitting huge applause.

The music stops, and Barry smiles as he addresses the crowd. "Aye, word. Thank you for coming to support some shit that DVS Mindz tryin' to do. And motherfuckers have somewhere to come out and kick it without the punk ass shit and dumb ass fakin' and that ho ass punk shit. And everybody can come out and kick it. I appreciate that shit. And I never thought we could do some shit like this in Topeka without somebody getting they ass whooped for bein' ignorant. I appreciate everybody keeping it real. Word *up!*"

"Top Town!" De'Juan says, exiting the stage. "Thank you. Love."

As the group members descend the short flight of stairs from the stage area, they are swarmed by a two-dozen strong line of well-wishers, exes, cousins, old friends, new friends, and friends of friends. The horde embraces the band with hugs, handshakes, daps, and drinks. A young male enthusiast slings an arm around Daymond's shoulders, points at him, and shouts to anyone who will listen, "DVS! This nigga's the coldest nigga in the Midwest, dog. All y'all niggas better recognize. Ain't nobody fuckin' with this nigga."

ON SET

1436 SW Byron Street, Topeka, Kansas, April 15, 2000

Stu and I stand in the outdoor stairwell to Randy's apartment building in Topeka. We're on the second floor, getting ready to shoot the first take of DVS Mindz's debut music video for the song "Tired of Talking." The track represents a departure from a band that once prided itself on their lack of commercial conventions. "Tired of Talking" follows a standard songwriting structure: verse, hook, verse, hook. Each verse consists of thirty-two bars. The four MCs each rap four lines until everyone has gone around twice. "Tired of Talking's" hook features the four MCs trading lines and rapping in unison.

The video will emphasize the group members' distinct personalities and rhyme styles. We shoot each MC's verse in a separate location and give each of them a unique look. This idea came from my childhood heroes, the heavy metal group Kiss, whose four "characters" were distinguished by costumes, makeup, and signature colors. In the "Tired of Talking" video, the group members will not just stand and recite their verses. Instead, they will constantly move toward the camera, adding forward motion and momentum. For inspiration, we draw from iconic movies such as *The Shining*, where a young boy glides on a tricycle through a hotel's hallways. "Tired of Talking's" hook will bring the entire group together for an explosive display of collective energy.

Our first setup consists of Stu rushing up a winding staircase, rapping directly to the camera as he ascends. The shot was inspired by the James Bond movie *A View to a Kill*, where the British agent does battle up and down the stairs of the Eiffel Tower. Stu is to begin rapping his lines at the bottom of the staircase, ending just as he reaches the top step. My friend Eliott will operate my video camera, walking up the stairs backward to get the shot. De'Juan stands off to the side, holding a boom box, which he will use to play the track as Eliott videotapes.

"Come on up to the front of the stairs," I instruct Stu, who takes a few steps forward. He's dressed in baggy blue jeans over tan Timberland boots and a white DVS Mindz T-shirt under a black DVS Mindz windbreaker. This is topped off by a black White Sox cap, brim turned 180 degrees backward. None of us have shot a music video before, but if Stu is anxious, he's not showing it.

I demonstrate the shot for Stu and Eliott, climbing the stairs backward as I go. "What we're gonna do is back up, all the way around the corner, and all the way up here to the top. And hopefully you can get through one verse in that shot."

Everyone is ready, so we try the first take. De'Juan presses play on the boom box, and "Tired of Talking" rattles through the apartment complex. Stu does not mime along to the track; instead, he raps in full voice. The goal is to get the entire verse in a single, smooth shot that will require no cuts or edits. The first take is good, but Stu ascends the stairs too quickly, backing Eliott into a railing at the top as he completes the last line. Instead of a constantly moving camera, everything snaps to a halt. "I didn't think it was going to be that fast," Eliott says. We rewind the tape and watch the take on the camcorder's flip screen. The beginning is solid, but the second half is unusable.

"That was good," I say, nodding.

From the courtyard below, Daymond, Barry, and assorted Crew members lounge on a pair of picnic tables. They call up to us and jeer, ribbing Stu for "messing up" the take.

I ask Stu to do it again, this time climbing the stairs a bit slower but using more arm movement to convey energy. We do the shot again, and Stu nails it.

"That was good," Eliott tells him.

Stu is professional and cooperative. He will do as many takes as we want, whatever we ask.

We try the verse a third time. It's good, but Stu comes up the stairs too fast again.

Take four has a wobbly start but ends with Stu powerfully gesturing as he raps directly into the camera. Take five is more of the same: the beginning is not great, but it ends well. "That was good," I tell Stu after each take. We shoot it again and then another time.

Stu gives it his all, and each take has good moments, but we have not captured the single flawless shot that I had hoped for. I'm reluctant to call for an endless number of takes because the band might think I don't know what I'm doing. I decide that I will edit Stu's verse together, using the best moments from two or three of the takes.

"I think we got it," I tell Eliott.

"We were just trying to get the first part anyway," Eliott replies.

We decide to shoot it one more time, just for good measure.

"Hey Stu," Aunt Tang yells from the courtyard. Stu looks over. "Put that energy in it that you're pissed off and tired of talking! Get pissed off!"

Tang is right. "Energy," I tell Stu.

"Energy," Stu smiles, motioning with his arms, like a boxer working a speed bag.

"That's good," I say, "but serious."

Stu completes another take, this one more intense than the others. "That was cool!" Eliott enthuses. We agree that we have what we need and move to Stu's next set of lines.

The second part of Stu's verse has an easier setup. The MC will stride straight down a walkway, rapping directly into the camera. Eliott, operating the camera, will walk backward, shooting Stu as he advances. We do five quick takes and move on.

Eliott and I are making up the shots as we go, using parts of the apartment building that seem like they will make good backdrops. We want to mix it up visually as well so that each of Stu's four sets of bars has a distinct look. For the third setup, Eliott holds the camera high in the air, simulating the angle of a security camera. Stu advances towards the lens, rapping as he looks up at it. We try a few different setups for Stu's fourth and final set of lines, but none of them are satisfying. We settle on shooting Stu from the ground as he raps from a second-floor balcony. To simulate forward motion, Eliott does a steady pan out.

Stu's verses are complete. We agree that we can always reshoot something if it doesn't work out. A few days later, we return to try more takes of Stu's third set of lines.

Low-budget music videos are frequently taped in a single day, but "Tired of Talking" is put together piecemeal. Over the next several weeks, I shoot the rest of the footage for the video, with Eliott or another friend, Doug, working the camera. We videotape De'Juan high atop Burnett's Mound, overlooking Topeka. We record Daymond in Lawrence, inside an underground walkway that annexes a grade school. We tape Barry indoors, using black lights and an elaborate set put together by Barry, Eliott, and me.

For the song's hook, we shoot the entire band rapping together in an alley behind 1137. Eliott and I are still putting away the camcorder when DVS rushes off to DJ's, a Topeka nightclub where they are booked to play a show. Daymond is the first to arrive at the venue, and the band's start time has already passed. Undeterred, he delivers a pair of solo numbers before being joined by Stu, Barry, and De'Juan, who rush straight from the parking lot and onto the stage.

HIP HOP HYPE

KJHK 90.7 FM, Lawrence, Kansas, April 21, 2000

The mood is celebratory in the control booth at KJHK 90.7 FM, where the four members of DVS Mindz are gathered for an on-air interview with Kareem and CGz, cohosts of a popular Friday-night show, *Hip Hop Hype*. KJHK is a student-run radio station at KU. It takes up both floors of a small standalone building located far from the campus center. "Nutmeg" by Ghostface Killah blasts at top volume as DVS crowds around a shiny silver microphone. Shelves filled with neat rows of alphabetized CDs cover every inch of three walls, floor to ceiling.

The fourth wall houses a soundproof glass window that looks onto another studio.

Outside the control booth, members of the Crew stand in an adjacent room, drinking, chatting, and listening to the interview. The Crew members fill the space and spill outside, smoking cigarettes on a concrete patio atop a set of narrow stairs. They are joined by the director and the camera operator for *Fusion*, a music-themed TV show that airs on a local cable station. *Fusion* is featuring DVS as part of a special on the Midwest hip-hop scene. *Fusion*'s producer makes plans with Randy to shoot footage at DVS's upcoming CD release concert. A photographer from KU's student newspaper circles around, snapping pictures.

As "Nutmeg" winds to a close in the control booth, Daymond, who is seated at the console between the cohosts, greets the radio listeners. "Eleven-Third, that's my word. Call in and request DVS Mindz. We up in here." Daymond adjusts a pair of over-the-ear headphones. He wears a tan baseball cap with Japanese lettering, turned backward, and a small earring in his left ear.

The phone rings. On the line is a KU student named Eve who gives shout-outs to her sorority sisters from Alpha Kappa Alpha. "I just want to say what's up, and we want y'all to play that 'Country Grammar.'"

"Country Grammar" is a track by a hot new St. Louis rapper named Nelly. The song was released a little over a month ago and is starting to cause a stir on college and urban radio stations. Nelly's full-length debut album is slated for release this summer on Universal Records.

De'Juan jokingly acts offended by the request for Nelly. "What about DVS Mindz?" he admonishes, teasing.

Barry steps in and helps, "Midwest, you know!"

"It's all gravy," De'Juan says. He sports cornrows and a long-sleeved orange T-shirt.

"Aye, big ups, thanks for calling," Kareem tells Eve.

"They wild for the night," Daymond says.

Barry asks, "Where are all the scri-geons hanging out drunk, like the ones called in? What is *really* going on!"

"Scrigeons?" CGz asks.

"Scrub pigeons," De'Juan explains, and everyone breaks up.

Daymond looks mildly annoyed and steers things back to band business. "Album dropping May the second," he says into the mic. "The first hundred is limited edition of *DVS Mindz: The DVS Experience from '94 to 2000, Volume One.*"

"Where our peeps gonna be able to pick that up at?" Kareem asks.

"The major chains," Daymond replies. "Blockbuster Music, Hastings, Sam Goody, Streetside, Seventh Heaven. Get online and come check us out at www.DVSMindz.com. We got the hottest site out, right now. And you can peep out the 'Tired of Talking' video online."

Kareem plays "Tired of Talking," from the band's first music video. The video is part of a flurry of activity that occurred just after De'Juan officially joined the lineup last year. The group enjoyed a run of successful shows in Topeka and Lawrence. DVS's debut CD is about to be released on the group's own No Coast label, the band just launched a website, and their first music video is a hit with the Crew.

To top it off, the current issue of the *Pitch*, Kansas City's preeminent alternative weekly newspaper, features a complimentary story about the group's forthcoming debut. In it, the writer lauds DVS's "smooth lyrical style" and suggests that DVS Mindz is "the area's best rap group." There is also praise for the band's recent opening set for Das EFX and Black Sheep, when "most audience members felt DVS Mindz was the best group on the bill."[3]

Two months earlier, the *Pitch* had run a standalone review of that show, singling out DVS as the top band of the night. Like my review of the U-God show, the upshot was that the headliners were outmatched by the opening act.

> Topeka's DVS Mindz took the stage fired up to perform for a crowd that seemed to know most of its songs. DVS Mindz write great lyrical hooks and have a knack for structuring their live performance around these crowd pleasers. . . . Those who paid the full ticket price for this concert and somehow missed seeing DVS Mindz should have asked for a refund. Unfortunately, a combination of the strength of the DVS set and the not-ready-for-prime-time feel of the headliners' performances made the rest of the evening anti-climactic. . . . Most headed for the door with a sad, sedated look in their eyes and DVS Mindz lyrics still running through their minds.[4]

Everything is coming together. After years of paying dues, DVS are finally getting the respect they deserve.

I pull Stu aside for an interview in KJHK's basement, which is used to store thousands of 12-inch vinyl records. Stu wears a red T-shirt over long denim shorts, a black baseball cap turned backward, and a necklace of small metal beads. "This is what DVS is *now*," he tells me. "When I had the thought of putting a group together, there wasn't any million-dollar contract, I wasn't worried about moving records. I just wanted to make music. And I went to the cats who I felt could do it. One of them was Barry. We did our thing. Daymond, he fell in in '93 and it blossomed to De'Juan. I never thought in a million years it would be where it is now. And right now we're just *here*. We got work to do."

Stu is realistic about the road ahead, but there is a prevailing sense that DVS Mindz is on the verge of hitting the big time. The group has yet to release their debut CD, but already there is talk of million-dollar album deals, Platinum sales awards, and cross-country tours. "There's a couple of heavyweights that's known in the Midwest for bringing some shit, and we one of them," De'Juan tells me. "I just hope for the same respect when the units start moving. No matter how many Platinum [albums] we drop—'cause we could drop two times Platinum after we drop the first one—we're still gonna always have that potential to get a little bit better." Hanging out at my apartment on a recent Sunday night, talking to De'Juan, Barry says, "The shit's that's so crazy—and it keeps me up at night, that's why I'm an insomniac—we are so close to just being straight *paid*, dude."

This excitement is contagious, infecting the entire DVS constellation: the band, Randy, their girlfriends, families, friends, and assorted Crew members. I interviewed Randy around this time and asked him to predict the future of DVS Mindz. "Success. Success. Out of control," he says, laughing and shaking his head. "It's gonna be off the hook. Niggas ain't ready. It's our time."

Randy describes how the band has moved forward year after year, slowly building momentum that is now coming to a peak. "I first came across them in '93, '94. As time went on and we was in this game longer, everything from songs to shows just kept getting better and better. Each time it reaches a certain point it's like, we've been thinking it can't get any better, everything keeps getting better. Just think of what could be going on in three months. It's going to be so much better than from where we are here. Everything's just going to keep getting better and better."

The group members' ambitions have grown in conjunction with the band's rising stature. Daymond now aims to be a celebrity rap mogul along the lines of Sean Combs or Jay-Z. "I don't want to rap for life," he tells me during an interview around this time. "I want to keep producing, and I want to own businesses for real. I want to model for Tommy Hilfiger. I feel like we're just using this rap shit for a avenue to get where we really want to be. All my adult life, I want to be a rapper, but that ain't all I want to do. I want to get on the big screen, I want to make movies. I want an R&B bitch, too. I'm serious. I want all that shit."

Stu also has grand ambitions, but they are not material. What Stu truly craves is respect and recognition from the rap music industry. "In the end, when we get fifty, when the Source Awards or any other award show come up, or the hall of fame for the rap music like they have for LL Cool J and all them niggas, that rap museum with all the shit in it, we want to be in that. You damn right. And be respected. And be sitting in that motherfucker like, 'Yeah. Them niggas put it the fuck down. On the real. They did the damn thing.' That's real. We *want* that."

Upstairs at KJHK, "Tired of Talking" concludes, and Kareem plugs DVS Mindz's upcoming show at the Bottleneck, opening for critically acclaimed Brooklyn act the Arsonists. "That's where the *real* hip-hop heads will be," Barry promises. Kareem asks the group to make introductions.

"DVS Mindz in the house, Midwest representatives," Barry says. He wears a white T under an unbuttoned Hawaiian-style shirt. He sports a navy-blue Dodgers baseball hat cocked to the right and placed over a black skull cap. There are small earrings in both ears, a big gold watch on his left wrist, and a thick gold chain and crucifix medallion. Barry's in a good mood, talking on-air in a beatific patter. "We all in here representing the Midwest, Top City, Cop City, holding it down like Frank Nitti." He roars with laughter.

The phone lines light up with listeners requesting De La Soul, Black Rob, and Dead Prez. There are calls from Crew members in

Topeka, who dial the station and ask the DJs to play DVS songs. "Top City is representing," Kareem enthuses after back-to-back DVS calls from Topeka. "We need that support in the Midwest. Support that DVS Mindz, support that *Hip Hop Hype*."

Daymond plugs the new album again and adds that the CD release party will take place at the Granada in downtown Lawrence. The Granada's proximity to KU's masses of hip-hop-loving college students makes it an ideal location for the CD launch.

Kareem asks the band, "How long y'all been ripping it?"

"We been ripping forever," Daymond replies. "As DVS Mindz, our first show was November the fourth, ninety-three. We been on the scene for a minute."

Kareem nods, responding, "Some people, they think they rappers, but they only been on the mic for like two weeks."

De'Juan says, "Put it this way, we been heavyweights since ninety-three."

"Without the belts," Barry adds. "We don't need 'em."

Stu adds, "If you've been rhyming for two weeks or you just started rhyming last year, and you think you can run up on a group of this caliber, you're losing your mind. You better stop it. 'Cause I'll slice you by myself."

"You'll get mad and it'll get on some street shit and you'll want to fight," Barry muses. "So don't do it, don't go there."

DVS's multiyear involvement in rap music is evidence, the group believes, of their status as elder statesmen. "We been doing it for so long," Daymond tells the radio hosts. "I'm twenty-six, I've been doing it for eleven years. Our first show was back in 1993, and here it is six years later. I think about all the shows that we've seen and everything that we've done since back then 'til now. A lot of groups, whether they want to admit it or not, they feel like we the grandfather of this whole shit. 'Cause when we was doing it and keeping it real, a lot of these motherfuckers was still sitting at home thinking about doing it. Now I'm like a Jay-Z to this shit, kind of like a godfather to this shit. That's what everybody knows me from, my face—that man that raps. A lot of people look up to us. So it's gotta be professional. We gotta keep DVS Mindz alive, the same buzz going. We gotta keep rolling with the shit, we can't slow down."

De'Juan concurs that the band's time is now, that the window of opportunity is open. But he warns that the band is busier and more distracted than ever. DVS have to set that aside and grind their way across the finish line. During a recent late-night conversation at my apartment, De'Juan says, "We gotta do this shit. Motherfuckers is dedicated. It ain't gonna stop. We got all the elements right now. We have to push it."

Rap is a youth-dominated genre, and DVS Mindz are no longer brash upstarts but senior members of the regional rap scene. Typically, adults still making rap music in their thirties are hobbyists who are busy with parenting, education, and/or career pursuits.[5] DVS are going in the other direction, doubling down on their ambition to make it as the group members inch closer to their thirties.

HEADHUNTERS

The Bottleneck, Lawrence, Kansas, April 26, 2000

The adrenaline flows backstage at the Bottleneck. A steep set of stairs leads to a 12′ × 15′ shoebox consisting of four wood-paneled walls that are caked in years of band stickers and magic-marker scrawl. The only furniture is two ratty futons and a pair of dollar-store coffee tables.

DVS and the Crew pack the tiny room, chatting excitedly about the show. CGz, one of the *Hip Hop Hype* hosts, is on hand, as is Barry's girlfriend Stacy, a petite, gum-snapping blonde with sculpted eyebrows and heavily manicured nails. She chats with Stu's girlfriend, Jessica, a striking brunette.

A photocopied schedule, written in black Magic Marker, is taped to one wall.

8:00 DJ Just
9:45 Mac Lethal and Approach
10:30 Sevenfold Sympathy
11:15 DVS Mindz
12:00 Arsonists

It is 10:20 p.m. Downstairs, DJ Just spins old-school records while a group of break dancers shows off their moves. Mac Lethal, an unknown eighteen-year-old white rapper from Kansas City, just wrapped up his opening set, where he mesmerized the audience with sharp wordplay and intense, crystal-clear delivery. Within a few years, Mac Lethal will develop into one of the most successful independent rappers to emerge from the KC region.

DVS's second-place spot on the bill, just behind the headliner, is an indication of the band's stature. "We don't look at ourselves as openers no more," Daymond tells me. "It don't matter when we go on. That's the exact thing that we take to the stage. If we go on first, if we go on last, this motherfucker's over."

A member of the Crew sits at a coffee table and splits open a thick cigar. He empties its contents onto a discarded paper plate and rolls a giant blunt, which he then lights and passes around. "It's getting ready to jump off, dude," De'Juan tells me, taking a huge toke. "Once we hit this motherfucker, it's getting ready to pop."

Daymond and Stu don't smoke pot, so they trade freestyle raps instead. Improvising, Daymond incorporates the names of everything around him. Stu, sporting a black T-shirt with a Superman logo, throws out a few improvised lines but stops to double-check tonight's setlist.

"I'm a sweaty palm cat," he says. "I get nervous when I have to bust a new verse for any one of these cats," he says, looking over at Daymond, De'Juan, and Barry. "Because those are my biggest critics. If they don't like it, I did something wrong. I want to impress these cats. That's coming from my heart, really."

Daymond explains, "We feed off each other, we know each other's lyrics. I can take any of their verses and make a song like I wrote it. A lot of groups can't do that. We can do that with each of us. We freestyle, I do some of his shit. Nobody lyrically can fuck with DVS Mindz. That's bottom line. I don't care who you go get. You can pay to go get Jay-Z, Redman, Ice Cube, whoever. We're gonna destroy 'em. They spend too much time worried about glamour and glitz. We ain't got glamour and glitz. If anybody ever asks me right now who's the illest motherfuckers that you would put money on, I'd put money on my team over anybody. Can't nobody fuck with my niggas, and I know I'm arrogant for saying it, but fuck it."

"That's not arrogant, that's telling the truth," Stu concurs.

The Bottleneck is almost at capacity, and the college-student crowd eagerly awaits the arrival of the Arsonists. The Crew has been pumping up DVS all week, telling the band how the audience at this show will consist of true hip-hop heads, aesthetes with sophisticated taste in rap music. DVS will need to bring their lyrical A-game. Barry immediately began concocting a novel way to open the concert.

Backstage, the energy remains high as Stu calls the room to order. "Yo, let's go ahead and get this prayer off," he tells the guys. The four members of DVS Mindz and Randy form a tight huddle and sway together rhythmically. Stu speaks softly; no one outside the circle can hear what he's saying. The room is silent. CGz and the others bow their heads solemnly. Then, from within the circle, there is laughter. The guys straighten up and place their fists together. Stu gives a three count and they all shout "DVS!" before returning to their clusters of friends and lovers.

"We get in this mode," Stu says of the band's preconcert ritual. "We're amped up, but we always calm down and get in our circle and pray to god. Everything's alright, even if the show is bunk."

A Bottleneck staff member appears on the staircase, a Black guy with cornrows and spectacles. "How you doin' man?" Stu asks, giving him daps. "You about ready for us?" "Five minutes," the staff member affirms and hurries back down the stairs.

De'Juan alternates between freestyling and large inhales from a second blunt that is going around. More people are coming upstairs, trading high fives, handshakes, daps, and hugs as they enter. Another Bottleneck staff member appears on the staircase, delivering a pitcher of cold beer.

De'Juan and Barry shadowbox with each other. In a booming announcer voice, De'Juan intones, "Let's get rrready to rumble! In this corner, we've got the real MCs with the heavyweight, middleweight, welterweight championship."

"We're serious when it comes to mic time," Barry says. "That's what it is. Don't play with me. I do this shit for a living; I do this shit 'cause I live it. Don't fuck around with me."

The band members bounce up and down at the top of the staircase, itching to descend and take the stage. "It's one thousand, one hundred and thirty-seven degrees!" Stu bellows.

A few minutes later, the room empties as DVS, followed by the Crew, winds their way down the steep staircase and toward the stage entrance.

Kareem from *Hip Hop Hype* announces the band to the audience. "Sunday night, CD release party for these people right here in the house. DVS Mindz, y'all. Make some noise!"

Daymond bounds to center stage, grabs a microphone from a stand, and shouts, "What's up! All you real live hip-hop motherfuckers, make some noise!" He draws out the last word for several seconds. There are a few murmurs from the crowd, but the reaction is largely staid.

"Y'all motherfuckers ain't ready," Daymond huffs. "I said all the real live hip-hop motherfuckers in the house, make some noise!" He draws the final word out even longer. This generates a somewhat larger response.

"The heads is in this bitch," De'Juan says to no one in particular.

"Real live heads," Daymond adds. "That's what I *like*."

De'Juan continues, "When we booked this show, they said there's gonna be nothing but heads there. Shine us the fuck up. That's what we want to rock with."

Ever the showman, Daymond tells the crowd, "Yo, we gotta warm up our motherfucking vocal cords right quick though. Lyrical fitness, you know. Come on, let's warm up right quick."

Barry begins rapping, a cappella, at breakneck speed, the words flowing together in a buttery jumble. The song is "Head-hunters," an ode to the group's own lyrical prowess that features no hook, just bar after bar of the MCs trading four-line stanzas. As Barry raps with no musical accompaniment, the rest of the band circles him, listening intently. Daymond plays the moment theatrically, placing his hands on his hips and leaning forward in an exaggerated pose. Stu follows Barry's verse in his signature rat-a-tat style, getting approving nods for rhyming Cyrax, a cyborg assassin character featured in the video game Mortal Kombat, with Air Max, a shoe manufactured by Nike.

As Stu raps, the other group members listen closely, bobbing their heads and looking at each other in mock disbelief, wincing at Stu's ability to put together intricately interlocking rhymes. De'Juan steps in immediately after Stu, followed by Daymond. It then goes back to Barry, who begins round two.

With no beat, a circular song structure, and MCs who are focused on one another rather than the audience, this is basically a cipher onstage. The purist heads in the audience are eating it up, oohing and aahing at the best punchlines, and nudging each other at deepest inside references. By the third round, DVS Mindz is spitting furiously, each MC trying to outdo the others. The song's structure begins to fall apart when Stu goes for eight bars, twice as long, on his third verse. Undeterred, De'Juan takes over and raps for sixteen bars, doubling Stu's time.

"Whoa," Daymond exclaims, feigning to be so impressed that he cannot continue. "I'm not even following that one. That nigga's *ill*!" The audience agrees. Having won over the hip-hop purists with their verbal prowess, DVS can now take the show anywhere they care to go.

"I heard the heads is in the house," De'Juan proclaims. "This one's called 'Rowdy Hip Hoppers.'"

A review of the concert in the *Pitch*, offers a series of back-handed compliments:

The now-veteran crew from Top City threw down its usual set of intense rhymes laid over a few simple beats. There are two schools of thought on the Mindz: those who think DVS Mindz is the area's tightest rap group and those who think their rhymes are unoriginal and their beats add nothing to the songs. There's some merit to both arguments. Lyrically, DVS Mindz rarely venture into uncharted territory, but few people have covered these topics with the same level of ferocity and emotion. As for the beats, not everyone wants to sound like the Fresh Prince when they take the stage, and the raw edge DVS Mindz possesses when it takes the stage proves more than parents just don't understand.[6]

Four days from now, DVS Mindz will host a release party for their debut CD at the Granada, a larger venue located a few blocks away. Tonight's thirty-minute set, however, is for the true fans, and DVS does not perform a single song from their new CD until the show is almost over.

8

THE CREW

1419 Ohio Street, Lawrence, Kansas, April 28, 2000

Barry and De'Juan arrive at my apartment first, along with two members of the Crew. Stacy, Barry's girlfriend, drove everyone from Topeka. Stacy is not only Barry's significant other but also a diehard Crew member, attending every show, pressed up against the stage, rapping along to every word at the top of her lungs, and responding with enthusiasm whenever the four MCs engage with the crowd.

"They crazy, they ain't like nobody else," she says in an Ozarksian drawl, shaking her head. "They rap *real* shit. It's *true*. Ain't too many rappers out there that rap true shit. But the ones that do, I mean, it's real. They holdin' it down for real."

Stacy's younger brother, Josh, tagged along tonight. Josh is a skinny eighteen-year-old white kid sporting a Tar Heels cap, wire-rim glasses, and a plaid button-down shirt. New to the band's music, he's already a superfan. "I think DVS is gonna drop a bomb on the Midwest, dog. They're cold blooded," he tells me. "I'm just hearing it, but I'm feeling all of it. They're coming on tight for real. Y'all should be watching out 'cause they're gonna come out and they're gonna be poppin'. Everybody's gonna wish that they'd heard them sooner."

I rent a funky one-bedroom apartment located just off the KU campus in a neighborhood dominated by fraternities, sororities, student housing, and a couple of bars and pizza places that cater to KU students.

The five of us settle into the living room, Barry, Stacy, and De'Juan on the couch and Josh and me sitting cross-legged on the floor, facing them. Screwdrivers and beers are distributed, and a joint is going around.

Barry is ebullient. He sits on the arm of the couch and pitches De'Juan his latest show idea—to begin the band's upcoming CD release party with a skit that involves an armed standoff, and concludes with a simulated gunshot sound.

"I wanna hear that shot *ring* through them speakers when it's inside of there," Barry exclaims. "I want it to pop off where it'll scare the shit out of motherfuckers, 'cause they don't know it's coming, just catch somebody off guard. You hear a shell drop, where you make everybody be like, 'Oooh shit.'" As Barry says this, he flinches theatrically. "All the sudden, *pow*! I want one of *them* sounds coming through all the speakers. Spook ya." Barry spreads his arms open wide. "You hear that shit ring out, I guarantee, all the chicks in there, you know you'll see a couple of people hit the dirt. 'Cause motherfuckers gonna be blew out. I know it'd get me. If I didn't know it was coming and a big-ass *kakow*, nigga. 'Whoa! That was realer than a motherfucker.'"

Still perched on the arm of the couch, Barry leans back and takes a long swig from an Olde English forty-ounce bottle. He's wearing a blue and white Esco 67 sleeveless jersey over a white T-shirt and blue jeans. A thick braided gold chain is draped around his neck, Jesus piece hanging to his navel. Atop his head is a black skull cap, and he sports a neatly trimmed goatee. Barry drains the beer bottle and continues.

"What I really wish we could do, but that'll get us arrested, I'd like to just go ahead and get a pistol. But there's too many people [that] get in accidental deaths. I ain't going out like Brandon Lee.[1] Otherwise, that'd be hella sick. Motherfuckers would be like, 'Now they're really tripping.' 'Cause you know it'd scare the shit out of some people." Barry smiles at the thought.

De'Juan nods in agreement. Seemingly, he's on board with Barry's standoff skit. De'Juan is dressed in dark brown, baggy corduroy pants topped by a light brown check-patterned polo over a white T-shirt. His hair is braided in cornrows and pressed to one side, and he wears a diamond earring in his left ear. "A lot of people think of the ideas, but we'll show up and do it. That's where you draw the line between them cats and us."

"Ain't nobody fuckin' with us, man," Barry concurs, taking a drag off the joint. "We been telling 'em for the longest. Not even hating. You just don't understand how serious we are when we put our mind to getting on something to do it. And it's *sick*. We be on what we trying to do, to be different from everybody else and make this shit live, instead of just some boring shit— you go hear somebody rap."

De'Juan nods. Rap's lack of energetic, creative live performances is a sticking point for the entire group. "Everybody knows Jay-Z's cold and he's selling Platinum, but how was the show? He walked about forty-five laps," De'Juan says. "We're vibing off each other. The shows come from shit like that, from just thinking we gotta do *something* that's live. And not knowing what to do because I'm broke. Still putting this shit together. We're just a local group. No, fuck all that we're DVS *Mindz*. And when DVS Mindz show up, we want motherfuckers to talk about that shit."

De'Juan looks over at Barry and continues. "Our man starts to bless us with ideas, and the cheapest way to do it, and the quickest way to make it live. But knowing in yourself that you can do what the fuck you want to do as long as you get down and do it for real, that's why hip-hop has no boundaries."

"We ain't scared to do shit," Barry says. "We know whatever we're doing that's different from somebody, it's gotta be gravy."

I ask Barry about his tattoos, and he offers everyone a tour of his ink. "This is my very first one," he says, pointing to a figure done in black lines that covers most of his right bicep. Barry explains that it depicts what was supposed to be the cover of a planned DVS Mindz cassette. "It's a little cartoon dude with a stocking cap that says DVS. He's pouring out a forty for his homies. He's got a little blunt." It was the first of Barry's three DVS Mindz tattoos.

Barry switches to his left bicep, where he has a tattoo that says "Killa" in black cursive lettering. Killa the Hun stands for Kansas is Lynchin Lyrical Adversaries To Help Elevate Hip-Hop's Underground Nation. "It's not just a catchy name for shock value," Barry insists.

Barry is in a boisterous mood, laughing and raising the volume of the proceedings. He gets up and shows off the 1137 tattoo that arches across his stomach. He then moves over to my turntable and begins flipping through a stack of LPs. Barry swigs a beer and smokes cigarettes as he spins records by LL Cool J, Tupac, Ice Cube, and then N.W.A.'s "Gangsta Gangsta." The 1988 banger is a classic to everyone in the room. Even Josh, just five years old when N.W.A. released their first single, knows every word. Off to the side, De'Juan watches, nodding intently in time with the music. "That's the *V* in versatile," De'Juan says, looking over in Barry's direction. "MCs on the turntables."

DANGEROUS MCs

Daymond arrives at the door, along with his wife, Sandra, his brother Kevin, Randy, and longtime Crew member, Casey. They tote brown paper bags filled with forty-ounce bottles of malt liquor, cans of beer, and a bottle of Crown Royal.

De'Juan and Kevin sit next to each other on a bench at my small kitchen table, passing the last of a joint back and forth. Kevin, who is nicknamed the Wolf, is laid back and chill. He alternates drags from the joint with a cigarette. Kevin is at the marrow of DVS's inner circle, brother to Daymond and cousin to De'Juan. He is also a member of the Crew, attending every gig, acting as a body man, security, roadie, whatever. Kevin is trying to establish himself as a producer, too, He created an eerie backdrop for Barry's solo song, "Murdarous Verses," which features De'Juan on the hook. Kevin and De'Juan, best friends since childhood, do a complicated series of twisting handshakes and daps, a routine that goes on for half a minute. You can tell they've been carrying out the ritual since they were school kids.

Over by the turntable, Barry and Randy are discussing recent dealings with a local promoter named Ken Wheeler. Randy says he's waiting for a callback from Wheeler to secure a venue for the band's CD release party in Kansas City. "We can't get in touch with him to confirm whether or not we got it," Randy says, sounding more bemused than upset. "He's missing in action, once again."

But Barry is angry. He says that Wheeler screwed the band over when he did not invite DVS to open for Raekwon (a member of Wu-Tang Clan) at a recent show. A competing band was asked instead, and Barry took it as a snub. Furthermore, Randy had proposed that Wheeler host a premiere party for the "Tired of Talking" music video, and the promoter has not responded. In

Barry's view, any promoter in town would jump at the chance to host DVS's video premiere, and he was dismayed that Wheeler had ignored them. "We can't even get an answer for that," Barry gripes. "So I feel where you're coming from when you say your boy's bullshittin', only double what you're feeling, 'cause I didn't even know about that, but that's fucked up."

Randy, sensing Barry's growing ire and wanting to keep DVS on the promoter's good side, backtracks, deescalating the situation. "He's probably busy," Randy says. "But we need to go ahead and lock [the venue] down with the owner so we can have that copacetic."

DVS's debut album is slated for release during a year filled with new CDs from a slew of Topeka-based aspirants: Versatial, Thug Moffia, Mannkind, Xtended Klip, and Fat Cat. Every one of these artists was inspired by DVS Mindz, and every one of them would gladly take the band's position as the kings of Topeka rap.

Barry goes back to playing records. I'm in the kitchen with De'Juan and Kevin, mixing screwdrivers and filling flutes of champagne. Sandra, Stacy, and Josh sit around the coffee table, playing cards. In my bedroom, Randy and Daymond are hunched over a desktop computer, checking out the band's new website.

DVSMindz.com was created by Chris, a KU student and electronica DJ who lives two doors down from me. Chris, who had recently started designing websites for fun, put together a simple but effective site for the group at no charge. It included the band's logo, a biography, the music video for "Tired of Talking," some of my live video clips, and samples of three DVS songs. Wary of having their music stolen, the band only allowed thirty-second snippets of their new album to stream online.

"Our website is tight, just how it has all the little icons," Randy says, clicking through the site. He is wearing a navy blue ball cap and a baseball jersey that says "Brown Pride" on the front. "It's just one of them things where you really got to get in there and learn how to do your thing. Nowadays with this website, you can do almost anything."

From the living room, Barry spins "Dangerous MC's," a posse track featuring the Notorious B.I.G., Busta Rhymes, and Snoop Dogg. Daymond begins rapping his own lyrics over the song, removing a dark corduroy jacket to reveal a purple Dada Supreme Damani long-sleeved T-shirt. He holds a glass in his left hand and gestures with the right, a silver chain swinging lightly across his chest. Daymond's hair is cropped neat, and he wears a wedding ring.

Daymond has a white-collar job, working as a customer service agent at a call center run by TeleTech, a local company that contracts with GTE (now Verizon). "I'm on the phone a lot," Daymond told me when I first met him. "We handle phone service all over the country and shit."

Daymond is also a barber on the side. He attended barber school but never finished the coursework. An ex-girlfriend who works for the state hooked him up with a temporary two-year barber's license. Daymond earns great money cutting hair, all of it paid in cash. He does not have a bank account, so he stores the proceeds in a Nike shoe box he keeps on the top of a closet. The box reportedly holds more than five thousand dollars.

Daymond needs all the money he can get. He has full custody of his son, Daymond Jr., who will turn six years old this year. In 1996, Daymond Jr.'s mother was sentenced to ten years in prison, and Daymond became the two-year-old's primary caretaker. Daymond's mother helps by watching the boy when Daymond has gigs or other music-related business.

Daymond, who entered the band with significant experience as a musician, has been on a producing kick lately.

He invested in some home studio gear a while back and has produced several DVS tracks: the original "Tired of Talking," a stellar remake of "No Coast," and the recent live staple "Madness." He is also working on a solo album that he plans to start recording soon. "Fifteen tracks," Daymond tells me. "I [produced] fourteen of those. I'm going to call it *If You Wake Me, Don't Forget Me.*"

Barry marvels at Daymond's artistic energy and output. "He's evolved into some new shit on the rhyming," he tells me. "Plus, now he's working with beats, so apparently he's comfortable enough with his writing that he's feeling 'I can do something else.' That's a hard feeling to come by, when you feel you can spend your time doing something else 'cause you got your other craft down pat. When he goes back to concentrating on straight rhyming again, people are gonna be in trouble." I sense some underlying tension here. Is Barry damning his bandmate with faint praise, insinuating that Daymond has lost focus or prioritizes his solo career?

One of Daymond's nicknames is the Invisible Man, an epithet that has dual meanings. Daymond calls himself invisible as a boast—his skill level is so far above other MCs that they literally are unable to see him. At the same time, Daymond is invisible in the sense that he is rarely around.

I mix Daymond another screwdriver, pulling him into the kitchen for a brief interview. He tells me about his early days as MC Hitman and recounts his time in prison. "I was a wildcat," he says, shaking his head and smiling at the memory:

My mom asked me did I believe in God. I said no. And God was like, "Nigga, you don't believe in me? Well, I'm about to show you something." Basically, he took me from my surroundings and my livelihood, and put me in a cage. I got in a few fights and shit like that, but nothing really bad happened to me. No matter where I was at or what I was doing, he sent an angel down to protect me. He let me know that, "I gave you a gift to rhyme. You need to use your gifts and make a living out of it." I was only gone for like fifteen months and I got out and that's when I got with DVS Mindz. It's been real ever since. Now it's where I'm supposed to be. This is the beginning of my lifetime with DVS. This is just the beginning.

The addition of De'Juan last year capped an era of change for DVS Mindz. 1137 Washburn is no longer the official headquarters for the band—in fact, no one in the group lives there anymore. For years, Stu had ignored the property tax bills that were mailed to the house, and a sizeable debt piled up. Eventually, the county threatened to repossess the property unless Stu came up with eight thousand dollars to cover the unpaid taxes. Having blown through his $50,000 windfall, Stu had no way to settle the bill. The county repossessed the house.

By then, Barry, De'Juan, and his cousin Kevin had already gone their separate ways. Daymond spent most of his days working and his nights raising his six-year-old son, and Stu didn't even live in Kansas anymore. "There's been a couple of shows where we hadn't seen each other in about two weeks," De'Juan told me during an interview around this time.

Without everyone living and collaborating at 1137, the band's writing methods have changed too. The once inter-active process now occurs in separate spheres. "It's been a long time since we sat at a table and wrote a song together," Daymond says. "We used to sit down together and really do it," Barry adds. "But a lot of times how we progressed and been in this a while, we're away from each other and know what's going on."

Daymond adds, "Members changed, the sound changed, our beats changed, everything changed. We had to tune up the machine and now it's hot. 'Cause when it was us three—me and Str8, and 40—it was just diehard writing rhymes every day. We didn't have shit else to do. We didn't have jobs. That was our jobs really, was just write rhymes, eat chicken, and drink beer. That's all we did. Now, all of us, we got kids, we got families, now we got studio shit. Now basically we can do what we want to do."

SONG OF THE YEAR

DVS was recently informed that they were nominated for the second year in a row for a "Best Rap/Hip-Hop" Klammy. The Klammies, or Kansas City Lawrence Area Music Awards, were bestowed annually upon local musicians, music industry workers, and venues. The Klammies were created by the *Pitch*, the KC-based alternative weekly newspaper.[2] Each Klammy award had five contenders, who were selected after the *Pitch* sent out a call for nominations from those working in the regional music industry—musicians, promoters, journalists, radio disc jockeys, and others. Physical ballots were then circulated to the public, primarily via the newspaper. Voters filled out ballots by hand and either mailed them in or dropped them off at designated nightclubs and retail stores. An awards ceremony is held each spring at a historic theater in downtown Kansas City.

This year, DVS is up against Tech N9ne and the 57th Street Rogue Dog Villians (RDVs)—acts that are enjoying significant radio airplay throughout the region, have CDs in the local stores, and street teams that plaster KC with flyers, posters, and stickers. "This is just my prediction, I'm not even hating," Barry says, taking a long drink from a mason jar filled with vodka and orange juice. "We should win every year. We're not gonna win this year. You know why? Politics. Whoever wins it's a joke 'cause you know who should have. I keep telling everybody, we're not winning. They're gonna give it to somebody else."

That somebody else is likely to be either Tech N9ne or the RDVs. Tech N9ne has built a rabid fanbase in Kansas City that has voted him winner of the best rap Klammy every year since the awards began in 1997. He is a hometown hero, beloved by everyone from the counter help at the local barbeque joints to the program directors at Kansas City radio stations. "KPRS been rotating the *shit* out of Tech and the Rogue Dogs these last two weeks," Barry gripes. "I mean playing it ridiculous, at the damnedest hours. That's what I'm saying about the politics of things. All of the sudden they got somebody to play those motherfuckers."

In addition to air time on the radio, Tech N9ne's single, "Planet Rock," is nominated for a song of the year Klammy, almost unheard of for a rap track. Barry complains that "Planet Rock" is an old song that should have been disqualified from consideration. "I heard it way before motherfuckers riding his dick. We can't even get our shit on the hometown radio at nine o'clock on Friday. Motherfuckers hating on us so bad. We're nominated for best hip-hop/rap act two years in a row, and they still won't play our shit. And we got three radio playable songs."

Daymond nods, agreeing. "Everybody in Kansas City sounds the same."

De'Juan walks over, beer in one hand, blunt in the other, smiling as he tells the group about a friend who is supposedly planning, the night of the Klammies, to "test drive" a limousine for a few hours. He grins at the thought of it. "Hey man, we might fuck around and win," De'Juan says to Barry.

"I think we *can*, dude," Barry replies, suddenly hopeful. "I thought we shoulda won last year. I know politics is going to fuck with us. But I'm telling you, we won already. Our shit ain't even hit the street yet. That's why I say we won already. I don't need a fuckin' award. If we win, we actin' a fool. If we lose, we actin' a fool."

MILLION DOLLA BROKE NIGGAZ

The Granada, Lawrence, Kansas, April 30, 2000

DVS Mindz storms the Granada stage, opening with an energetic take on "Rowdy Hip Hoppers." The band members look like stars tonight, accenting their usual jeans and T-shirts with an array of bandanas, gloves, and more jewelry than usual. The group follows the opener with an equally animated "Real MCs," by the end of which Barry is shirtless and sweaty.

Although the concert takes place in a college town on a Sunday night during finals week, a capacity crowd is on hand for DVS Mindz's CD release party. To ensure a turnout, the band added Tech N9ne and the 57th Street Rogue Dogg Villians to the bill. KC band the Zou, issuing their own debut CD, was invited to get things started.

At DVS's first live performance in 1993, the band opened for Tech N9ne, who was then a hot up and comer. Seven years later, Tech is a bona fide celebrity in Kansas City and is poised for national stardom. He recently appeared on Sway & King Tech's hit, "The Anthem," which was released by Interscope Records and featured legends such as Eminem, RZA, and KRS-One. In November 1999, Tech released a CD titled

The Calm Before the Storm on a local label, Midwestside Records, but he had also started his own record company, Strange Music, Inc.

Strange quickly established itself as an ambitious independent label. In the pre–social media era, Tech and his business partner, Travis O'Guin, amassed a "street team" of fans willing to go all out to promote Tech N9ne's brand. As a local journalist noted in the *Pitch* around this time, "Every night, its members pass out promotional materials such as CDs, posters, T-shirts and caps to the prospective hip-hop heads it encounters outside clubs, malls and retail music stores. The crew has already hit twelve other cities, including Atlanta, St. Louis, Houston and Indianapolis."[3]

DVS's profile has continued to rise, and they hope to follow suit. Over the past two years, the group has become a larger and more complex business. The band established their own record label, No Coast, and are represented by Randy as manager. Now they aim to take it to the next level, to transform the ragtag posse from 1137 into a multifaceted business operation. As De'Juan puts it, "Niggas trying to get our money right, get our whole situation right."

Money is a continual source of concern. The group's live performances generate modest revenues—fifty or one hundred dollars for an opening set if they are lucky. That is used to repay the costs required to get everyone to the show and maybe buy a few burgers and a round of beers. And that is when DVS gets paid at all. "You got to make sacrifices, even if that means doing shows for free," Randy tells the guys. "Once we get the name recognition with the local promoters and we start to build a fanbase, *then* we can start talking about how much we're going to charge if they want us to perform."

The cost of getting the band to concerts and recording sessions is dwarfed by the mountain of expenses related to No Coast, the band's independent record label. Lack of funding is the primary reason it took No Coast more than two years to issue its first CD. DVS Mindz had to cover the substantial outlays related to *Million Dolla Broke Niggaz*: purchasing beats from local producers, recording, mixing and mastering, and printing the first round of one thousand CDs. The band has amassed dozens of tracks over the years, recorded piecemeal with a myriad of producers and sometimes without written documentation. There are clearance issues with some of the instrumental tracks, which required hiring a lawyer to review what contracts and paperwork existed. Some of the beatmakers are refusing to sign off on their productions without substantial concessions; others have disappeared. DVS plans to distribute the disc personally, hand-delivering their debut to area record stores, to be placed on consignment. At a minimum, that requires logistics, tens of hours of time, and gas money. The band members are willing to pitch in to varying degrees, with the assumption that a big payday is around the corner.

As a business enterprise, DVS Mindz faces high overhead and low revenues. Randy and the guys are expected to make up any difference as part of their investment in the group's future. Daymond, Stu, and Randy work full-time and contribute money from their paychecks to subsidize the band. But Barry and De'Juan are employed less frequently, if at all, and have less to give. When it comes time to cover a DVS-related expense, they might not have enough to pay their share. This means that everyone else has to chip in more or let the band suffer. Randy regularly takes out payday loans to keep things afloat, while Barry struts around in brand-new Air Jordans, chatting into the latest cell phone. All of this has led to resentment, bickering, and accusations of laziness.

"When we got into it, it was about rhyming," Stu says.

The business has kicked in now. If we want to do this full-time, we got to think of it as a business. If you don't have your business right, you're going to be out there like a lot of these major cats, selling millions of records and filing bankruptcy. Ain't getting paid shit. Getting fucked over because they didn't look at one line or two lines of their contract. I'm not trying to be that motherfucker. Fucking with my dinner table. "What's up with the publishing? I don't like the way that's written in the contract right there. Let me have my people look at it, and then we are going to get back to you." I'm not trying to get fucked. I don't want to be just some lyrical skilled motherfucker, out there making records for somebody and making them money, so they can drive around in big Benzes.

The band's desire to earn money is heightened by pressures to support their growing families. "We've changed, we were younger back then," Stu explains. "All of us have families now. I got kids. Pay me. I got to get paid."

Money matters are complicated by an aura of mild bedlam that permeates the DVS organization. The band's day-to-day operations are hindered because Barry and De'Juan do not own cars. Substantial time and energy are involved in everyday tasks like getting the band members to someone's home studio for a recording session or to a venue for a gig. Those hurdles multiply when the recording studios and concert venues are located outside of Topeka. Logistics are often difficult and require a mixture of begging, pleading, waiting, getting stood up, and endless phone calls and messages in an era when mobile services are limited.

For example, De'Juan was recently invited to guest on a song at the Granada with Lawrence-based party band, Phat Albert.

He showed up midway through his number, sprinting from the parking lot directly onto the stage and grabbing the nearest mic. After the show, catching his breath backstage, De'Juan explains, "I got a ride that said they could bring me to the show. It happened to be 40-Killa's girl. She comes up missing. Doesn't pick him up from work at six, seven o'clock. Calls me about eight o'clock. Then, I got outside to get my phone— 'cause I only got a car charger 'cause I'm broke. And my aunt left with my fuckin' phone in her car. So I shoot back past her to get my fuckin' phone out of the car. Then we stop by motherfucking Walgreens to get some cigarettes, 'cause we're already fuckin' running late. And then I get out to change right then 'cause I don't have time and I'm cussing everyone else out 'cause I'm fucking late. So I change in the parking lot and lock the keys in the trunk. That was about nine o'clock, nine-thirty. Show started at 9:45. I was twenty miles away."

As manager, Randy keeps everything running as smoothly as possible, but there are many moving parts to the DVS organization. The band's stature is rising on the regional rap scene, but conflicts within the group are increasing too. The band's creative drive and vision are undeniable, but there are also ego battles and jostling for position—energy expended with little to show for it. This leads to tensions and arguments that are increasingly a feature of the DVS environment.

"We go through the brotherly shit," Stu tells me. "There's behind-the-scenes shit that goes on. If we agreed on every motherfuckin' thing, we got a bunch of fuckin' yes men. I don't want a bunch of yes men. My point of view may not be right, but if I got you telling me it's tight, come on, man. We go through that. We get mad and I mean *mad* at each other. 'And another thing!' It goes through that."

ME AGAINST MYSELF AND I PREVAIL

At the CD release party, Stu takes position at the front of the stage and addresses the crowd directly. "I was sitting at home one night, and I started thinking," he says. He sports a sleeveless gray T-shirt with a skeleton hand giving the middle finger. A blue bandana is wrapped around his head, and his hands are covered in Reebok athletic gloves.

"What was you thinking, baby?" a guy in the audience yells back.

Stu grins and continues. "I've battled motherfuckers from California to Florida. And I started thinking, what the fuck would it be like to battle myself? I wrote a song about it. Y'all wanna hear it?"

The audience cheers.

"Well, here it go."

The beat kicks in, and Stu launches into "Me Against Myself and I Prevail," a solo track featured on DVS's new CD.[4] The song is a six-minute high-concept piece where Stu assumes three personalities–Stuart, Str8jakkett, and Wrexx—who trade verses and battle one another. Even knowing this, "Prevail" has a steep learning curve and is filled with complexities that are difficult to digest upon first listen. The song's appearance at the Granada concert marks its live debut, so it is unfamiliar to almost everyone on hand. As Stu begins, the rest of the group fades into the background, leaving the MC out front to fend for himself.

Behind Stu, the back half of the stage swells with Crew members, friends, fellow musicians, hangers-on, and a teenager hoisting a No Coast banner above his head. Some stand, holding drinks and watching the proceedings. Others lean against the drum riser, talking and hanging out on the stage like it's their living room. Still others stand on the drum riser on either side of the DJ, passing around shots, smoking cigarettes, and chatting. The result is a stage that is crowded, visually confusing, and distracts from the performance.

The merits of "Me Against Myself and I Prevail" are lost on the Granada concertgoers, and the song ends with muted fanfare. The rarely played "DVS Mindbender" and the popular "No Coast" follow but fail to take flight. Daymond then performs back-to-back solo tracks, neither of which are featured on DVS Mindz's debut CD. Despite his best efforts to ignite the hundreds-strong audience, Daymond's songs conclude to barely a hint of applause. His frustration is palpable. "They ain't ready for the real live shit," he says dismissively to no one in particular.

"We fitting to get live for y'all," Daymond tells the audience. "What y'all want to hear? Y'all want to hear 'Niggaz'?"

His question generates a murmur and some halfhearted applause.

"That's what niggas was waiting on," Daymond laughs. "Somebody told me they want to hear 'Tired of Talking' though. The Zou still here so you know we gonna do 'Bust Somethin'.' They screaming out 'Bust Somethin'.'"

Stu and Daymond confer briefly, away from the audience.

"Wait a minute," Stu asks. "What you want to do?"

"'Tired of Talking'," Daymond replies.

"Daymond," someone yells from backstage. "It hits the stores May ninth, let 'em know."

"Yo," Daymond tells the audience, "DVS Mindz album, *The DVS Exxxperience, Million Dolla Broke Niggaz*, will be in every major retail store May ninth. Seventh Heaven, Blockbuster, Blockbuster Media, Hastings, wherever you can get a tape, DVS Mindz is gonna be there."

CHANGING SOUND

The recent triumphs of Tech N9ne and the 57th Street Rogue Dogg Villians may have influenced DVS's thinking about the best path forward. Rather than pursuing a major label deal, the band followed Strange Music and Hogstyle's blueprint: start their own record label and self-release a CD. DVS's musical style is also changing. The group's early songs might be described as energetic, bouncy, or funky, but much of their recent output is ominous and foreboding. The beats are slower and hit harder. As MCs, DVS remain as lyrical as ever, but gone are the complex metaphorical descriptions of verbal beatdowns, often replaced by plainspoken descriptions of real violence.

These modifications are evident on DVS Mindz's debut CD, *Million Dolla Broke Niggaz: The DVS Exxxperience, 1994–2000, Volume One.* By the time DVS released the disc, the band had amassed years of studio recordings, and they were eager to release as much of it as possible. Initially, it was going to be a double album with thirty songs that filled two discs. But contractual headaches, budgetary considerations, and common sense won out, and the group went with a single CD instead. This meant eliminating half the songs.

From the group's original three-man lineup, only three S.G.-produced tracks ("DVS Mindbender," "Misrepresenters," and "Unsigned Hype") survived. Seminal early numbers such as "Rowdy Hip Hoppers," "Central Time Zone," "Real MCs," and "No Coast" were axed. The Crew was pained by these omissions, but the band favored newer material that showcased their changing sound and lineup.[5] The most recent songs, recorded just months before the album's release, had, as Barry puts it, "a whole different production and just a whole different outlook on it." This included the menacing, hardcore rap of "Bust Somethin'" and "Niggaz (1137)," both of which were produced by longtime associates, Boogieman and Rock, members of KC rap act, the Zou.

"Bust Somethin'" was a posse cut that paired the original three-headed dragon, Stu, Barry, and Daymond, with members of the Zou. "Bust Somethin'" was more overtly violent than DVS's earlier material. The title has dual meanings—to "bust something" means to shoot a gun but also refers to MCs spraying the room with killer verses. Grand in scale and polished to a shimmer, "Bust Somethin'" marks a noticeable upgrade in production. It sounds big-budget compared to the indie stylings of the earlier material. Boogieman and Rock completely overhauled "Tired of Talking" in the same vein, slowing it to half speed and stirring it into a witch's brew that bubbles with fire and venom. The "Tired of Talking" remake does not appear on *Million Dolla Broke Niggaz*, but DVS used this version for their first music video and performs it at nearly every concert.

Then there was "Niggaz (1137)," DVS's ominous ode to self. Slowed to a thudding crawl à la Tech N9ne and the RDV's "Let's Get Fucked Up," the song became an instant standout at DVS Mindz shows. In the prebroadband era, when the music of obscure, underground acts is difficult to find online, "Niggaz (1137)" is the closest thing DVS has to a hit—a song that local concert audiences recognize and responded to.

"A lot of people said we sound East Coast and we're on the East Coast dick," Barry tells me a couple of weeks after *Million Dolla Broke Niggaz* is released. "That's not the case. So we decided, 'Okay let's do something. Everyone says we never rap over slow beats and don't really talk about gangster stuff. We're not gangsters. We're just real niggas. So let's make a song called "Niggaz" and we'll make it the song that everybody wants to hear. We'll give them what they want to hear but still keep it real and give it from our perspective.' And niggas dug the *shit* out of it."

COMMERCIAL PRESSURES

The new material produced by Boogieman and Rock is part of an effort by DVS Mindz to expand their appeal. This does not mean going commercial or trying to score a novelty rap hit à la "Who Let the Dogs Out?" But even Stu, who built an identity around his refusal to sell out, concedes that he wants to earn money from music. "You have a hit and you get paid," he says in reference to a rapper who recently landed a goofy song in a Burger King commercial. "That's real. 'Cause all of us got kids that need to eat."

For rap musicians, making money serves as a stamp of professionalism and authenticity. "Money equals power, and making money is celebrated as long as it happens on the artist's own terms."[6] But reaching larger audiences requires that DVS make stylistic and sonic adjustments to the original three-headed-dragon concept of all-night ciphers at 1137.

Hardcore gangsta rap dominated the nineties. N.W.A., Ice Cube, Dr. Dre, Snoop Dogg, Tupac, the Notorious B.I.G., Big Pun, and Jay-Z became some of the genre's most prominent figures, often without significant radio play. These artists were credible, skilled, and famous. Plus, they sold a lot more records than critically acclaimed lyrical acts such as De La Soul, A Tribe Called Quest, Talib Kweli, and Mos Def.[7]

DVS badly wants to make it, yet the group also operates under an ethos of artistic purity. Selectively adopting certain gangsta styles, sounds, and lyrical imagery allows the band to toughen up their image while remaining true to their anticommercial ethos. "We are dope whether or not [it sells]," De'Juan says of *Million Dolla Broke Niggaz*. As for selling out, "It's going to cost more than they paid Mase. It's going to cost more than they paid the Lox. 'Cause I'm for real about my shit."

The phrase "million dollar broke niggas" first appeared on the 1998 Method Man track, "Cradle Rock."[8] Using it as the title of DVS's debut album was Barry's idea, a nod to one of his personal heroes. DVS Mindz was never going to be mistaken for N.W.A., but being an edgier version of the Wu-Tang Clan seemed within reach.

In the end, Stu believes that *Million Dolla Broke Niggaz* showcases DVS Mindz's commitment to independence and artistic integrity. The album's centerpiece is "Niggaz (1137)," a song that has no chance of being played on the radio. "The most beautiful thing about this album to me is that everything we put on this album and everything that we did on this album is what we want to rap about. Other artists are under pressure from A&Rs and executives that cater to certain people, that cater to this audience or that audience. We never went into the studio with that goal. We just did what we felt like we wanted to do."

THE POOL ROOM

While Tech N9ne and the RDVs were ruling Kansas City, and DVS was toughening up their sound and image in Topeka, Lawrence's rap scene was moving in an alternate direction. Project Groove was a weekly hip-hop night held at the Pool Room, a dive bar located far from the popular downtown venues where Tech N9ne and DVS performed. The Pool Room became home base for a new generation of up-and-coming hip-hop acts that included SoundsGood, Archetype, Approach, and Johnny Quest from Lawrence, and KC-based artists Mac Lethal, Ces Cru, the Guild, Sevenfold Sympathy, and Deep Thingkers.[9]

Several of the Pool Room hip-hoppers met while living in the KU dorms. Most of them are a decade younger than DVS, and their brand of socially and politically enlightened rap is far removed from DVS's gritty street yarns. DVS wears prison-issue orange and call themselves "niggaz," while nineteen-year-old SoundsGood leader Miles Bonny sports a porkpie hat and plays jazz trumpet under the alias Dino Jack Crispy. "Jazz is where I'm most at home, but I love hip-hop's energy and culture and beats and essence," Bonny tells me during an interview around this time.[10] The Pool Room acts are friendly and nonthreatening, perfect for a Midwestern college-town audience that wants to have a good time, drink a few beers, and hopefully hook up.

Over time, the Pool Room began attracting larger crowds. "I love the fact that on a Wednesday night with relatively no promotion, you can draw a couple hundred people to a venue to watch you perform," says Sean "Approach" Hunt, whose recent CD *Ultraproteus* features down-to-earth poetics and no curse words.[11]

The Pool Room acts are also media-savvy in a way that DVS is not. Bonny and some friends launched a website, (now defunct) LawrenceHipHop.com, that heavily features the Pool Room artists. The site's forums buzz with opinion and debate. There is open disdain for Tech N9ne and the 57th Street Rogue Dog Villians, who are derided as fake thugs that create bland corporate rap. Pool Room icons such as Mac Lethal mercilessly poke fun at gangsta rap stereotypes in songs such as "My Mom Izza Thug." Perhaps unfairly, acts such as DVS Mindz are lumped in with the gangsta rap set, dismissed as out of touch compared to the Pool Room's supposedly sophisticated fare.

"It's really poppy or popular, like some gangsta shit or some R&B shit," twenty-year-old Archetype frontman Isaac "ID"

Diehl tells me when I ask him about the local rap scene. "People are there just to be mindless and chase each other around. I'm not talkin' shit or anything. I just don't think our music has that kind of vibe. It definitely lacks a lot of the content of those kinds of music."[12]

The local music press praised Project Groove to the heavens, with one scribe avowing that the weekly event "single-handedly transformed the Pool Room from a good-ol'-boys watering hole to one of the most respected hip-hip hop venues in the Midwest."[13]

LAST CALL

On stage at the Granada, the opening chords to "Tired of Talking" ring out. DVS is now eight songs into their CD release party set, and the band has only performed two tracks from the disc. The "Tired" remix is followed by "Bust Somethin'" and "Niggaz (1137)," completing the trilogy of the Boogieman and Rock–produced material that forms the core of the release party setlist. "Niggaz (1137)" continues to be DVS's most familiar song, and it gets a big reception, followed by a Granada staff member interrupting the concert to announce last call.

Barry's solo number, "Murdarous Verses," arrives next, with Barry performing the song from high atop a tall riser located to the right of the stage. This is followed by "Do or Die," a solo track from De'Juan that was not included on the album.

"Y'all make some noise," Daymond says as De'Juan's song bangs to a close. A few female voices holler back. "That's it?" Stu asks, sounding surprised. "I know we got more ladies in the house than that."

THE CREW ❧ 155

"All the fine-ass ladies, be quiet," Daymond yells. The line generates a mild laugh but little else.

Stu and Daymond are joking around, but De'Juan is upset at the audience's lack of response. To him, it is a sign of disrespect. "Y'all acting a punk-fucking fool," he yells at concertgoers in the front row, voice raspy. "Topeka got a whole bunch of crazy-ass niggas, man. Ya'll niggas don't want to say shit! What the fuck you come out here for?" De'Juan is met with silence.

Looking to defuse the situation, Daymond quickly steps in and delivers an a cappella rhyme. He performed the same verse about two months earlier at the same venue. At that show, it was well-received, but this time around, less so. DVS is still on stage, but the audience seems to have moved on. The group finishes out the concert with a cappellas from De'Juan and Stu. Stu gets a big reception on his last line, and De'Juan holds the index finger of his red Nike athletic gloves to his lips. "Hey, don't tell nobody. 'Cause they act like they don't fuckin' *know!*"

"This ain't no motherfuckin' game," Daymond says, trying to lighten the vibe. "DVS Mindz holding down real hip hop. We got one more nigga to go."

Frustrated, De'Juan refuses to back down. "Niggas start going to sit down like this shit was wack. Lace these niggas, man. We don't need a fuckin' beat!"

Barry raps a cappella for a couple of minutes, followed by a short scratching session from the DJ. The CD release party, which began with vigor, ends in enmity.

9

HEAT

1436 SW Byron Street, Topeka, Kansas

Barry slouches in the front seat of a late-model Buick, brandishing a silver .357 magnum in his right hand. I'm sitting directly behind him in the back. "That's the kind of shit we got to get down on tonight," Barry drawls to Daymond, who is seated next to him up front.

Barry's Topeka twang sounds thicker tonight, more pronounced than usual. "Niggas don't understand," he says, dragging out each word as he waves the pistol around. "They think that this rap shit is sweet and don't think shit is real in the streets." Barry's voice is rising now, getting louder. "We might have to do that shit tonight and risk some motherfuckin' pen time. Are we gonna go in here and handle this shit?"

"Yeah," Daymond says, nodding, "What's the plan though?"

Barry lowers the gun towards the seat. The Buick is stationed in the well-lit parking lot of an apartment building, and Barry doesn't want to attract attention. "I'll tell you what," he says, leaning back and lighting a Kool with his left hand. "I got these niggas that's gonna go ahead and take this shit off our hands. Shit's just so hot, you know we tired of holdin' on to it. We can also get other motherfuckers around this motherfuckin' Midwest connected, get this shit poppin', and get niggas paid. But come down to it, it might take certain motherfuckers to do it. Are you the nigga that's ready to be the nigga to do it?"

"Yeah," Daymond affirms immediately. He's draped in an opulent brown leather jacket, clutching a dark gray mobile phone in his right hand. "I got kids to feed and a wife to lace. I'm gonna call this motherfucker, tell him to meet us here in five minutes." Daymond looks at the phone and shakes it. "Five motherfuckin' minutes, nigga!"

Barry and Daymond give each other daps and exit the car, Barry cocking the pistol as he goes.

There is silence for a beat.

"That was good," I say, hitting the stop button on my camcorder. "Let's do another take, but this time let's have Barry say something about the briefcase."

Murdarous Verses is the title of an eight-minute movie DVS and I are in the midst of creating. The short film is part of Barry's vision, his most ambitious concept for a show opener yet. It will take place at the Granada and, in Barry's mind, it will go something like this: As DVS Mindz waits in the wings of the Granada to perform, the house lights dim, and our movie begins to play on the stage's massive backdrop screen. In the film, the members of DVS Mindz are trying to get to a gig at the Granada but encounter various obstacles and enemies along the way.

To create the music video for "Tired of Talking," the band and I looked to movies such as *A View to a Kill* and *The Shining* for inspiration. For *Murdarous Verses*, we use a similar strategy, paying winking tribute to more of our favorites. The entire thing will look like the ending of *Goodfellas*, when Ray Liotta drives around, coked out of his mind and convinced he's being followed by helicopters. In our movie, DVS Mindz possesses a mysterious briefcase that belongs to an enigmatic mob boss whose face is never seen, plot points taken from *Pulp Fiction*. Our film climaxes with a standoff and gun battle inspired by *Reservoir Dogs*, followed by a car chase that culminates with our heroes screeching to a halt behind the Granada and rushing through its backdoors and towards the stage. As the movie concludes and the screen fades to black, the Granada's house lights flare on, and DVS Mindz strides onstage for their opening number. Having witnessed the screen come to life, the audience will be positively blown away.

DVS's vision for the movie motivates everyone to get to work. I recruit my friends Jeff and Eliott to help with the taping. The band enlists various Crew members to play enemies and heavies. Randy is cast as the faceless mob boss. We shoot Barry driving around Topeka in a convertible, making calls at a pay phone, looking up overhead for helicopters. We record Stu outside my apartment in Lawrence, playing Special Agent Wrexx and instructing the guys to call in using access code 1137. We videotape the quartet driving around, parking, and jumping over a wall behind the Granada, banging on the back doors to be let inside. In a nod to our best-loved mafia movies, we record a scene in my apartment kitchen where the guys prepare an Italian meal, boiling linguini and slicing razor-thin slivers of garlic for "the gravy." There is no script; everyone just improvises their lines.

Over a series of nights, we videotape in and around Randy's apartment complex in Topeka. We shoot in the parking lot, with Eliott recording from the roof of a moving vehicle. We tape in an exterior alleyway and at the front security gates. We capture multiple takes of De'Juan effortlessly springing over a six-foot fence.

Randy's apartment is located on the underground level of the building, accessible by walking down a flight of stairs. We shoot outside his front door and in his living room, kitchen, and bedroom.

One Saturday night, the band puts out a call for everyone to come to Randy's with their guns so that we can record the standoff and shootout finale. The Crew delivers and then some, arriving with an armory's worth of Glocks, gats, shotguns, and AR-15s. They also bring alcohol and weed, and Randy's living room is soon transformed into a crowded and boozy barroom loaded with firearms. As Eliott and I set up the cameras, Barry drunkenly wrestles with a friend while one of his buddies tries to take a pistol from another guy. Crew members continue to arrive, adding more artillery, booze, blunts, and bodies to the mix.

Eliott and I prepare to tape the standoff, pleading with everyone to double-check their weapons to make sure they are not loaded. We begin taping. In the scene, Barry enters the apartment, gets into an argument with one of the Crew members, and pulls a pistol on him, prompting everyone else in the room to whip their guns out and aim them at Barry. This, in turn, prompts Stu, Daymond, and De'Juan to burst into the room with rifles cocked and ready. We tape from numerous angles, with everyone's guns pointed directly at Barry's head. Barry improvises new dialogue each time, ratcheting up the volume with every take. Between shots, the guys suggest lines of script while Barry tells jokes and doubles over with laughter.

I edit all the footage together, bringing the guys individually to my apartment to record voiceovers and additional dialogue. We set the movie to a backdrop of DVS instrumentals and mix the sound. *Murdarous Verses* will not win any Oscars, but it is a fun tribute to some of our favorite films. It's a low-budget action flick that simultaneously pokes fun at the Pool Room purists who decried DVS's turn towards harder sounds. The movie will be a creative way for the band to open a show, something they've never tried before. The Granada audience will not know what hit them.

SOUNDMAN SABOTAGE

Club 301, 301 S Water Street, Olathe, Kansas

"913 representing. Y'all enjoying this shit tonight or what?"

The hosts's microphone sends sharp feedback squeaks through the speaker, nails on a sonic chalkboard.

The host winces and tries again. "If you enjoy this shit say 'hell yeah,'" he calls to the audience.

"Hell yeah," the crowd responds dutifully.

"Say fuck yeah."

"Fuck yeah."

"All right, we really like that. DVS Mindz is about ready to represent, showing they mad skills. You know what I'm saying? Put your hands together for DVS Mindz!"

There is not much of a reaction. Unless you count Randy, no one from the Crew made it to the show tonight. The white, mostly teenage audience from Olathe, Kansas, a suburb of KC, has never heard of DVS Mindz. The band is appearing tonight as part of a concert put together by local promoter BigStinky Productions titled Show Me What You Workin' With. Tickets cost $10, and the lineup features more than twenty regional rap artists. Most are unknowns, but there are some bigger names on the lineup, including the Popper and the night's headliner, Tech N9ne. The concert is open to those sixteen and older and drew mostly high-school students who are here to see Tech N9ne. They are ambivalent about trudging through an assembly of opening acts.

The host hands the mic to Barry, who walks onstage saying, "Midwest representatives. And if you don't know and if you ain't been there and the mic sounds nice. Holding it down for the Midwest."

As Barry addresses the crowd, the other DVS members walk on to the stage, testing their microphones. "Check, one," De'Juan repeats. "One, two, one two," Daymond intones. The testing goes on a beat longer than it should. Barry explains to the audience, "We're just making sure the mics right and we'll jump it off."

After a few more moments, Stu says, "Let's make it happen." The DJ nods at him but cannot get the music started.

"Yo, where my real live hip-hop niggas?" Daymond yells. "Make some noise!" There is a mild response but not much. The crowd mostly just stands there.

From the left, Barry peers at the audience, looking to an area beyond the stage, where a handful of small groups are seated around a set of tables. He can't believe it. "None of y'all standing over here? *None* of y'all? You'll get live when I get hype then."

"Wait a minute," Daymond says. "I said, where my real live hip-hop niggas? Make some noise!" There are a few more cheers, but the overall response remains chilly.

Finally, the music begins. Stu motions to the club's sound engineer to turn up the volume. The engineer ignores him. Barry launches into his verse, barreling into the song with gusto. The volume on Barry's microphone is set lower than the others, so it's hard to make him out. When the other three MCs chime in with backing vocals, they instantly overpower Barry's lead.

De'Juan holds his microphone in the air, pointing to it and nodding to the sound engineer. The engineer cranks up the volume on De'Juan's microphone, causing it to emit squalls of feedback. He instantly turns it all the way down. De'Juan begins to rap his verse, but his microphone is turned off, and the only sound that can be heard is the group's backing vocals. Daymond walks up behind De'Juan and, in a single fluid motion, passes De'Juan a microphone over his shoulder. Without averting his eyes from the crowd or acknowledging Daymond, De'Juan takes the mic with his free hand and swiftly switches over to using it, not missing one syllable of his verse.

Unfortunately, De'Juan's replacement microphone feeds back, and the sound engineer turns it down too. De'Juan still cannot be heard. As the group takes over for the song's hook, De'Juan holds up the two microphones sideways, hanging from their cords like dead fowl at the end of a pheasant hunt. As De'Juan raps the hook, he alternates between the microphones, trying to gauge if either is producing sound.

While De'Juan was completing his verse, Daymond scrounged up another cordless mic. Now it is his turn to rap, but when he launches into his verse, the mic is turned so low that Daymond cannot be heard. In a sweeping arm motion that resembles a high five, Daymond immediately grabs one of De'Juan's two mics so that by the end of his first line, he's rapping into the new device. The handover occurs so quickly that audience members who weren't closely watching would never even know it took place. Daymond plows through his lyrics, trying out both mics and eventually settling on the new one, which produces no sound at first and then begins squealing and feeding back as the sound engineer makes adjustments. Daymond looks dismayed.

Stu attempts to bring order to chaos by walking up to Daymond and urging him to rap harder. "Come on!" he encourages. "What?" he yells and then backs up Daymond along with the rest of the group.

The band makes it to the end of the song, but the sound is a mess the entire way. DVS did their best under trying circumstances, but the audience is entirely unmoved by anything it just witnessed. Most of the spectators seem confused. Daymond looks dispirited, the wind taken out of his sails. "Wait a minute," he says angrily into the mic.

De'Juan interrupts, speaking into his microphone and directly addressing the sound engineer located on the other side of the room. "Hey, hold the fuck up, man. Can we get some volume on this bitch?"

Barry piles on, shouting, "Can we get the fuckin' mics right because apparently they're not 'cause nobody's moving. And I am and that's *bullshit*!"

"Come on, man." Daymond yells to the sound engineer. "Get my shit right, man!"

"Niggas didn't pay they money to hear that bullshit," De'Juan admonishes.

"Let's get it right," Barry adds, annoyed. "Let's keep it moving. Nobody paid to hear feedback. Let's get the shit jumping off. I want to drink and get bombed and get the fuck off here if nobody's feeling me. And I know you are. Let's jump it off, let's run to the next shit."

"No no no no!" De'Juan yells, stopping Barry. "My shit's not ready, dog. My shit's still not ready." De'Juan turns to the sound engineer. "I'm gonna keep talking until you check my shit. Please turn up the volume on my motherfucking shit."

"The cordless mics suck," Stu says to no one in particular.

The sound engineer looks hopelessly lost, adjusting knobs and dials on the soundboard to no avail.

De'Juan continues to rap about his lack of volume, his mic alternating between total silence and piercing feedback blasts.

"Come on, man," Daymond yells to the sound engineer, furious. "These people paid for a fucking show. Let's give 'em a fucking show. These mics is wack."

More than a minute has passed since DVS finished their opening number.

"My man trying to get his mic up a little bit," De'Juan says to the sound engineer. "I know you got some juice. Our shit's real shit. You got to hear the words *and* the beats. We ain't rapping over no motherfucking words nigga, we came to bang. Top town!"

"Come on, man," Daymond implores, "Let's get this shit sounding right, man. DVS Mindz is professional. We want this shit to sound like we professional."

Daymond's plea is met with more shrill feedback. Someone's microphone is causing it, but the sound engineer cannot tell where it's coming from.

"That's not my shit either," De'Juan says. "Somebody's shit feeding back. And it's not my shit. Somebody's else's shit fucked up. It's not my shit."

"It's not mine," Barry says. "Mine's not feeding back. Goddamn it I want to get full and stand like everyone else. Mine's good. Can you get my man's correct, so we can start the shit? Please."

Two minutes have now elapsed since the band played a song.

"I'm straight," De'Juan says finally, his mic working to his satisfaction for the first time. "Sometimes you just got to get your shit right. Ain't no point in doing it if it don't sound right."

The beat for "Niggaz (1137)" kicks in, and Stu takes the helm. He can't be heard. De'Juan hands him his mic, which is marginally louder but overpowered by the music. Daymond is up next, and his microphone is substandard too. Without looking at each other, Daymond and Stu trade microphones in a fluid, over-the-shoulder motion. The sound is not much better. A few lines later, Daymond and Barry trade microphones. It's only a slight improvement.

As De'Juan starts his verse, Daymond hands him his cordless mic. A few lines later, De'Juan passes the corded mic to Daymond behind his back. At the start of his verse, De'Juan and Barry trade microphones. These slights of hand are barely noticeable. The song comes to a close, and the band immediately starts up the next number, "Tired of Talking."

Bemused at the train wreck, Barry says, "The mics are out of control, but we're gonna keep it rolling." "Tired of Talking" goes much like the first two songs, with the haphazard sound keeping the show on the edge of disaster.

Everyone departs the stage except for Daymond, who closes the set with an a cappella, the same one he's performed at most of the group's recent shows. The crowd is statuelike. Daymond concludes his verse to complete silence. "DVS Mindz, No Coast representative," he says. "Y'all pick up the fuckin' CD in the back, ten dollars. Here's a free one." Daymond tosses a CD into the crowd, turns, and walks offstage, stooping to place the microphone on the stage floor as he departs.

The host implores the crowd, "Give it up for DVS Mindz, y'all."

There is no response.

"Show your love, no doubt. Show your love."

A few people clap. Some others boo.

Backstage, the band is fuming. "Soundman sabotage!" Stu bristles. "The soundman is a fuckin' dickhead. Now I know why the song 'Sound Bwoy Bureill' was made. Fuck him!"[1]

It was a miracle Stu even made it out that night. Earlier that day, his live-in girlfriend, Jessica, came home from work and found a set of divorce papers on the kitchen table. Jessica was stunned to discover that Stu was married. It was a long story.

In the fall of 1993, back when he was living at 1137 Washburn, Stu met Renae, a woman who lived in nearby Lawrence. With a string of failed relationships in his recent past, Stu was wary of getting involved with anyone. But a bad case of "the lonely bug" convinced him that Renae was a good match. Renae was soon living in Stu's room at 1137. The honeymoon was short-lived.

"We got along at first and then just started having trouble, arguments. Fighting like cats and dogs, and the next thing you know we're swapping spit. And then fighting like cats and dogs."

The tumultuous relationship became even rockier after Renae discovered she was pregnant. The birth of Stu's third daughter, Awtiawna, did not stabilize the situation. Instead, the couple's fighting escalated. Renae and Awtiawna moved to Wichita to live with Renae's father. Stu stayed in Topeka for the rest of 1995 but moved to Kansas City to crash with his cousin, Earl, the following year. Stu and Renae kept in contact and eventually reunited. They married on Valentine's Day 1997, moving into an apartment in KC. It lasted about a year. By the time the pair finally divorced in 2000, Stu was already living with Jessica in Lawrence.

Everyone in the group has children. Randy is the primary caretaker to his two sons, Randy Jr., six, and Dre, two. Daymond is the primary caretaker for six-year-old DJ and has another son, Brandon, who lives with his mother. Randy and Daymond work full-time and rely on their parents for help with child-care. Barry has two sons, and De'Juan has one. All of the group members have to balance their musical ambitions with the realities of single fatherhood: parent-teacher conferences, doctor's appointments, child-support payments, drop-offs and pick-ups, visitations, and custody hearings.

Everyone in the band is adamant that their motivation to make it stems from wanting to provide for their families, particularly their children. Even Daymond, so vocally opposed to the commercial music industry, indicates a willingness to compromise his art if it means moving up financially. "I want to own my own business, something I can leave my kids," he tells me. "Because my dad, he wasn't there, he didn't really do it for me. I got two sons myself, so I ain't trying to be in this shit and be broke. If I got to put on some shiny pants and get jiggy with it, hey."

SWEATING BULLETS

Barry and Lisa's apartment, Topeka, Kansas

In the bedroom, Barry strips the comforter from a queen-sized mattress as *Million Dolla Broke Niggaz* blasts from a CD player in the living room.

"Just doing some house cleaning, being as I haven't been here in days," he says in a raspy drawl. Barry sports an unbuttoned blue Hawaiian-style shirt with a white floral print that nearly matches his sheets. "I've been running around doing a bunch of shit trying to make this music shit happen. Trust me, it's not all sweet like a bunch of people think. You still have to deal with this shit. Room fucked up. Clothes all over the place."

Barry is not exaggerating. Clothing is piled everywhere, and at least five pairs of Nikes are strewn across the light brown carpet.

Barry shares the apartment with Lisa, the mother of his six-year-old son, Marcus. There is also two-year-old Devon, born to a different woman named Lisa. Then there is Stacy, Barry's on-and-off girlfriend. It's a complicated situation.

"This is actually, even though it sounds weird, my down time to relax," Barry says, fluffing a pillow. "Cleaning, believe it or not. Plus, I can't sleep unless the bed's straight."

Barry tucks the corners of the sheets and spreads the comforter across the top, smoothing everything over with two hands. Beads of sweat glisten atop his head, which is shaved bald.

"This is about as far as I'm going on this room," Barry says, wiping his brow. "Sweating bullets, I'm done fucking with it. Bed's done. That's my shit over in the corner." He points to a pile of clothing and shoe boxes on the floor.

"It's organized confusion. I know where my shoes are and my Timberlands, that's all I need to know. As long as all this is together, I'm organized."

We walk to the living room, where Barry plugs in a vacuum cleaner. The walls of the small room are covered with framed photos of Marcus taken over the years. There are also mementos from DVS Mindz hanging throughout the apartment. In a prominent spot in the living room, a 24-by-36-inch gold frame features photographs of Barry performing in concert, the CD covers and discs for *ICU The Revival* and *Coast to No Coast*, a compilation issued by DVS's No Coast label. The band's *Mag* cover and the two-page article "spread" from inside the issue are also featured in the collage.

Barry proudly produces his latest DVS Mindz artifact, a receipt from the Topeka Hastings store. It shows the words "Million Dolla Broke Nigg" and a price of $14.99. Barry has the CD, too, still wrapped in cellophane with the Hastings bar code, which also features the group's name and a portion of the album title. At last, a DVS Mindz CD sits alongside the legends of rap music. I ask Barry what sort of response the group received over the debut's changing sound.

"Shit, it's been a pretty damn good one. I expected a good response, and I was hoping for one, and we did it. It shocked people. Like they were getting something they weren't expecting or something. But I mean, hey, if they'd been listening for years, it shouldn't have been no surprise. Thing is, the next volume is going to be a surprise, and everything from then on is going to be a surprise. It took some people a little more time to feel us, but they do and that's tight. So, whatever formula we using is a good one and we need to stick to it. And if anything build on it and make it progress. But I dug it. It was a good response. It made *me* feel good."

Barry is the emotional lightning rod that runs through the center of DVS Mindz. When Barry is in a good head space, he is the most outgoing and engaging member of a group that is characterized by big personalities. But Barry also has a dark side that can appear out of nowhere and scorch everything in its path. It is this volatility that led Barry to punch the drunk guy in front of a nightclub when I first met the band. By contrast, De'Juan, with his history of violent crime and incarceration, comes across as completely in control.

Barry describes this unpredictability one night while hanging out at my apartment: "That's one thing about DVS Mindz, we're all cool and shit, we're fun as hell. Only thing that we cannot stand is bullshit. There's just no discrimination with DVS Mindz and bullshit. Whether you're Black, white, woman, man, kid, we can't take it. And it makes us just *snap*. There's been many incidents I'm not proud of where shit has happened where bullshit's been involved. I can't be held responsible for my actions. I can't take it. I'm allergic to it. If there was a plastic bubble to be away from bullshit, I'd be in one, twenty-four, seven."

Today, cleaning his apartment, Barry is relaxed and easygoing. He vacuums the living room carpet in a state of near zen, moving furniture and straightening up along the way. He finishes and grabs a bottle of blue-tinted soda from the refrigerator, taking a long slug.

Barry says he's tired from all the running around. DVS continues to perform anywhere and everywhere. On May 29, Memorial Day, DVS is booked to play two out-of-town concerts on the same day. One is called the Memorial Day Bash 2000, a showcase featuring ten Topeka rap acts. It will be held at the Granada in Lawrence at night.

Barry is more excited about the earlier show, the Mayday Beach Concert and Party 2000, an outdoor "summer jam" headlined by Black Rob, the Ying Yang Twins, and Nelly. The Mayday show has been heavily advertised on KC radio stations, and flyers promoting the event are plastered all over town. DVS and other local acts had to cough up a two-hundred-dollar "promotional fee" for five minutes of stage time. Paying to play was a hard pill to swallow, but the band could not pass up the chance to perform at a high-profile event in front of a festival audience.

"That one definitely is going to be fun," Barry says. "We only got five minutes but we make the most of whatever time we got. We're going to make them five minutes seem like fifteen, just to keep the crowd moving."

Given the short performance time, I wonder what songs DVS will choose to play. "Shoot, we still don't know, we ain't really decided," Barry tells me. "With situations like that, we go ahead and pretty much wait until we get there. See what it's like, see how the feel is going. And then we usually decide. 'This will be a good one. Let's do this one.' We'll wait until Monday and decide. Depending on how the crowd is and how damn hot it is."

JIM ROME

5150 Mental Productions, 920-1/2 Massachusetts Street, Lawrence, Kansas

The recording booth at 5150 Mental Productions features soft lighting, hardwood floors, and walls comprised of linen sound panels and strategically placed maple. A professional-grade condenser microphone with a metallic grille is affixed to a silver stand. Next to the mic is a black metal music stand with a thick white towel draped over it. Stu peers down at a spiral-bound notebook containing his lyrics. He fiddles with a pen and dons a pair of large headphones that cover his ears.

Stu is dressed in gray track pants, a navy-blue T-shirt that says "West Coast" over the left pectoral, white tennis shoes, and a black baseball cap, turned backward to reveal the word "Str8jakkett" in white lettering. Stu sports a few days of stubble and a gold watch that is more "retirement" than "bling."

Stu peers through the studio glass at producer Will Wilson, who is scrutinizing the sound levels on a long, rectangular mixing board. Will sits before a pair of dual computer monitors flanked by two pairs of speakers, an Akai MPC 2000 drum machine, a keyboard, and an array of digital boxes and gadgets. Barry sits off to the side, watching intently.

Inside the recording booth, Stu runs through his verse a few times to warm up. He finishes, and Will, who Stu can hear through headphones, asks him to do another take. Stu looks surprised and annoyed. "Is he *recording*?" Stu asks Barry through the glass. Stu had been running through his verses to get the flow down; he didn't know Will was taping. He gives the producer a stern look. "Hey man, you was testing levels. You didn't say 'record,' nothing. I thought we was still testing levels."

Will tells Stu that he had been recording the entire time. Stu is pissed. "Oh, okay, well shit, man. Son of a bitch."

Will asks Stu to make an adjustment to the placement of a word in one line.

"I doubt if it's gonna work," Stu says dismissively.

Will fiddles with some knobs on his computer.

"You still checking levels?" Stu asks, eyebrows raising. "Oh *boy*."

Finally, everyone is ready, and Stu fires off his first verse, a forty-five-second tongue-twisting volley. He finishes and turns a palm upward, looking at Will. "Okay? Yeah?" he asks. He does a second take, then a third, each better than the one before. Stu's warming to it now, smiling a bit and lightening up.

The song is called "Jim Rome," and it pays tribute to a California-based sportscaster with a growing audience. *The Jim Rome Show* began on a San Diego AM station but was tapped for national syndication in 1996. Rome was a prototypical "bad boy" radio host, launching his program each weekday to Guns 'N' Roses' "Welcome to the Jungle." A plug from Rome could help a band like DVS, which is why Stu and Barry are here tonight. The idea is to record a rap homage to Rome, embedding the lyrics with inside references to the show in hopes that Rome might play it on the air. It's not a total long shot—Stu and Barry have an inside connection. Jim Rome is friendly with the linebacker-sized man currently sitting next to Will at the mixing board.

Keith Loneker is a Lawrence legend who made a name for himself as a member of the KU football team a decade earlier. Keith then spent five years as an offensive lineman for the Los Angeles Rams before charming his way into Hollywood. At 6'3" and 325 pounds, Keith has a menacing look that makes him a perfect big-screen villain. His first film was Steven Soderbergh's *Out of Sight*, starring George Clooney and Jennifer Lopez, and he went on to play small movie roles alongside A-listers, such as Samuel L. Jackson, Mark Wahlberg, and Jennifer Aniston.

Keith, who never moved away from Lawrence, channeled some of his NFL and movie earnings into his latest venture, the music industry. He founded a production company, 5150 Mental Productions, and a record label, Lock-N-Load, tapping Wilson as an in-house producer. The pair envisions a music production and management company that specializes in street-level R&B and rap. At its downtown Lawrence recording studio, framed posters of Al Pacino in *Scarface*, Robert DeNiro in *Taxi Driver*, and Frank Sinatra's Rat Pack give some indication of the aesthetic 5150 is aiming for.

Another poster at 5150 is H. Jackson Brown's "21 Suggestions for Success," with life advice such as "marry the right person" and "work at something you enjoy that's worthy of your time and talent." For Keith, it's all part of a larger philosophy—to approach life with integrity and effort, whether one is playing football, filming a movie, or raising children.

"It's more than the music," Keith tells me. "I want these guys to come out of it being better people too. It's the same thing with a football coach. The game is everything, but you want to draw things out of the experience and out of your work that's gonna kick back into your life too. That's something that Coach Mason was always on us about that I've always held pretty dear."[2]

Keith is a DVS Mindz fan. Initially, he wanted to build his record label around the group and had offered to sign DVS numerous times. Concerned that they might be taken advantage of, the band has remained friendly with Keith but kept their distance. Instead, Keith put together Bombsquad, a Lawrence-based septet with a sound and image that closely resembles DVS with one key difference: Bombsquad's music is deliberately commercial, built around radio-friendly, singalong hooks that are intended to attract the widest possible audience.

"You can be an MC and still produce good songs that people want to listen to for a whole album," Keith tells me. He doesn't say DVS's name specifically, but we both know who he's talking about. "You get on some MC stuff, and it's like, 'All's I need is a drum beat and a snare drum and I can rap.' And they *can*! We got a lot of MCs around here who, shoot, you can beat box for 'em and they can entertain you for hours. But when it comes to paying the bills, you do have to sell some records to the masses. It's a business."[3]

Keith is entrepreneurial and energetic. The Jim Rome song was his idea. Given Keith's background in sports, it just makes sense. Keith and Wilson wrote the song's hook and tapped Bombsquad member Cassanova to rap it. Always looking for ways to connect 5150 and DVS Mindz, Keith called Stu, who also lives in Lawrence.

"I really liked how you and Killa sound together," he told Stu. "I got a song that I think would really fit you and Killa. How hard do you think it would be to get Barry up here?"

"It wouldn't be hard at all," Stu replied. "I just got to call him and tell him to come on up. Let's do this thing."

That night, knowing almost nothing about the track, Barry and Stu appear at Keith's studio. He plays the instrumental for them and pitches the Jim Rome idea. "I want you guys to write a theme song about this guy and his show." Stu has never heard of Rome, and the name only vaguely rings a bell with Barry. Keith hands the two MCs a four-page printout that contains keywords, catchphrases, and characters from the program and urges them to write and record the number on the spot. Stu instantly agrees, but Barry is hesitant. He has no interest in Loneker's "cheat sheet," and is unsure about being thrust into a collaboration with Bombsquad, who clearly aspire to DVS's crown.

The two MCs go outside to smoke cigarettes and confer.

Barry tells Stu he doesn't want to do the track. "Man, fuck all that. That dude [from Bombsquad] is doing the hook, it should be one of DVS's people. Why do they have me and you on a song when his group has three, four other rappers? Why are they calling us?"

"It's just business," says Stu, ever determined to advance DVS's career by any means necessary. "Apparently they called us for a reason. [Bombsquad] can't do what DVS do. You know what? How you feel right now. Tap into that when we record this damn song."

Barry sees Stu's point. "Alright, I got you," he nods, and the pair go back inside.

"Play the beat one more time," Barry says to Will and Keith.

As they listen, Barry takes two pages of Keith's printout and hands the other two to Stu. The pair sit down to write, hunched over the recording console, sketching out lyrics on yellow legal pads. Twenty minutes later, they are ready to tape, each having written twenty-four lines of lyrics based on Keith's sheet.

Stu completes his takes, and Barry steps into the booth. He sports a skull cap topped by a navy-blue wool hat and a plain white T-shirt over baggy blue jeans. A diamond nose piercing twinkles from his left nostril, and a long silver chain hangs from neck to navel. Around his wrists are two loosely hung diamond-encrusted watches. He runs through his lines a few times, using a pen to make changes to his lyrics, written in a notebook and laid open on the music stand.

"I'm gonna rap how you want it," Barry says, looking up at Will. "I'm just making sure I got the rhyme right and getting my breath where it's supposed to be."

They try a take and then another. Whatever hesitation Barry was feeling earlier is gone. The MC throws himself into each line, gesturing as if he's onstage performing for an audience. Barry finishes and looks dissatisfied. "I tricked a couple of 'em off," he says. Will comes into the booth and makes a few small adjustments to the microphone stand.

Barry runs a third take but rejects it immediately. "I can do better," he says. "I need to do it again."

Will comes back into the booth. The studio's highly sensitive microphone is picking up noise from Barry's necklace, which swings like a pendulum as he is rapping. "We're probably gonna have you double it," Will says to Barry. "And then we'll probably have you double that one. You know how we do."

They run a fourth take, and Barry nails it. "Man, I'm mean!" he enthuses.

"Hey, Mr. Mean Guy?" Will says, smiling. "Give me one more."

Barry fires it off again.

"Hey, Barry, one more time," Will says. "Run it straight back." Barry nods and goes again.

"Ready to tag?" Will asks. Barry nods and does a "backup" track where he raps along with the main vocal, emphasizing certain words or phrases.

Barry finishes and peers through the glass.

Across from him, Will and Keith sit side-by-side, conferring. Moments later, Keith gives Barry a thumbs up. "Let's go to the other one."

Barry nods and steps to the mic for the next sixteen bars.

FROM THE GROUND FLOOR UP

DVS Mindz's years of hard work are finally paying off. *Million Dolla Broke Niggaz* is availed to a handful of KC, Lawrence, and Topeka retail stores in May 2000. The overall response is positive. Local music critic Andrew Miller labels the CD "essential," while another scribe dubs the album "stellar," adding that "Tired of Talking" and "Niggaz (1137)" are "two of the best hip-hop singles ever to come out of this area."[4]

The band is riding a creative peak, with freshly recorded material being generated on a regular basis. One afternoon, Barry walks in with a brand-new song that blows everyone's minds. A one-listen classic called "Heat," the track represents an even tighter embrace of full-blown gangsta rap. Maybe Keith's more commercial approach is having an influence. "Heat's" singalong hook lends the track a catchiness that DVS has historically taken pains to avoid.

The group continues to perform regularly throughout the region, including two shows on Memorial Day. On June 24, the band headlines "Hip-Hop Live—Straight Underground Flava" alongside other regional rap acts at a four-hundred-capacity theater in Junction City, about sixty-five miles west of Topeka.

As further evidence of DVS's rising prominence, the group is offered the opening slot for the most anticipated rap concert of the year, Wu-Tang Clan at Lawrence's fabled Liberty Hall. Tech N9ne and the RDVs will have to watch enviously from the sidelines as DVS shares a bill with one of the most legendary bands in rap history. During a group interview around this time, I ask the members of DVS how they got the gig.

Stu: We got it because we're the livest hip-hoppers in the Midwest!

De'Juan: Who else would you call in the Midwest if Wu-Tang showed up? Who would you call to rock that? If a cipher was going to fuck around and jump off in the Midwest, who would you call?

Stu: We got it because of that. The Wu-Tang Clan, they had openers from different cities and the livest motherfuckers was going to get picked. Who would you think would be the livest around here? DVS Mindz. Quote-unquote.

Daymond: Who's fucking with us? Nobody. Stage show-wise, nobody fucking with us, for real.

Barry: If you got eight hundred thousand motherfuckers and midgets flipping and all of that, you'll probably turn us out. But us four you're not fucking with us. We don't need tight ropes and cannons.

Stu: We don't need bitches, we don't need flashy clothes, we don't need ice. We rock. We get down. All the respect and any props that we get, we've earned it on stage. We earned that shit. We came from the ground floor up. From no one knowing us, to people knowing us, to people disrespecting us, to opening for major acts, to the point where we're opening the Wu show.

Stu Tidwell, pictured here in 1976 at age six, was adopted by parents who separated when he was a year old. This fueled a lifelong quest for a stable family.

Photo courtesy Stuart Tidwell

Barry Rice, pictured here in 1976 at age six, was adopted as an infant. Barry's adopted father was an organist who died in a car accident when Barry was five years old.

Photo courtesy Barry Rice

Daymond Douglas, pictured here in 1986 at age thirteen. When Daymond was in second grade, his parents divorced. "We go from this four-bedroom house, having everything, to the complete opposite," he recalls.

Photo courtesy Daymond Douglas

De'Juan Knight's parents struggled with addiction and fought constantly. His teenage years were marked by gang membership, drug dealing, and violent crime. He is pictured here at age sevent[e] in 1995.

Photo courtesy De'Juan Knight

Barry, right, attended a private high school where he was the star basketball player. He is pictured here with longtime friend Casey Burnett.

Photo courtesy Barry Rice

Barry (left) and Stu (middle) met as children in the Head Start program. They are pictured here as twenty-two year olds in 1992. The early versions of DVS Mindz featured members such as Stu's cousin Earl (right), who rapped under the stage name Sandman.

Photo courtesy Stuart Tidwell

Daymond was a seasoned performer with years of experience when he joined DVS Mindz in 1993.

Photo courtesy Stuart Tidwell

VS Mindz in 1994.
rom left to right, Stu, Troy
Def DJ" Owens, Will-E,
aymond, Barry.

hoto courtesy Stuart Tidwell

Carla Daniels, DVS Mindz's first manager, 1994. What Carla lacked in music industry experience she made up for with courage and ambition.

Photo courtesy Stuart Tidwell

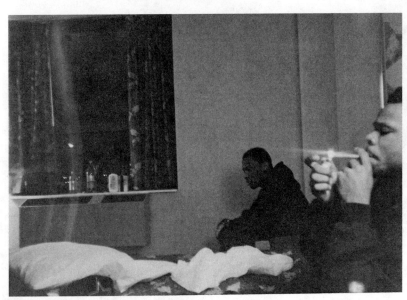

Daymond and Barry relax in a hotel room, 1994. DVS Mindz spent two years traveling the country, seeking a major-label record deal.

Photo courtesy Stuart Tidwell

Barry, Daymond, and Stu performing in Miami in 1995. "Nobody believed we was from Kansas," Daymond says. "They thought it was a gimmick. 'There's Black people in Kansas? They got hip-hop in Kansas?'"

Photos courtesy Stuart Tidwell

Stu, Randy, and Barry at 1137 Washburn Avenue, the house where DVS Mindz lived and created music around the clock. Randy met Barry and Stu in high school and later became DVS Mindz's manager.

Photo courtesy Barry Rice

De'Juan was a troubled teen who took refuge at 1137 Washburn Avenue, where he learned how to write lyrics and rap by watching DVS Mindz.

Photo courtesy De'Juan Knight.

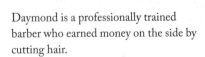

Daymond is a professionally trained barber who earned money on the side by cutting hair.

Photo courtesy Daymond Douglas

Barry performing in concert, backed by Bryan "DJ Skee" Lyons, left, and Troy "Def DJ" Owens.

Photo courtesy Stuart Tidwell

Kansas City–based producer Steve "S.G." Garcia listens to the tracks he and DVS Mindz just recorded in a Topeka studio. DVS Mind's collaboration with S.G. resulted in some of the most lyrically potent songs of the band's career.

Photo courtesy Stuart Tidwell

DVS's rejection of songwriting conventions resulted in material that had little chance of appealing to mainstream audiences or garnering significant radio play. Instead, the band prioritized intricate rhymes delivered with power and precision.

Photo courtesy Stu Tidwell

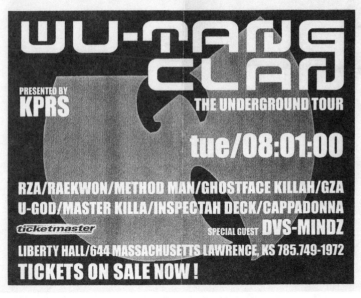

DVS Mindz opening for Wu-Tang Clan at Liberty Hall in Lawrence, Kansas. The band's live performances earned it opening slots for some of the most renowned artists in rap history.

Photo by Sean Spinelli

DVS Mindz's CD release party featured three Kansas City acts: Tech N9ne, the 57th Street Rogue Dog Villians, and the Zou, who also released a CD that night.

Photo by Sean Spinelli

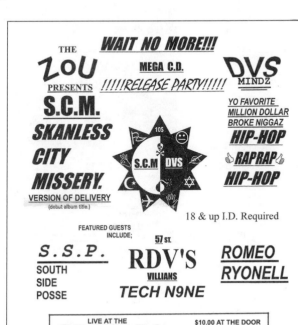

Daymond in the "Tired of Talking" music video, which drew visual inspiration from Kiss, James Bond, and *The Shining*.

Stu and Barry stand outside Lowman Hill Elementary School, March 2000, in a clip from *DVStory: The DVS Mindz Documentary*.

De'Juan reminisces in front of 1137 Washburn Avenue, March 2000, in a clip from *DVStory: The DVS Mindz Documentary*.

Barry in the short fictional film *Murdarous Verses*, which drew inspiration from movies such as *Goodfellas* and *Pulp Fiction*.

DVS Mindz and the Crew pay a visit to 1137 Washburn Avenue in 2000. From left to right, Casey Burnett, Daymond, Kevin "The Wolf" Douglas, Stu, De'Juan, Randy, Barry.

Photo courtesy Stu Tidwell

Barry, right, with Joseph "Scorpeez" Johnson II, a musician, collaborator, and longtime Crew member.

Photo courtesy Barry Rice

Randy and Stu circa spring 2003. Randy managed DVS Mindz at the peak of their popularity. "He started like how we started, so we learned all this shit together at the same time," Barry says.

Photo by Geoff Harkness

Barry was the emotional lightning rod that ran through the center of DVS Mindz. He was a talented MC and charismatic performer, but Barry had a dark side that appeared out of nowhere and scorched everything in its path.

Photo courtesy Barry Rice

Daymond produced several DVS tracks: the original version of "Tired of Talking," a stellar remake of "No Coast," and the live staple "Madness." In concert, he was DVS's ringleader, interacting with the crowd and directing the proceedings.

Photo courtesy Daymond Douglas

Randy stands by as De'Juan, Barry, and Daymond wait to go on stage in 2001.

Photo courtesy Barry Rice

The *Million Dolla Broke Niggaz* CD. DVS Mindz spent years pursuing a major label deal without luck. In 2000, the group self-issued their debut album on their independent label, No Coast Records.

Photo by Geoff Harkness

DVS Mindz occasionally created and sold small batches of merchandise to their fans. Pictured here are a windbreaker from 2000 and a T-shirt made in 2001.

Photos by Geoff Harkness, Sean Spinelli

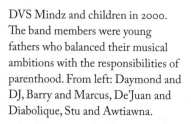

DVS Mindz and children in 2000. The band members were young fathers who balanced their musical ambitions with the responsibilities of parenthood. From left: Daymond and DJ, Barry and Marcus, De'Juan and Diabolique, Stu and Awtiawna.

Photo courtesy Stuart Tidwell

Stu on his thirtieth birthday, July 31, 2000, with his three oldest daughters: (from the top) Britnea, 11, Tahnae, 8, and Awtiawna, 5.

Photo courtesy Stuart Tidwell

Barry, right, is pictured in 1994 at twenty-four years old with his son Marcus, and his mother, Barbara Rice.

Photo courtesy Barry Rice

Daymond, left, is pictured in 1996 at twenty-three years old with DJ and his brother Kevin "The Wolf" Douglas.

Photo courtesy Daymond Douglas

Stu continued to make music after DVS Mindz disbanded, releasing hundreds of songs and more than a dozen solo albums.

Photo by Geoff Harkness

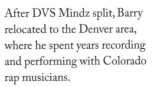

After DVS Mindz split, Barry relocated to the Denver area, where he spent years recording and performing with Colorado rap musicians.

Photo courtesy Barry Rice

Daymond met his future wife, Desirae, while working in Dallas, Texas. The two married in 2010.

Photo courtesy Daymond Douglas

De'Juan in prison in 2011.

Photo courtesy De'Juan Knight

Barry in Topeka, Kansas in 2014.

Photo by Geoff Harkness

in Grandview, Missouri in 2014.

to by Geoff Harkness

st of the members of DVS Mindz
ame grandfathers in their forties.
mond is pictured here in 2018 at
45, holding his grandson Eli.

o courtesy Daymond Douglas

De'Juan performing in Topeka in 2014.

Photo courtesy De'Juan Knight

Three-fourths of DVS Mindz reunited in 2019 to record tracks for *Modern Warfare*, their first album in twenty years. From left to right, De'Juan, Barry, and Stu.

Photo courtesy Stuart Tidwell

In early 2020, De'Juan was in a car accident that nearly took his life. Doctors were uncertain he would ever walk again.

Photo courtesy De'Juan Knight

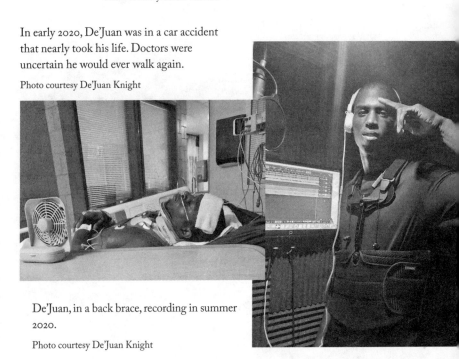

De'Juan, in a back brace, recording in summer 2020.

Photo courtesy De'Juan Knight

Stu and his seven children and two grandchildren in 2012. Whether it was in the band or at home, the one thing Stu—an adoptee from a broken home—always craved was a solid family. Top row, from left: Tahnae (daughter), Tyla (daughter), Nikki (wife, holding youngest son Nyko), Awtiawna (daughter), Britnea (daughter). Bottom row, from left, Stu (holding son Stuart Jr. and grandson Terrell). Stu's mother Christine is holding grandson Xavier and daughter Keely.

Photo courtesy Stuart Tidwell

Barry in Aurora, Colorado, 2020.

Photo courtesy Barry Rice

ymond in Dallas, Texas, 2022.

oto courtesy Daymond Douglas

De'Juan in Aurora, Colorado, 2022.

Photo courtesy De'Juan Knight

DVS Mindz, May 2022.

10

KILLA BEES

Shawn Edwards is a writer-newscaster and a rising star in the Kansas City metropolitan media. A handsome, charismatic African American in his early thirties, Edwards was born and raised in KC. Edwards focuses on Black stories, including music and movies that feature African Americans. Edwards is a major rap music fan and references hip-hop culture frequently in his work. DVS Mindz has met Edwards on several occasions, and though he had never written about the group or mentioned them on the air, he has always been friendly and encouraging.

On July 20, 2000, one week before DVS is slated to open for the Wu-Tang Clan, Edwards publishes a cover story in the *Pitch*, an exposé on the dubious tactics of a local concert promoter named Chancellor Cochran.[1] In May, Cochran hosted the Mayday Beach Concert and Party 2000, the festival where DVS and other local artists were charged $200 for five minutes of stage time. By most accounts, the event was haphazard, held on a scorching afternoon at a treeless outdoor raceway with no water or tents for shade.

In Edwards's *Pitch* article, his assessment of the concert is dismissive. "Twenty local rap groups that had paid for the opportunity to perform delivered second-rate sets," he wrote.

None of the groups, including rap veterans DVS Mindz from Topeka, captured the crowd's attention. They paced the stage, spewing out unintelligible lyrics. The audience wasn't rude—but it clearly was unimpressed.

As they tried to capture the crowd's attention, most of the artists began calling the people in the audience "motherfuckers" and yelling "Suck my dick!" They started talking down to people in the audience, calling them "haters" for not responding to their music, and they invited women to dance explicitly on stage. The crowd briefly got excited as young women flashed their breasts, but the strip-club antics grew tiresome as each group tried the same stunts.

Because DVS Mindz is the only band Edwards names in his negative assessment of the concert, the group feels ambushed by the story. Edwards's description of rappers cursing at audiences and bringing female dancers onstage are behaviors I had never witnessed from DVS Mindz and seem out of character. By singling out DVS Mindz in a critique of twenty bands, Edwards makes it sound as if DVS was the most distasteful act at an offensive, failed event. This infuriates the group, which has built a reputation on top-notch live performances. They decry the fact that Edwards has always been affable in person but is suddenly venomous in print.

"My whole thing ain't even with the article that he wrote," Daymond tells me. "My whole thing is that when he sees us, he congratulate us, but when he don't see us, he player hate us. He always all up in our face talking about like, 'Oh give me a tape, y'all niggas cool.' For years, even before we were doing major shows. For him to write something like that is just beyond me. It's like he stabbed us in the back. Fuck the article, nigga, keep it real. That ain't even keeping it real."

Stu agrees, adding, "We take it personal because we've known Shawn and we've talked to him on different occasions. If he felt the way the words he put in that article for this long, he could have been realer about it. We're men. If you didn't like a certain song or whatever, you could have said that, instead of shaking my hand and being one of those shady individuals I have to look out for now. He could have told us like that instead of just taking a stab in the back and shooting us in the press."

The band questions the timing of the article, published so close to the Wu-Tang concert, DVS's biggest show to date. The group's ire is understandable, but the *Pitch* article is a tempest in a teapot. Edwards's derisive description of the concert is a small part of a larger story about a shady promoter not an indictment of DVS Mindz. Moreover, in this prebroadband era, the story is not circulated via social media nor disseminated beyond the *Pitch's* readership. Those readers probably gave little thought to its throwaway line about DVS. To the band, however, this is headline news. They vow to get even from the stage at the Wu-Tang concert, which they are sure Edwards will attend.

WU-TANG CLAN

As DVS prepares to take the stage at Liberty Hall the night of the show, it is not to their usual instrumental music but to De'Juan ranting about the article. "How many of y'all know about the *Pitch*? Who read that shit?" De'Juan bellows to the crowd as DVS begins their performance. The spotlights have not been turned on yet, so it is dark, and De'Juan is speaking from backstage. This just confuses the audience, which consists primarily of hip-hop-loving college students who are eager to see the Wu-Tang Clan. A few concertgoers cheer, likely in recognition of the local newspaper's name. Most everyone else is silent, impatient to get on with the show.

De'Juan continues. "Who knows about DVS Mindz? Who read about them niggas?" There are some loud cheers from the audience. "Shawn Edwards said, 'DVS Mindz paced the stage, spewing out unintelligible lyrics.' What the *fuck* is going on?"

The audience has no reaction. Almost no one has any idea what De'Juan is talking about. He continues anyway. "DVS Mindz always comes to work. You understand? We ain't mad, we let the crowd be down. As long as the crowd good, we are. So let's make some motherfuckin' noise if you know what's up!"

The audience cheers louder this time, ready to get on with the concert. The band's intro music begins, and the spotlights flare to life. Across the back of the stage runs a massive banner of a painted cityscape with the words "Wu-Tang Clan" in bold yellow graffiti-style letters.

De'Juan, Daymond, Stu, and Barry enter one at a time. "We from the T-O-P-E killer assassin," they intone in unison. The group launches into their new song, "Heat," and delivers one of the strongest performances of their career, pummeling the audience with rhymes and energy. On the big stage, with professional sound and lights and a sold-out crowd of hip-hop fanatics, DVS Mindz gives their all.

"Heat" is followed by a vigorous take on "Madness," which culminates in a dazzling a cappella breakdown that the band put together especially for this show. In it, Stu revives his old beatboxing routines, and the entire squad creates a spectacular rap soundscape using nothing but their four voices. The hip-hop fanatics in the audience eat up every second.

DVS's performance is superb, but the band's focus on Edwards mars what is otherwise a crowning achievement. Throughout the set, Stu and De'Juan repeatedly target Edwards, who they assume is watching. The MCs incorporate the journalist's name into almost every song. At one point, De'Juan tries to get the entire crowd to chant, "fuck Shawn Edwards" but it does not catch on. Virtually no one in attendance knows who Shawn Edwards is or why the band has such a problem with him.

DVS closes their set with an a cappella from each member. Stu goes first and begins by discussing Edwards again, telling the audience, "We've been receiving some bad press from a writer named Shawn Edwards. I know you heard us saying his name. Fuck Shawn, fuck you forever if you're in here. And if you know him, slap him for me. That's real. I wrote this for him." Stu wears a sleeveless T-shirt with a skeleton hand giving the middle finger. This is accompanied by baggy denim shorts, white tennis shoes, and a black DVS Mindz ball cap turned backward. Stu raps a cappella for about ninety seconds, accentuating his words with points and pokes from his hands, which are sheathed in athletic gloves. Stu's verse doesn't mention Edwards, and his precise, rapid-fire delivery leaves the audience impressed, as always.

"My man pissed us off," Barry tells the crowd nonchalantly as he saunters toward center stage to begin his a cappella. He is resplendent in a billowing orange jumpsuit worn over a white T-shirt and Nikes. Barry's watch, chain, and bracelet sparkle in the spotlights. He wins over the crowd with an a cappella packed with sports and pop culture references before handing it off to Daymond.

"Yo, I got some shit to get off my chest for real," Daymond tells the crowd. He sports khakis, a plain white T-shirt, a backward ball cap, and not a hint of jewelry. "I'm so fuckin' tired of the industry sleepin' on the fuckin' Midwest!" Daymond rattles off a list of Midwest artists before launching into a two-minute a cappella rant against the music industry.

De'Juan goes last. He wears baggy black track pants and a tattered sleeveless white T-shirt that has one of my video still images of the band printed on the front. His hair is frayed upward, and he's wrapped a white towel around his neck, like a boxer catching his breath between rounds. For his a cappella, De'Juan blends together pieces of "Flamethrower" and "Madness," ending with a line about how Shawn Edwards is not ready for a band of DVS's caliber.

The group's obsession with Edwards during the biggest show of their career is lost on almost everyone in the audience. But members of the local music press know exactly what is happening, and DVS's war on Edwards is mentioned in the *Pitch*'s concert review the following week. Music editor Andrew Miller praises the performance, opining that "Topeka's DVS Mindz, delivered a fierce set teeming with intensity and emotion. Using stop-and-start beats and group recital in an impressive fashion, the crew spit fire on tracks such as 'Tired of Talking.' . . . This was the group's big-time showcase, and it proved to a tightly packed crowd and two touring bands that it deserves major-label interest."[2]

Miller also notes, "DVS treated fans to some 'real live a cappella hip-hop lyrics,' with one rant that blasted the music industry for sleeping on the Midwest and several others that brutally lambasted *Pitch* writer Shawn Edwards, who the group felt gave it a bum rap in his piece 'One More Chance.'"

Despite exacting public revenge at the Wu-Tang show, DVS remain miffed about the Edwards situation. They decide to write a diss track about him. "He basically put us out there under the gun and took shots at us," Stu tells me. "We didn't understand why, but we weren't going to lay down for it. So we licked shots. And it ain't over. We're gonna keep licking shots. We got a song to make about it. It's not gonna be done until *we* say it's done."

The Edwards situation aside, the Wu-Tang show is a triumph, the high point of a year filled with hard-earned victories. Not long after the concert, I ask Stu how he would describe the past twelve months. "We've definitely had some positive moments," he replies. "The Wu-Tang show, opening that, that's a hell of an accomplishment right there. They don't need an opener. They got nine members with solo albums. We were picked to do that, so that's an accomplishment. We got nominated for the Klammies a second time in a row. We didn't win, but we're not gonna get into that. But that's an accomplishment, that was a thumbs-up. From the shows to the songs to the release of our album, and how well it has done, considering, it's been a phenomenal year."

In the *Pitch*'s annual roundup of local music, "Niggaz (1137)" and "Tired of Talking" make the list of best local songs, while *Million Dolla Broke Niggaz* is lauded as one of the "Local Records of the Year." In praising DVS's debut album, the paper even disses hometown heroes, the 57th Street Rogue Dogg Villians: "Eschewing Kansas City's hardcore sound might have been easy for DVS Mindz to do, given that the crew hails from Topeka, but its collection of raw, tough-talking, and introspective songs on *Million Dollar* [sic] *Broke Niggaz* showed K.C. listeners that rap could be about more than simply getting fucked up."[3]

Despite these achievements, DVS Mindz's debut CD is still not widely available. There had been a problem with the original manufacturer, causing a last-minute delay in the release date. There were no discs for sale at the CD release party, and fans who went to area stores to pick it up found that it was not on the shelves. The band scrambled to have a few hundred copies printed by a manufacturer in California, but the rush order came at a significant markup.

DVS is relieved to finally have a CD in hand after years of delays, but the disc's limited distribution means that it is difficult to find. Even now, it can only be purchased at a handful of independent retailers and a single Best Buy location. The band had hoped for wider circulation; the album was supposed to make a huge splash. There is frustration and finger-pointing. "It didn't hit the shelves like we wanted it to," De'Juan tells me. "If we don't get it out everywhere, I'm going to jump off a bridge. It's just been some bumbaclot fuckery going on too, trying to run all this shit ourselves. Got to handle a lot of different shit. We got a lot of people on our team, but some people is in the way. They won't shut the hell up."

Stu predicts further success in the coming year but cautions, "We got a lot to learn. We damn sure want to get established and get our feet planted so we can move forward with different projects. We want to do a whole lot more outside of music and keep the music thing going too, but you can't make them kind of promises until you get yourself established."

DVS MINDED

The Bottleneck, Lawrence, Kansas, February 21, 2001

The vibe backstage at the Bottleneck is tense. "Where the fuck is Stuart?" De'Juan says to no one in particular. He's wearing a sleeveless navy-blue DVS Mindz T-shirt with a matching headband that pushes his hair upward in all directions. De'Juan is trying to get in the zone, to get his head right for the show. It's crowded in the Bottleneck's tiny backstage tonight. The Crew is here along with the entire Zou contingent, accompanied by an entourage of half a dozen women. Alcohol flows liberally, with 40-ounce bottles of beer and fifths of hard liquor going around. "We need to be going on *right now*, dog," De'Juan fumes. "Where the fuck is Stu?"

De'Juan's question is lost in a swirl of backstage clamor. Blunts are being passed around by some of the Zou members, and Barry says, "I gotta hit one of them motherfuckers on stage." Barry is wearing a white T-shirt imprinted with an image of the *Million Dolla Broke Niggaz* compact disc. His head is shaved bald, and diamonds sparkle from each ear.

Beside him, Daymond raps a quick a cappella, but an MC from the Zou steps in and cuts him off. No one's really in the mood for rhyming right now anyway. Everyone is talking about the Klammies.

DVS Mindz was nominated for Klammy awards the last two years in a row, a major achievement for a group that had not released an album. The Klammy winners are determined by mail-in vote. Both years, DVS was beaten by Tech N9ne, whose massive fan base submitted stacks of ballots. It is seemingly impossible for any local act to prevail over Tech N9ne's army of followers.

In April 2000, just as DVS Mindz was preparing to release its debut CD, Tech N9ne won his fourth consecutive Klammy. Tech showed up to the awards ceremony that night with the 57th Street Rogue Dogg Villians in tow and the word *bane* painted across his forehead in white lettering. As if Tech's showboating wasn't humiliating enough, later that night, he won the most prestigious Klammy award of all, Musician of the Year. "I told you we were going to be back up here!" the rapper gloated to the tuxedoed attendees as he accepted the crown prize. Tech N9ne later told a reporter for the *Pitch* that he kept his growing collection of Klammies alongside his wine glasses.[4]

Despite Tech's formidable streak, DVS feels hopeful about their chances of winning a Klammy award this year. The group had been handpicked to open for the Wu-Tang Clan, the biggest rap show in recent memory. They finally have an album in the stores, their own website, and a growing catalog of live and conceptual music videos. Furthermore, the preliminary voting panel liked *Million Dolla Broke Niggaz* enough that it ranks among the five finalists for the Best Local Release award. With a second nomination in the Best Rap/Hip-Hop category, DVS feels that some sort of Klammy award is a virtual guarantee.

Backstage at the Bottleneck, Stu is finally located. It turns out he has been here all along, sitting alone in a corner of the room, hand covering eyes, bobbing his head and rapping softly to himself in a trancelike state. He wears a navy-blue DVS Mindz ball cap and a black T-shirt with a large star on the front and white lettering that reads "Hollywood 2000 U.S.A."

Randy tells the band it's time to go. "I'm ready," Barry replies. "I'm waiting on the intro music so I can walk down."

De'Juan says, "I told the DJ ten minutes before he went downstairs to fuckin' start the music."

"That's what I'm waiting on, the intro music to start," Barry says, sounding annoyed. "What the hell I want to stand down there and keep doing the same shit?"

Randy announces to the room, "We got some group shit we gotta handle real quick. Everybody gotta go downstairs."

The Crew starts gathering up their belongings, but as it does, the intro music begins playing from the stage below. DVS's traditional preshow prayer is nixed, and the band, the Crew, the Zou, and their entourage hurry downstairs. DVS takes the stage to "Tired of Talking," produced by Zou members Boogieman and Rock. Over the course of the song, three members of the Zou walk onstage. They stand alongside DVS, adding backup vocals and performing for the crowd. The number itself is disjointed. Daymond is having problems with his microphone. The entire group gets out of synch with the music. Some lines from the hook are missed.

The song is threatening to collapse, but Daymond resuscitates things with a call and response. "When I say DVS, y'all say Mindz," he hollers. The crowd takes the cue while the background music is adjusted. Order is restored.

The group moves immediately into "Madness," elbowing for room among the growing throng of Zou members filling the small stage. In the middle of the song, someone in the crowd passes a blunt to De'Juan. He takes a huge toke, exhaling a cloud of smoke from center stage. Barry is distracted. He turns his back to the audience and confers with the DJ at the rear of the stage. He stands there for the rest of the song as the other guys perform.

The area near the stage has become hazy with blunt smoke. "Whew, shit. I'm catching a contact. I don't even smoke weed," Daymond says to the crowd, laughing and adjusting his backward ball cap. "You know what, when I was rapping and shit, taking my breaths and shit, I inhaled a whole bunch of weed. I was like, god-*damn!*"

"I'm trying to *find* that motherfucker," Barry says, interrupting. He walks to center stage and peers into the spotlight, looking for the blunt. "I'm trying to find it. Where's it at?" He looks from left to right. "You," he says, pointing to a guy standing in the front row. Barry makes a weed-smoking gesture, and the man passes the blunt to him. "Everybody gonna see it now, it's up here," he tells the audience. He takes a couple of deep hits, exhaling plumes of smoke.

Daymond tries to wrest control back from Barry. "Hey, who got that new DVS Mindz album, make some noise." There are a few cheers.

"It should be louder than that," Stu admonishes.

Daymond continues, "I know more people got it than that 'cause we had to re-cop a few times. Y'all be ready for that new DVS album to drop, for real. It's hot rocks. Yo, who want to hear some new shit?"

There is a murmur from the audience.

"Y'all don't want to hear no new shit?" Daymond implores before laughing and adding, "We ain't even got no new shit. No, I'm just fuckin' with y'all. Come on, let's run 'Heat.' That's some new shit. This is going on the next album for real. This is called 'Heat.' I know some of y'all heard this, y'all know the hook."

The band churns through a perfunctory take on "Heat." "If y'all like that new shit, show love," Daymond says as the song closes. It gets a response, partly drowned out by De'Juan and Barry, who are having a conversation about beer that is being picked up by their microphones. As they talk, Daymond stands in front of them, addressing the crowd. "Who wanna hear some more new shit?" Barry interrupts, yelling to the bartenders at the other end of the room. "Yo, can I get a Bud Light or some fuckin' water? Anybody?" There is no answer. "I'll come get it," Barry says, handing the microphone to Randy as he exits the stage.

Daymond continues to talk around Barry, speaking to the audience. "We gonna do some new shit on one condition, y'all got to do it with us. Who heard of KRS-One? Show love. Who know who KRS-One is?" There are some claps and shouts of recognition for the Boogie Down Productions pioneer. "Who remember 'Criminal Minded?' Y'all remember that hot shit in the '80s, well this shit is called 'DVS Minded.' Listen to the hook, it's real easy."

Daymond raps the hook slowly so that everyone can hear the lyrics, bounding back and forth in time with the beat. The crowd is into it, playing along with Daymond's call-and-response routine. "Y'all a ill-ass crowd," Daymond beams. "That make my dick hard!" As Daymond says this, Barry returns to the stage, beer in one hand, microphone in the other. A beat kicks in, and the band launches into "DVS Minded," a newly written number that decries the current state of rap music. The song marks a return to DVS's lyrical style of yore.

As Daymond spits a fiery verse, Barry sits down on a large black monitor positioned at the front of the stage, near the center. When Barry's turn to rap comes, he puts down his beer and does most of his verse seated, rising to stand only near the end. But "DVS Minded" closes strong, with the entire band standing front and center and delivering the song's catchy hook.

It generates the loudest applause of the night, which draws Barry's ire. Suddenly pissed, he snaps at the crowd, "That's why we didn't win two years in a row, getting nominated for the Klammies. That's shit that nobody's heard but y'all because you guys are our personal friends. So we won't win this year too. That's why I'm not going. Fuck 'em. They hated on us and the Zou, they can suck a dick. I like Rogue Dogs and I like Tech N9ne, fuck that. I do not like fuck shit. We got fucked. Just keeping it real. Period. That's why I'm not going this year. Fuck 'em. And I'm gonna piss on Shawn Edwards."

De'Juan tries to lighten the mood, laughing, "Forty Killa says he not going to the Klammies this year. And we're gonna win this year."

"No we're not," Barry fires back angrily. "We're gonna get fucked again."

Eventually, the rest of the Zou band members come to the stage and join DVS for rowdy takes on "Bust Somethin'" and "Niggaz (1137)." The last song crushes, as always. The Zou loves the song as much as the Crew members in the audience, and it seems like everyone in the Bottleneck is rapping every line.

The number ends, and moments pass with nothing happening onstage, which is overflowing with members from both bands and various Crew members.

"This is our last song," De'Juan says.

"Y'all wanna hear some a cappellas?" Daymond asks the audience.

"They don't want to hear no a cappellas," De'Juan says.

"We're just about to make up something, fuck it," says one of the guys from the Zou.

"Hey, we want to hear the a cappellas, man," another Zou member adds. "Let's hear it."

Barry has wandered off stage and is nowhere to be found. "Hey, where the hell Forty Killa? He's always drunk," De'Juan says to the audience.

Eventually, Barry is located at the bar, where he stands chatting with some friends, freshly topped beer mug in hand.

"Y'all want to hear some a cappellas or not?" Daymond asks from the stage. The audience is listless; there is little response.

"Fuck that," Stu says, walking over and grabbing a microphone from a stand. He launches into a verse. Barry is still talking to his buddies at the bar. De'Juan recites his a cappella as Barry slowly makes his way back toward the stage, entering as Daymond begins rapping. The stage is filled with members of DVS and the Zou. Daymond's a cappella is followed by a member of the Zou and then a self-proclaimed "thug nigga" whose amateur-level curse-laden rhymes crack everyone up.

Doubled over with laughter, Barry walks to center stage and slings an arm over the rapper's shoulder. "I was ridin' with you 'til you went ahead and just acted a total fool," he says into the microphone. "But you know I got your back. I'mma come off the wig tight like that 'cause you kept it hella real. How many 'fucks' was that?" The two go on chatting into their mics for a while.

Finally, Barry slowly begins to rap. He flubs a line about ten seconds in and stops. "Damn it," he exclaims. There is laughter

from the audience. "I didn't say 'fuck' enough. Hold on, I got it."
Barry begins again, making it shakily through several bars before
losing his way a second time. Barry throws his fists downward in
frustration. There are some taunts from the front row.

A couple of college students in the audience, standing toward
the back, turn and look at each other, unamused. They are hip-
hop fanatics, seeing their first DVS Mindz concert. One of the
guys shakes his head. Without saying a word, they turn and walk
toward the door.

* * * *

The next several months are a rocky time within the group, a
period characterized by personal turmoil and internal squabbles
between band members. Stu lives in Lawrence, and Daymond
is nowhere to be found. Stuck in Topeka without cars, De'Juan
and Barry are adrift. There are some bright spots—including
a killer performance opening for Digital Underground—but
anger and frustration are commonplace.

The group remains united, however, in their quest to win a
Klammy at the upcoming awards ceremony in KC. Nominated
for two prizes, DVS are certain that they will leave the ceremony
with a trophy in hand. The Klammy awards will also bring
the band face-to-face with Shawn Edwards. DVS relishes
the opportunity to call out the journalist from the stage while
accepting an award from the same publication that ran his
offensive story.

In conjunction with the Klammy awards, DVS has been
tapped to perform at two Klammy showcases, one held in
Lawrence and one in Kansas City. The KC event will be hosted
by none other than Shawn Edwards himself. The thought
of two forces colliding at a small music venue the week of the
Klammy awards ceremony is almost too much to bear.

11

HATERSVILLE

The Granada, Lawrence, Kansas, April 2001

As the stage lights flare to life, all eyes are drawn to a large Black man strapped to a refrigerator dolly. He wears a matching Sean John jeans and jacket combo, the lower half of his face obscured by a blue bandana. His hands are bound behind his back, and duct tape is wound tightly around the trunk of his body. A sign hangs around his neck by a cheap-looking gold chain. It reads, "Shawn Edwardz, H.A.T.E.R."

Over the sound system, De'Juan intones, "Lawrence, Kansas. Granada. The *Pitch*. What you are now experiencing or will experience is simulated life in Hatersville. Topeka knows it best—triple six zip code.[1] Welcome to Hatersville. Hey look, it's "Shawn Edwards.""

A beat begins to slap, and De'Juan takes the stage rapping the opening lines of a new song, "Hatersville." The venomous track was produced by Vandon "DJV" Pittman Rias in his Topeka studio. It chronicles DVS's long list of adversaries and describes the punishments the group intends to dole out to each. Stu enters second, rapping directly at the figure strapped to the dolly. Joseph "Scorpeez" Johnson II, an MC and longtime

Crew member, plays the role of Edwards dramatically, shaking his head in shame. Stu is followed by Daymond and then Barry, each of them serving up choice lines for the offending journalist.

As "Hatersville" ends, a member of the Crew wheels Scorpeez offstage. "Bye Shawn, you bitch!" Barry says sharply.

"All my real live hip-hop heads make some noise," Daymond cries, but only four or five people clap. There's almost no one here. The Granada is a cavernous venue, a massive open space where the lack of seats and high ceilings make the sizeable room feel even more expansive. Save for a handful of patrons sitting at the bar and a few Crew members standing in front of the stage, DVS is playing to an almost empty house; their verbal torching of the Edwards effigy is falling on deaf ears.

"I know y'all didn't come to just sit down and look like you're the shit," Daymond pleads to the people at the bar. Busy chatting, they ignore him.

The night has already gotten off to an inauspicious start. Betting that the Klammy showcase would be a high-profile event, DVS chose this performance to premiere *Murdarous Verses*, the eight-minute movie we shot the previous summer. The film was supposed to be the band's most incredible show opener to date, but it is plagued by technical issues. The Granada's movie screen is located at the rear of the stage, buried behind piles of sound, lighting, and stage equipment. The house lights are not dimmed for the screening, making the movie difficult to see, and the film's dialogue and voiceovers are barely audible after being churned through the Granada's reverb-heavy concert sound system.

Murdarous Verses is supposed to be a smart action film that pays tribute to some of our favorite mafia and mobster movies and does not take itself too seriously. But any such nuances are lost at the Granada showing. All the few attendees see is DVS Mindz on-screen, yelling and waving a bunch of guns around.

As the film plays, I stand behind two of the only people in the venue who are watching, elite members of the Pool Room scene. The pair do nothing to hide their contempt for our cinematic effort, cackling with laughter and elbowing each other every time a band member appears on screen with a weapon, deriding the group as wannabe gangsters. *Murdarous Verses* seems to confirm the criticisms that DVS Mindz's changing sound and image is a ploy—some guys from small-town Kansas trying to pass themselves off as gun-toting gangstas.

The band's reputation begins to be questioned by the press around this time as well. In March 2001, the *Pitch* runs a feature story about the group titled "Mindz Control." The story's writer, journalist J. J. Hensley, notes, "Over the past year the group's public persona hasn't reflected such self-assured, we're-in-demand confidence. Its profile certainly has risen because of what is perhaps the best live hip-hop show in the area. Instead of resorting to the crowd-involvement gimmicks and strip-club antics that turn a lot of rap shows into endurance tests, DVS Mindz keeps it simple: four MCs trading rhymes over haunting beats. . . . But it is about respect, and the members of DVS Mindz have publicly admitted to being a little pissed off that they aren't getting more of it."

Hensley describes the Edwards kerfuffle and DVS's perception that they have been unfairly singled out. He adds that the band "took time out at every show to preach from the pulpit about the evils of the local music bureaucracy. Over time, these diatribes snowballed into full-blown conspiracy theories."[2]

Hensley also quotes Barry and Stu making farfetched accusations about the *Pitch*. Barry insists that recent changes to the newspaper's distribution strategy are "a direct conspiracy to keep us from ever getting nominated [for a Klammy] again." Stu avows that Klammy ballots with DVS votes are being intentionally thrown away to prevent DVS from earning an award.

The group's conviction that various nemeses are actively plotting against them is not limited to Shawn Edwards, the Klammies, and the *Pitch*. De'Juan tells me that two KC radio stations conspired to keep DVS's name out of advertisements for the Wu-Tang Clan show. "Fuck KPRS that put that Wu-Tang show on and Hot 103 Jamz. Fuck them for not putting our name on the commercial. They knew we'd be there." Barry adds Topeka's hometown newspaper, the *Capital Journal*, to the list. "They also have an advertisement for it, and we're from here so fuck them too. I forgot old girl's name who wrote the article, but I'm gonna email you and cuss you out."

According to Barry, the media's desire to limit DVS Mindz stems from embarrassment. The group is so talented that it makes everyone else look bad by comparison, causing resentment and a desire for revenge. "We're from town and everybody else in the town's wack and we be showing up and blowing 'em out, so they get tight."

As the band's short set at the Granada comes to a close, a smattering of spectators congregate in front of the stage, spread around the venue's sizeable main floor. This includes a college student whose ingestion of psychedelics has him flopping and twirling like he's at a jam-band blowout. "Y'all make sure to vote for DVS Mindz best rap group for 2000," Daymond says as the final notes of "Tired of Talking" ring out. There is no response from the tiny crowd. The jam-band guy keeps dancing, oblivious. The band turns it over to a DJ, who scratches at his turntable as the group members linger on the stage, eventually departing separately and in different directions.

HURRICANE BARRY

The Hurricane, Kansas City, Missouri, April 5, 2001

"How many of you out there like a little hip-hop?" Shawn Edwards asks the audience at the Hurricane. He holds a microphone in one hand; half a dozen T-shirts are slung over his right shoulder. Edwards is a solidly built Black man dressed casually in jeans, a T-shirt, and a baseball cap. He sports eyeglasses and a small diamond earring in his left lobe.

"We got a real hot group coming up. My name is Shawn Edwards, representing the *Pitch* and the *Source* magazine. I been waiting a looooooong time for this one. Got my main peeps in the house, DVS Mindz. Mad love to them. Giving a nigga much props in the house. They got some hot shit for you. They coming up next. We about two minutes away from showtime. We'll be right back at y'all to introduce DVS Mindz, all the way from Topeka, Kansas. We about to set this motherfucker off. Go get your drinks, go get your spot on the floor. Move up close to the stage, we about to tear the Hurricane up tonight. Back in a minute."

The Hurricane, which has already reached about half of its three-hundred-patron capacity, is arguably the premier music venue of Kansas City's oldest entertainment district, Westport.[3] With a history that dates to the early nineteenth century, contemporary Westport features an eclectic mix of live-music nightspots, dance clubs, restaurants, cafés, coffee shops, clothing boutiques, hair salons, record stores, and tattoo parlors. With its bohemian vibe and urban setting, Westport attracts throngs of boozy partygoers seven nights a week. On weekends, the streets sometimes overflow with crowds, venue-hopping in search of sex, drugs, and music. In subsequent years, Kansas

City has developed upscale urban entertainment zones, including the Power and Light District, located north of Westport in the heart of downtown. In 2001, however, Westport is ground zero for local music, its multitude of venues catering to fans of live rock, blues, punk, heavy metal, and rap.

Tonight's concert at the Hurricane is part of a five-venue showcase featuring Klammy award nominees. Local music-lovers pay a five-dollar cover charge, which allows them to see any one of twenty-five bands performing at five neighboring clubs—the Hurricane, the Beaumont Club, Blayney's, McCoys, and the Mill Creek Brewery. Attendees can cast Klammy ballots for their favorite acts at any of the venues. The Klammies live-music showcase is the first of what organizers hope will be an annual event to preview the awards ceremony. The 2001 showcase attracts four thousand attendees, averaging one-hundred to one-hundred-and-fifty people to each act's performance.[4]

DVS is slated to play second on a bill of five Klammy nominees, including two DJs—DJ PMS and DJ Roland—and a pair of regionally popular alternative-rock bands, the Casket Lottery and Season to Risk.

The Hurricane features a small stage, and there is no backstage area at all. So the members of DVS huddle in the wings, waiting to go on. Barry distributes bottles of water to his bandmates, studiously ignoring Shawn Edwards, who is standing mere feet away. A couple of minutes later, Edwards introduces the group, taking the high road. "I need y'all to do me a favor real quick. When I say Topeka, you say Kansas." The audience, hovering close to the stage and ready for the show to begin, responds eagerly. Edwards and the attendees go back and forth a few times, and then he shouts, "Live from Kansas, I bring you DVS Mindz!"

As Edwards yells the group's name, the four MCs enter from each side. "What's up Hurricane!" De'Juan hollers, while

Daymond yells, "Where all my real live party people at? Throw your motherfuckin' hands up." De'Juan urges the audience to move forward, to press against the stage. "This shit should be tight, packed. That's how the Wu-Tang show was. It was hot shit."

The band immediately launches into "DVS Minded," their recently penned disavowal of commercial rap music. There is a sizable turnout from the Crew, and everyone in the front raps along at top volume. This is followed by a rousing rendition of "Heat" that has half the Hurricane bouncing up and down in time with the band. Playing on Edwards's home court in front of the man himself, DVS is hitting every shot.

As "Heat" winds to a close, De'Juan leans forward to address the room. He's wearing loose black overalls over a plain white T-shirt, his hair braided into tightly pressed cornrows. "One love, Hurricane. One love for hip-hop. One love for all those who create. One love for all those who write, spend some time wracking your brain coming up with shit. Kids getting killed the fuck up. We spend half our day creating. That's what sets us apart from the rappers." De'Juan is directly addressing Edwards and others who overlook DVS's artistry and write them off as cookie-cutter gangsta rap.

Following a stellar version of "Tired of Talking," Daymond steps forward, exuberant and friendly in a white tank top with a matching Yankees ball cap. "Even though we in Kansas City, we gotta keep it to the Topeka Kan-*tricity*," he tells the Hurricane mass. "And you *know* we gotta keep it underground hip-hop. We gotta do some a cappella shit with no beat, just to let y'all know it's the skills. If y'all want to hear some a cappella, underground, raw dog hip-hop shit from DVS Mindz, let me hear you say fuck yeah!" The crowd roars its approval, and Daymond hands the mic to De'Juan, who walks to center stage and pauses. The audience goes mostly silent.

Dating back to 1137 Washburn, De'Juan has always assumed the role of the hard-working younger brother to the rest of the band. De'Juan's multiyear effort to be taken seriously by the older and more experienced members of DVS honed him into a razor-sharp lyricist. Today, De'Juan is DVS's most serious writer, and arguably their best, with intricately woven rhymes layered such that they must be unpacked a few times to be fully appreciated.

"This is the type of shit you ain't gonna get nowhere else," De'Juan tells the audience at the Hurricane. " 'Cause there's a lot of cats *rapping*, we lyricists. Fuck rappers. We MCs. I put my heart on paper. I talk about my soul on paper. Ain't gonna be no bullshit. Real shit."

The Hurricane crowd, out to party and enjoy a night on the town, is getting restless. "Come on!" one heckler says, semijoking.

De'Juan whips his head around at the sound. "Who said, 'Come on?' " he asks, scanning the front rows. No one answers. He moves towards the section where the jeer came from. "Check it out." De'Juan goes into his a cappella, a lyrical hailstorm referencing Jesus Christ, Martin Luther King Jr., Satan, witchcraft, and reincarnation. The audience applauds, impressed. "That's real shit. That's the difference between a rapper and a lyricist," De'Juan says, walking off.

This is followed by a dazzling a cappella from Stu that wows those who have not seen him before. After Stu is Daymond, who serves up a punchline-filled a cappella that has everyone in hysterics. In a review of the showcase the following week, *Pitch* music editor Andrew Miller will rave that DVS "unleashed a devastating lyrical exhibition complete with jaw-dropping freestyle flows."[5] Miller was not writing about Barry.

Barry trudges to center stage. "What's happenin' y'all?" he asks halfheartedly, beer bottle in one hand. An audience member says, "Let me hold your beer." Barry shakes his head. "No, you're the second person that wants to hold my beer." He mumbles something about tipping the bartenders and "my boy Chris."

Barry turns and hands his beer bottle to Randy and then begins rapping slowly, proceeding with caution like a drunk trying to walk the line. Barry is only a few bars in when he flubs a word. A few shaky couplets later, Barry's frustration gets the best of him. He turns and raps with venom, speaking the words through gritted teeth. Barry ends with a flourish, but the audience registers no response.

"Let me do something for real, that was too short," Barry says aloud to himself. "Let me think, let me see." Barry folds his arms in front of his chest and strikes an exaggerated thinker pose, nodding his head as if channeling divine inspiration. After a moment, he breaks form, turns his back to the audience, and wanders to the side of the stage. "Hang on," he says into the microphone. "Let me talk to my man real fast." Barry whispers something to De'Juan, and they converse for what feels like an eternity. Daymond stands next to them grimacing, incredulous over the onstage delay.

After nearly a minute, Barry saunters back to center stage, takes a long swig of beer, and calls out to the bartenders across the room. "I want another one, right after this," he says, pointing to his beer bottle. Barry then recites his verse from "Bust Somethin'," one of his finest recorded moments. It fails to take flight as an a cappella, ending to weak applause. Without a word, Barry turns and wanders off stage, handing his microphone to Randy as he passes.

The club is silent. No one knows what to do. The DJ looks over and, after a few seconds, starts playing an instrumental. Four minutes pass as the band coaxes Barry back to the stage. The group is about to begin their final number when the sound system stops working.

"We're having some technical difficulties," Daymond says to the crowd. "Y'all stand by. This is what's called live hip hop. This ain't no Britney Spears, choreographed dancing type shit." As he says this, the sound comes back to life and a beat kicks in. "This is called 'Madness,'" De'Juan says to the crowd, and the song begins.

Minutes later, as DVS exits the stage, Daymond says, "Thanks for showing DVS Mindz mad love, for real. The Klammies, we hope to see y'all there. And we'll be back next year, believe that."

Shawn Edwards returns to the stage, enthused. "One more time, give it up for DVS Mindz! Come on, they came all the way from Topeka, Kansas. One more time for DVS Mindz! When I say Topeka, you say Kansas."

THE KLAMMY AWARDS

Uptown Theater, Kansas City, Missouri, April 14, 2001

Nine days after the Hurricane showcase, DVS Mindz is decked out in their finest attire for the Klammy awards ceremony. This year, the event is held at the Uptown, an opulently restored theater that first opened in 1928. The band members and Randy mingle in the lobby briefly, cutting a dashing figure. Daymond sports a shirt-and-tie combo under a formal vest with a high u-shaped collar. Stu wears a black dress shirt with a banded collar, a thin silver chain draped over his chest. De'Juan is dressed entirely in black, completing the look with dark sunglasses worn indoors at night. Barry is bedecked in black leather with a matching Kangol hat, diamonds blinging from each ear, and a long silver chain that stretches to his waistline.

The band, Randy, and I make our way inside, setting up camp at a large round table to the immediate left of the stage. Like all awards shows, this one takes forever. KC newscaster Brian Busby is the host, and local celebrities come on and off stage to present awards. *Million Dolla Broke Niggaz* almost immediately loses in the best local release category to *Starless*, the third album from popular KC alt-rock band Shiner. At the table, DVS Mindz grumble over the loss but keep their cool. The award for best local release is not the big prize; the group is fixated on the best rap artist award, which Tech N9ne has won four years in a row. Tech is not here tonight, a sure indication in the band's estimation that he lost to DVS.

Shawn Edwards walks onstage to present the award, telling the audience that it is the "hottest" category of the night. Edwards opens an envelope with a flourish and announces Tech N9ne as the winner for the fifth year in a row. Immediately, the members of DVS rise in disgust, shoving their metal folding chairs backward with venom. The chairs create a huge racket against the Uptown's hard floor. Barry picks up his chair and heaves it toward the stage, where it crashes in a heap. The band stamps out of the room en masse, cursing loudly as they go.

Two members of the local press mention the incident in reviews of the Klammies. Andrew Miller, likely wanting to avoid the band's wrath, does not identify the group in his writeup for the *Pitch*. "After Tech N9ne was named the winner, crashing furniture and loud cries of dismay resounded from the floor as the other nominees bemoaned their fate."[6] Music writer Jason Meier is more critical, posting a review on a local music site, Synapsis: "DVS Mindz provided one of the nights most classless moves. Within seconds of hearing that they lost to Tech N9ne for another year, the group tossed their chairs high in the air, which made for a thunderous crashing sound as they stormed out of the theater."

One of the members of the 57th Street Rogue Dogg Villians accepts Tech N9ne's Klammy. The winner himself finally shows up around midnight, claiming that he had been caught in traffic. "Give someone else a chance!" Tech crows from the stage. Edwards, likely relieved to have all of this over with, expresses dismay over the "drama" and "circus environment" of the Klammies.[7]

DVS's good reputation opened many doors over the years. Now, those same doors have begun to close. It will be more than a year before DVS's name is printed in the *Pitch*, and then it is only a passing mention. Promoters and the local music press seem turned off by DVS's reactionary antics, their public reprimand of Edwards, and their behavior at the Klammies. Following the incident at the awards show, no local press outlet ever writes another feature story about DVS Mindz. The golden child that opened for the biggest headliners in town suddenly finds gigs hard to come by. And because the promoters, journalists, and other industry types serve on the Klammy awards committees and panels, the group is never nominated for another music award again.

TREMORS

Lawrence, Kansas, November 2001

Tremors is dark, which suits the mood onstage as well as tonight's setlist, mostly songs from *G-Coffee*, a compilation CD that features DVS Mindz alongside longtime associates, Zeem, Scorpeez, and Bronz. All the *G-Coffee* tracks were produced by DJ Kutt, who had been named DVS's permanent DJ. The four DVS MCs make appearances on *G-Coffee*, cropping up on solo numbers and posse cuts, but there is no track credited to the entire band.

DVS Mindz's debut album contained a few songs from their early days as nimble-tongued lyrical assassins, but *G-Coffee* revels in darkness, a hip-hop Goya painting. The Tremors show serves as a *G-Coffee* release party, with DVS Mindz and the Zou coheadlining. The opening act is Bombsquad the Lawrence-based rap group put together by Keith Loneker, the NFL lineman and movie actor turned rap producer. What Bombsquad lacks in talent and charisma, they make up for with catchy tunes, produced and polished in Loneker's state-of-the-art studio down the street.

The *G-Coffee* showcase lacks coherence. There is nobody hosting or directing the caravan of MCs who wander on and off stage, hanging out in the spotlight, a dozen deep at times, chatting to one another while rappers sweat and spit in the spotlights.

De'Juan positions himself front and center. He has been on a hot streak this year, recording features with two local groups that have raised his profile considerably. Phat Albert, a funky party band with a horn section, built an entire song around De'Juan. "Devious" features a standout verse from De'Juan, but also includes vocalist Arron D from the ska-rock band KB Posse. Arron D was impressed enough to invite De'Juan to record with his band, and De'Juan shows up on two tracks, "Damn Dirty" and the stellar "KBP." Both bands released the tracks as part of their latest CDs, with "Devious" topping the charts on a couple of local radio shows. De'Juan appeared onstage with both Phat Albert and KB Posse, including a college gig in Warrensburg, Missouri opening for pop-rockers Smashmouth.

At Tremors, De'Juan spends the majority of the night onstage, turning in one impassioned performance after the next. He is joined by artists from the *G-Coffee* compilation, but his DVS bandmates are nowhere to be found.

After several songs, Barry and Daymond join De'Juan for a posse cut that also features longtime Crew members Bronz and Scorpeez. Three members of DVS have appeared onstage tonight, but the group has yet to play a DVS Mindz song. No one has seen or heard from Stu.

Arguments over finances are at an all-time high, with everyone increasingly pointing fingers at Randy and demanding to know what happened to all the money. They were playing concerts, selling merchandise, and their CD was being sold in local stores. Where was the money?

"We don't understand the financials," the guys would complain.

Randy was incensed. He was taking out payday loans to pay for merchandise that the guys gave away half the time—or kept for themselves. "That you think I'm stealing from you already is an insult," he told them. " 'Cause I can go to the credit union for these payday loans that I'm taking out and paying off repetitively. I got receipts. Yeah, we made this [amount], but then you got these expenses. And add up what you contributed to the group aside from your talent. It's like you guys just don't really know. You're quick to slap on these jackets and shirts, but you guys didn't put in on this. I *did*."

At Tremors, De'Juan—joined onstage by Barry, Daymond, and members of the Zou—plays another *G-Coffee* cut, "Full Devils." He crouches down into a squat near center stage and orders the DJ to turn off the music. "Let me run it a cappella. 'Cause this right here is a piece of me, dog, you gotta hear this shit." In the verse, De'Juan describes various "devils" that haunt him: lust, envy, jealousy, self-hatred. As De'Juan concludes, Stu finally makes an appearance, and DVS plays fiery versions of "Heat," "DVS Minded," and "Niggaz (1137)."

"We got one more from this *G-Coffee* shit," De'Juan says. The DJ cues up the backing track for "Vengence," a posse cut that includes the four members of DVS Mindz. But Daymond is already gone. De'Juan continues, "That *G-Coffee* shit will be in stores in the middle of November. *Million Dolla Broke Niggaz* is still in stores."

As "Vengence" begins, a man stands behind the MCs, singing at the top of his lungs. "Da da da dum da da da," he repeatedly intones in an off-key warble. De'Juan waves his hand back and forth sideways across his throat in a "cut" motion, but the clueless crooner continues to stink up the joint. De'Juan raises his voice, trying to rap over the din, but the vocalist just sings louder. Furious, De'Juan stops rhyming and addresses him directly. "Please stop singing in the goddamn mic! Stop!" De'Juan hurls his microphone to the floor and storms off stage.

Eventually, Barry steps in and takes over for several minutes, followed by a few brief bars from Stu. As DVS Mindz concludes their headlining set, half the group is missing, with De'Juan still steaming somewhere in the club and Daymond long since departed. It was the last time I would see the entire group perform on the same stage. Not long after the Tremors show, Daymond quit the band.

SNAFUS

Topeka, Kansas, June 2002

Big Brawn John puts his hands on his hips and flexes his massive biceps, which bulge and ripple through his tight black T-shirt as Prince's "Pussy Control" rattles over the sound system. The bodybuilder has altered the track, recording himself singing "muscle control" in a squeaky falsetto over the song's hook.

"Twenty-one-inch guns from KC in the house," he booms to the audience, arching his back and gyrating his hips.

"Alright ladies, get your asses up there," the house DJ intones into a microphone. A couple of strippers make their way toward the stage, dresses glowing under the purple neon tube lights that flank a waist-high brass railing. Big Brawn John dances over, looking down at them from high atop the platform. The body-builder unfastens his belt, then unbuttons and unzips his black dress pants, pulling them down to mid-thigh.

A female Crew member runs up to the stage and waves a dollar at him. "Must be jelly 'cause jam don't shake like that," Big Brawn John laughs, taking the cash. Urged on by the strippers, he pulls his pants down to his ankles, revealing dark brown bikini briefs. A few females in the crowd hoot and holler.

After more dancing and hip grinding, the bodybuilder pulls up his pants and buckles his belt. He sashays around a brass stripper's pole that runs through the center of the stage and introduces himself. "What's up, what's up Topeka? Big Brawn John in the house. I ain't gonna swing on this pole or nothin' but we gonna get live tonight. Y'all ready to get this party goin'? Let me hear you say yeah! Ain't no party like a Midwest party tonight 'cause a Midwest party don't stop. Let's get it up! Y'all about to hear the baddest rap and funk, brothers and sisters, that you ever seen."

Snafus is an adult entertainment club located in an industrial area out by the Topeka airport, near an auto salvage yard and a scrap metal plant. On the stage, Big Brawn John raises one hand and thunders, "Let's get rrrrrrready to rrrrrrumble!" The audience barely registers a response. The Crew is on hand, as always, but most of Snafus' patrons are here to see naked women, not rap concerts. Dead air hangs in the room as Big Brawn John waits for the music to begin. The moments drip by.

Big Brawn can't take it any longer. "Can I have some music please, DJ?" he pleads. There is not enough room on the Snafu's stage for turntables, so the DJ works from inside the venue's isolation booth, located in a separate corner of the room. "Give me some hip-hop music, baby," John pleads from the stage. The music still doesn't start, so John stalls for time by doing his impersonation of Bill Clinton.

Daymond's departure from DVS Mindz and the downgrade in venue are not the only changes of late. DVS also parted ways with Randy, their longtime manager and friend to Barry and Stu since high school. The split with Randy was acrimonious, resulting in hard feelings on all sides. With Randy went No Coast, the group's record label. Randy had been covering the hosting fees for the band's website, which drifted offline in late 2001.

Stu, Barry, and De'Juan are weathering on, writing material for their sophomore album and recording new songs when they can. But the trio's efforts have been hindered by Stu's relocation from Lawrence to Grandview, Missouri, more than eighty miles east of Topeka. When Stu first moved from Topeka to Lawrence, he stopped coming around as much. Now that Stu is living in Grandview, the other guys barely see him anymore.

Barry projects total confidence, as always. "Two thousand and everything. We comin' and bringing it hella correct," he tells me at Snafus. "No Coast is now toast. DVS, that's the best!"

I ask Barry about Daymond's departure. He replies tersely, refusing to even say Daymond's name and suggesting that he was fired for lack of involvement in the group's day-to-day dealings. "We had to start fresh. Friends is friends, business is business. I got two niggas that got my back. There's been more people than the person you mentioned that has been excluded from the group for not handling they business. You can't be mad at nobody but yourself if you ain't handling your business. If you know what you gotta do, and don't do it, why be mad at somebody else? That's like me owning this club and all my workers—from the bodyguards to the bartender—ain't handling they business, and my people are walking out and I'm losing money. I gotta get rid of they ass or I gotta put a fire under they ass to do something. If that don't make 'em move, I gotta get rid of them and get somebody that can do that."

There are at least a dozen artists performing tonight: Scorpeez, Bronz, Dirty Mike, Chubby, Kasper, Killer Combo, and the Moffia Boyz. Some are longtime Crew members; others are new to the fold.

Scorpeez, a burly Black teddy bear, appears onstage decked out in a pink and white tracksuit. He is joined by De'Juan and members of the Moffia Boyz, a youthful Topeka trio that aspires to the DVS throne. "Much love to Snafus for having us out here," De'Juan says to the audience as they all take the stage. "All these beautiful ladies walking around out here," a member of the Moffia Boyz replies. "Dressed and undressed," De'Juan adds, nodding in agreement.

Scorpeez plays his most popular number, "Operatin' Pounds." The Crew loves the song and raps along to every word, while Snafus' stage fills with rappers, strippers, and even members of the audience. As Scorpeez raps, De'Juan cozies up next to a stripper in a schoolgirl uniform. She grinds up against him seductively and pulls up her tank top to reveal her bare breasts. I can't help but wonder what Shawn Edwards, who so offended the band by implying that it engaged in "strip club antics" on stage, would think.

Following sets from half a dozen artists, the club stops the show so that the strippers can attend to a group of impatient patrons. The DJ blasts Petey Pablo's "North Carolina" as the dancers peel off their clothes. Next up is "Slacker," the lead single from Tech N9ne's latest album *Absolute Power*, which was released on Tech's own Strange Music label and peaked at number three on Billboard's independent albums chart. Tech's career continues to soar to new heights. Last year, he toured the country with Cypress Hill and opened for Snoop Dogg at the twenty-thousand-seat Kemper Arena when he got home.

Tech has become a bonafide celebrity in KC, where it seems like everyone knows, loves, and feels a personal connection to him. It's getting to the point where he can barely go out in public. "At home everybody thinks they know you real well, so everybody wants special treatment," Tech tells me in late 2001. "Imagine 1,500 people wanting special treatment from you. So when you're talking to one and (someone else is pulling on your sleeve, saying), 'Boy, you know me!' It gets nerve-wracking sometimes. It's not you that changed, it's the people that changed: 'Aw don't act like you're all Hollywood and you can't talk to me!' And I'm like, 'I didn't even *see* you. What are you talking about?' I'm not changing, I've never changed."[8]

Back at Snafu's, the DJ plays "Niggaz (1137)" as a heavyset blonde in her late thirties dances topless onstage, pulling her G-string down to her knees. She bends over and inserts a finger into her rectum as Stu's verse rat-a-tats from the speakers overhead.

Larry, a Crew member who helped put together the show, surveys the scene and tells me, "We entrepreneurs, just trying to make this money lucratively. The reason we in a strip club tonight is because it's lucrative. This is where people are going around and spending their money."

The strippers finish, and the concert begins again. From the stage, the host, a local rapper who calls himself Spiceberg Capone, twirls languidly around a stripper's pole. "Snafus, Snafus, how y'all doin'?" he intones. "We got the infamous DVS Mindz coming up next. When I say DVS, you say Mindz. 'Cause I want my niggas to come out here and rock it, 'cause they rock every show they do." Capone attempts a call and response but the audience, save for the Crew, mostly ignores him.

"Get the fuck up!" De'Juan shouts into his microphone from offstage, entering the stage area to the opening strains of a new song, "Flamethrower." DVS Mindz is a different band now. With Daymond gone and Stu, Barry, and De'Juan up front, the group is a three-headed dragon once again.

The trio roars through "Flamethrower," a high-velocity throwback to the group's early caffeinated tempos produced by DJ Kutt, who helmed the recent *G-Coffee* compilation. Stu, De'Juan, and Barry spit their bars with ferocity and venom. Any resemblance to DVS 1.0 ends there. Whatever pretenses the group once had about metaphorical violence are obliterated by Barry's verses, which openly threaten to murder members of the Topeka Police Department, some of them by name.

The Crew already adores "Flamethrower" and shouts along to every line. Before the show, outside the venue, Barry told me that "Flamethrower" is his favorite of the group's new songs. He promised that it would be on the second DVS Mindz album. "I speak for those that are just like me, that don't have a mic or a voice to speak. I speak for 'em. I speak for real niggas trying to do the right thing," he says of "Flamethower's" call for violence towards police officers. "The cops is crooked around this motherfucker. I do not like police. I put that in my words on 'Flamethrower' and everything I said is the truth. So if the cops don't like me after they hear it, fuck 'em. Freedom of speech. I can say what the fuck I want. But if I were to yell 'fuck the cops' while they were standing there, then they woulda harassed me for something. That's why I don't like 'em."

As "Flamethrower" concludes onstage, Stu rocks out, buzzed. He looks like he's had a few too many. DVS's secret weapon is not in battle-ready form tonight. The band's second song is another new Kutt-produced number, "Genocide," with the three MCs spitting fast-paced apocalyptic rhymes over a triple-time beat. "Genocide" showcases the group's hyperspeed delivery, but the response from the crowd is mild. After the song concludes, Barry, exasperated, says, "Y'all ain't gotta clap. We doing our last one. You don't have to get excited for us."

"Everybody's tired by now, huh?" De'Juan admonishes the audience, listless and seated at tables.

DVS concludes their set with a third new song, "Desperados," whose Spaghetti Western guitar line was laid down by me in DJ Kutt's Topeka studio. The three MCs chant the song's sing-song hook in unison, but the audience isn't feeling it. "Get the fuck up!" De'Juan yells. "All the niggas I know that are sitting around need to get to the dance floor." No one moves.

After the show, standing in the parking lot outside the venue, Barry is magnanimous, feeling himself. He tells me that after the music thing takes off, he wants to act, to star in movies. "I'm a genius in some sorts," he muses. "There's a thin line between genius and insanity. I'm a little bit of both of those. I think of great things. They just come to me. I'm kind of an asshole, but I've learned being an asshole gets you kind of far. People don't bullshit you as much. The realer you keep it, the realer people keep it with you."

Barry continues. "Life is what you make it, and life is like a movie. I can do anything. And that goes for any person. You put your mind to it, you can do it. I ain't an actor. I don't need a trailer full of white flowers and forty-five CDs like J-Lo. All I need's a forty and a blunt. As long as I can smoke and drink, tell me what I need to do and I'ma give it to you and then some. *Believe* that."

On stage at Snafus, De'Juan says goodnight as DVS Mindz exits. It is the last time I will ever see the band perform. "Much love to Snafus for letting us be out here, dog, kickin' it live like this. All the ladies, all the homies. DVS. And we out."

III

2004–2020

12

THE DVS STORY

North Kansas City, Missouri, September 5, 2009

It's been six years since I've seen Stu, and we greet each other like old friends. We meet up in a basement recording studio in North Kansas City, where Stu has been working on new music. We pull up chairs next to a long rectangular table topped with a multiknobbed mixing board, two laptop computers, a tall rack of digital effects boxes, a pair of chunky gray speakers, and an assortment of electronic gadgets, cables, and microphones.

Stu plays "The DVS Story," a new track from his forthcoming album. In the song, Stu recounts the trials and tribulations of DVS Mindz with unsparing honesty, addressing the jealousy and frustrations that sometimes plagued the group. Stu's lyrics also mention money issues, problems with women, and drug and alcohol abuse as contributing to the band's demise.

The thirty-nine-year-old MC recorded the song two weeks ago, with production courtesy Boogieman, who coproduced three popular DVS Mindz tracks: the video version of "Tired of Talking," "Bust Somethin'," and "Niggaz (1137)." Stu doesn't look like he's aged much since I first met him. He bobs his head in time with the music, taking long slugs from a bottle of beer.

"Here we are in oh-nine, still on the grind," he muses. "It's oh-nine, time to do something different, gotta keep moving."

A DVS Mindz reunion was supposed to take place today, with the entire band back together and recording a new song. The group invited me to videotape the event for posterity, and I drove here from Chicago, where I had moved in 2003, to do so. But Stu is the only one who showed up. He is frustrated—another fuckup in a long list of DVS Mindz fuckups. Stu now lives about twenty minutes away in Grandview. Barry resides in Denver and texted to say he'd missed his flight. Daymond is in Dallas, and no one has heard from him. De'Juan still lives in Topeka, but he is not here today because he is currently in the Shawnee County jail.

I brought my video camera, so I decide to interview Stu anyway. DVS Mindz broke up not long after I moved to Chicago. Daymond had already departed, leaving Stu, Barry, and De'Juan at the helm. I ask Stu what happened.

"DVS happened to DVS," Stu says. "Things got rocky. After the Wu-Tang show is when a lot of shit started to go down. Drunkenness. It got to a point where didn't nobody want to be around nobody."

After Daymond left, the next to depart was Randy, the group's longtime manager and friend. "We fell out with Randy," Stu recalls. "We weren't seeing eye to eye with him. He was managing four different personalities. All kind of shit's going on, people showing up late. So there was a lot of shit put in his lap. But ultimately in the end, where he stopped managing DVS, it was a money issue. Where is the money? This is a business; you need to be watching your money. We have him watching the money and there was issues with the money."

With Daymond and Randy gone, the remaining three musicians toiled in bedroom and basement studios in Topeka and KC, recording tracks for a follow-up to *Million Dolla Broke Niggaz*.

The sophomore effort was tentatively titled *Paper*, and several new tracks were recorded and ready to go: "Flamethrower," "Genocide," "Open Season," "Colors," and "Just Us." But without management or a record label, the group had no way to finance the pressing of CDs. In the prestreaming era, physical discs were still the best way for independent artists to disseminate music, including availing copies to radio stations and music journalists. The *Paper* album never made it that far.

"It was leaked to the streets," Stu says. "Niggas pressed it up, put it in the streets, sold it, but it didn't have the professional package that *Million Dolla Broke Niggaz* had. I wouldn't call it an official release. We did a ton of work, but it went under the radar; people didn't hear about it. We weren't performing as frequent, but we was working. The whole time I'm trying to keep niggas together. *Trying* to."

Writing and recording songs, however, was never difficult for DVS Mindz. The issue was money and the fact that no one was making any. That was especially bothersome to Stu, who was juggling band responsibilities, a relationship, and being a single father to a teenage girl. "Money was my problem," he says. "How are we gonna get this money? I'm already unemployed, getting little punk money through the state. I just hurt my ankle. My oldest daughter came to live with me, so I gotta hold that down. My chick's here. And I'm bringing in unemployment money."

For Stu, the low point of the entire DVS Mindz saga was the show at Snafus, the Topeka strip joint where I last saw the band perform. "I'm onstage rapping and I'm seeing naked chicks over here, there's an ass in my face there. There's mirrors, glitter balls. How the hell do we go from Wu-Tang to this shit? What the hell are we doing? To go from the Granada, and there's six, seven hundred people there, we're opening for M.O.P., doing the thing. The Halloween show when we did the costumes, a sea of people. And then I'm looking up and I'm seeing naked chicks around me, and I'm rapping. I pride myself on never having to have a bunch of naked women on stage or in my videos. Where are we at in our career? Is this what we're doing? We're performing in *strip clubs* now? At that point right there is when I made up my mind that I was going to leave the group."

Stu says that he stuck with DVS Mindz for so long because they continued to score victories. The band was just successful enough to keep everyone motivated and striving to make it. "Daymond joins the group. A year after that, we're opening for Boss and Onyx. The year after that we're opening for Redman and Keith Murray. The year after that we're at the Granada, packed house. That was the motivator. 'We got to keep going, we're almost there. We can't give up now, we can't quit. I'm not going to let it go.' That's part of the reason that I kept going even after the group disbanded. I was like, 'I'm right there. I can't let it go.'"

But it never happened. Despite the group's many achievements, DVS Mindz never quite made it across the finish line. Nor had they planned for anything other than doing so. None of the four had gone to college or mastered a trade. There was no backup plan. Instead, DVS Mindz put all their chips on the table and lost everything.

WE DID THAT

"You can't cry over it," Stu says of the band's demise. "It was a great experience, good or bad. I wouldn't trade any of that time for anything." Stu tells me that his personal highlight was opening for Wu-Tang Clan. "We hit the stage and we weren't in a position where we had to familiarize the crowd with our music.

The reception that they gave us, how they reacted, it was just a live crowd from the beginning to the end. And it was opening for Wu-Tang Clan. That was a huge thing for us, us being fans of Wu-Tang and every member in it. That was just a wonderful thing for me and for DVS. Even the haters couldn't take that experience from us. We did that. You can't take it from us."

Stu bears no ill will towards the other members of the band. For him, there will always be an unbreakable bond among this group of longtime friends. In Stu's estimation, DVS accomplished a great deal and did it together. "I love every last one of them dudes. They're like brothers from different mothers and fathers. Even though it ended fucked up, there were still a lot of great times in there and lot of history that was made as far as this area for a Midwest group to even do. I was part of that. So I can't forget that."

After DVS split in 2003, Stu began working on a solo album. This was still an era when passing digital files back and forth was uncommon, so recording new material required that Stu book sessions in local bedroom and basement recording studios. Over a series of months and then years, Stu collaborated with area beatmakers, including Daymond, DJ Kutt, and longtime DVS producer S.G., traveling to Kansas City, Lawrence, and Topeka to record new songs. Stu also cut a track with Keith Loneker and the production crew at 5150. When Stu finally had enough songs for a full album, he spent his own money to have cover artwork designed and CDs professionally pressed.

Stu's solo debut, the twenty-one-track, seventy-eight-minute *Mood Swings*, was released in 2007. There was little reaction other than a lukewarm review in the *Pitch*, which praised Stu's rhyme skills but opined that "many of his beats sound like they've been sitting on the shelf for at least a decade."[1] Stu was stung by the criticism, partly because he agreed with it.

Like athletes, popular musicians have a window during which they can make it, typically during the teens and early twenties. Stu was thirty-nine years old and practical enough to know that he was never going to achieve his dream. This process, Stu says, involved "realizing that if it's gonna happen for me, it was gonna happen back then."

This hard truth forced Stu to confront himself and evaluate things anew. Was music still worth pursuing, even if it was not created in service of making it? "This is the time to look in the mirror. Being thirty-eight, thirty-nine years old and then having to ask myself, 'Why am I doing this? Are you in it to blow up? Are you in it for the women, the money, the fame? Or are you doing this because you love it? What are you in this for?'"

Stu concluded that, for him, the creative process and being an artist in the purest sense were all that mattered. "I love doing it," he says. "I like writing. I love coming up with the lyrics. I love to record. I still love performing, just the energy and everything that you get from that."

Stu believes that his age and maturity mean reimagining his artistic identity, tackling more serious themes in his song lyrics. "You're not twenty-one anymore," he told himself while writing songs for an album he would eventually title *G.A.M.E.*, an acronym for Grown Ass Man Experience. "You're a grown man: responsibilities, kids, wife, grown-folk business. Do that. You gotta write from a grown man's perspective. What the hell else are you gonna write about?"

Stu plays me another new track, "Scratch and Sniff," bobbing his head and rapping along quietly. I've been listening to DVS Mindz for almost ten years, and Stu's ambidextrous wordplay and trademark rat-a-tat cadence are instantly familiar. "DVS was my baby, from '91, '92 when we started it, so I'm still gonna hold that candle," Stu proclaims. "But at the end of the day, it's music. I'm Str8jakkett, same as it always reads. I'm still doing my thing. Until God decides to turn out *my* lights, I'm not going to stop doing it."

As Stu plays me another new track, his phone rings. It's De'Juan, calling from the Shawnee County jail. Stu puts his red Samsung flip phone on speaker, and we lean in to listen.

In the spring of 2009, De'Juan was arrested on charges of domestic battery and selling drugs. He bonded out and hid from the law, crashing on couches and working for cash. The sheriff began broadcasting De'Juan's mug shot on a local news feature called "Kansas Most Wanted." De'Juan explains over the phone, "These motherfuckers, man, they don't even try to come arrest me no more when they get to looking for me, they just put my ass on TV. I'm a high-profile boy out here. I'm not a big fish but I'm not Nemo."

Eventually, De'Juan was pulled over by police for a broken turn signal, leading to his arrest. He is currently awaiting trial. His bail has been set at $32,000, an amount the thirty-one-year-old says he cannot afford. Thus, De'Juan sits in the county lockup. His next court appearance is slated for September 16, eleven days from now. "Sometimes you got to bite the bullet," De'Juan tells me and Stu. "I'm just biting the bullet on that shit, otherwise I'd be there [with you]. It's all to the good. What they can't do is keep a nigga forever."

Stu and I had been reminiscing about DVS Mindz, so I ask De'Juan for a personal highlight. The Wu-Tang show, he answers without hesitation. "That Wu-Tang show was a beast. It was just us and them really. Armageddon click. After we came off stage man, just the look. There was a couple thousand motherfuckers out there. I had my hair all wild, looking crazy. Motherfuckers notice me on the side and they kind of rushed me. There ain't no feeling like it in the world, man."

A recorded voice interrupts, intoning, "You have sixty seconds left on this call."

We all say goodbye. "I'm about to get out of here," De'Juan tells us. "When I get out, I'm going to be in Kansas City throwing big shows. If none of the artists that supposed to be there show up, I'm taking the cash and running. Don't tell nobody. Hey, I love you all, man, take care. I have to get up out of here. Lockdown time."

13

UNITED STATES OF AMERICA VERSUS DE'JUAN KNIGHT

1924 Van Buren Street, Topeka, Kansas, June 22, 2014

Five years passed before I saw De'Juan in person again. When we got together for an interview in 2014, De'Juan was newly freed from prison and living in Topeka. I had messaged him on social media, and we agreed to do an interview at his place the next day. I had not seen De'Juan since 2003. De'Juan looked about the same, except that he was more muscular compared to the past, a physique sculpted by years of working out in penitentiary weight rooms.

The first time I interviewed De'Juan one-on-one, in May 2000, it was hard to get him to open up. "I'm always thinking," he explained. "I'm just a quiet motherfucker, naturally. I don't talk a whole lot on the regular. I don't even like to. I'd rather you not know what the fuck I'm thinking than tell you everything that's going on with me."

Today, I was a more experienced interviewer and De'Juan was ready to talk. "His years of writing experience turned him into a hell of a narrator," I wrote in my notes after the interview. "His stories were long and detailed but short on fluff and leading sharply from one point to the next. He was open, honest, thoughtful, and reflective."

At the time, De'Juan was renting a bed in a shared house. It was dark and dilapidated. Eight-by-four-foot plywood sheets were affixed to the walls, and there were gaping holes in the floor. The entire kitchen sagged under the weight of old appliances, including a washer and dryer squeezed between the stove and the refrigerator. De'Juan and I sat on two rickety chairs at a ratty kitchen table that held two boxy late-model televisions. Over the next three hours, De'Juan told me his story.

When DVS Mindz broke up in 2003, Daymond and Randy had already departed. Stu was living in Grandview and only came to Topeka once or twice a month. There were no more songwriting sessions and no new material to record. Bookings for shows had dried up. Tensions within the group began to escalate. "All the little bickerings and arguments, back and forth started to create distance," De'Juan recalls. "Stu stopped coming down so much and Barry fell out a little bit. Them being the original members. If Barry and Stu ain't rockin', what are the rest of us doing over here?"

De'Juan says that DVS Mindz did not so much break up as it did fade away. "It was like a long-distance relationship," he recalls. "It started to fizzle, and nobody actually called each other to say, 'Hey, I don't want to be together no more.' Everybody was going their own way."

The dissolution of DVS Mindz hit De'Juan hard. He had spent years fighting his way into the group, beating out every other contender in the Crew to become a full-fledged member. He had staked his hopes and dreams on the band's making it. "We were looking at it like this is going to save our lives and feed our family someday," he says. De'Juan's determination and talent had taken him all the way to the Wu-Tang Clan show, but now the dream was over. He was back to selling weed to make ends meet.

The change in stature affected De'Juan and everyone around him. Topeka is not a very big place, and De'Juan was still a well-known public figure. "You still got this persona in the streets, but I don't have five dollars for gas money. To be *that* guy, it's kind of a shock to the pride. After the DVS thing, I was still maintaining an image and still living the lifestyle. Used to being in the clubs, VIP, being backstage to now being the guy at the back of the line. And everybody's like, 'Why aren't you performing?'"

In the wake of DVS's dissolution, De'Juan began to run into serious trouble with the law. On October 29, 2004, he was arrested for possession of narcotics with intent to sell. There were also issues on the home front. De'Juan had been estranged from his mother, Charmaine, since leaving home at age sixteen. Now Charmaine's health was deteriorating. In 2001, the forty-two-year-old suffered a debilitating stroke. Unable to maintain her balance, Charmaine could no longer stand or walk and was confined to a wheelchair. She would require around-the-clock care.

In 2001, De'Juan was living in the fast lane, rapping in nightclubs with DVS, getting arrested for low-level offenses, and spending time in and out of the county jail. At just shy of twenty-four, De'Juan was the oldest of Charmaine's three children. With no other family members able to assist, De'Juan was suddenly prevailed upon to help. "It turned into six years' worth of dealing with retirement homes and independent living, the nurse's aides not showing up to her house to get her up and get her dressed. I didn't have no choice but to do that shit and handle that and make sure that those things were in place. I went from the stages and the nightlife to having to head that up. That was a transition on its own, kind of a grown-man situation. That also changed me as a man."

De'Juan never resolved things with his mother. Charmaine had an aneurysm and passed on December 15, 2007, at the age of forty-eight. "There was so much hatred and anger wrapped up in it," De'Juan says. "They say that anger comes from two places, hurt and fear. It was so much hurt and so much anger in it because there was so much love. It's just a twisted ball of shit and it was all fucked up emotionally and mentally."

Six weeks after Charmaine passed, on January 28, 2008, De'Juan was arrested for the sale of narcotics. In April 2009, he was arrested for domestic battery, armed robbery, and possession of a firearm. Not long after he called from jail during my 2009 interview with Stu, De'Juan was brought up on federal charges. He had spent his life scraping by on small-time offenses that carried relatively minor sentences—a few days in jail here, a couple weeks here, maybe a month or two there. This time was different. This time, the justice system was throwing the book at him.

THE DEAL

De'Juan arrived in court a seasoned veteran of criminal proceedings. He had been in and out of the Shawnee County correctional system for more than half his life. But this was a federal crime, with proceedings held in federal court. De'Juan was brought into the courtroom wearing shackles and protective gear. "They take you to court like you're a suicide bomber or somebody's going to kill you in court," he says. "They might as well put a bag over your head and tie it so you don't see where they take you to. It's also the whole intimidation thing, just the huge show that they put on. Your paperwork says, 'United States of America versus De'Juan Knight.'"

The Armed Career Criminal Act of 1984 (ACCA) is a law that enhances the sentences of individuals who carry firearms while committing a third felony. Due to De'Juan's prior convictions, he was charged as an armed career criminal, which carries a minimum sentence of fifteen years to life. De'Juan was stunned.

As De'Juan awaited his next hearing, he pored over legal documents, sure that the ACCA charges were unfounded. Advocating for himself was De'Juan's best option. His public defender was swamped with other cases, and fees for lawyers who handle federal criminal trials started at ten thousand dollars. Eventually, the federal prosecutor offered a plea bargain of ninety-six months, a total of eight years in prison, in exchange for De'Juan's pleading guilty to possession of a stolen firearm. According to De'Juan, the gun was not stolen but purchased legally by a friend. It did not matter, the public defender told De'Juan. This was the deal being offered. "You can take eight years today and lock it in," she said. "There's no way they'll give you more than that."

Public defenders frequently pressure defendants to take bad deals with terms that should not have been offered.[1] De'Juan was reluctant to plead guilty to trumped-up charges, but turning down the deal was a gamble that could result in fifteen or more years in prison. "It's hard when it's just you sitting in that room with your lawyer, and they're talking about fifteen years in prison, and there's paperwork on the table that you can sign. That's heavy."

De'Juan refused to sign the deal. The public defender urged him to reconsider. "Don't shoot it down," she said, "Talk to your family, and get some opinions." De'Juan didn't have any family members to talk it over with. His mother had passed, and his father had just been released from serving two-and-a-half years in prison on gun charges.

Eventually, the public defender returned with a new plea bargain, four years, with the potential for time reduced for good behavior. "They're offering you forty-eight months," she told De'Juan, handing him a pen. "Four years. You'll do two-and-a-half, three." De'Juan was due in court the following day. "Just sign this," she pressed him.

Confused and anxious, De'Juan took the deal: four years in the federal penitentiary.

De'Juan served his time at the Federal Correctional Institution—El Reno, a medium-security federal institution located in El Reno, Oklahoma. Built in 1933 and spanning four thousand acres, FCI El Reno houses 894 prisoners in two-man cells.[2] Its most notorious inmate in recent years was Timothy McVeigh, who set off a bomb in downtown Oklahoma City in 1995. Barack Obama made headlines in 2015 when he made a stop at FCI El Reno, the first time a sitting president visited a federal prison.

De'Juan focused on doing his time and getting out, looking ahead to the future rather than ruminating over the past or lamenting the present. "There's a phrase my man told me: 'Poor people are living for today. Rich people, they're living for tomorrow, next year. Wealthy people are living for five years from now, ten years, twenty years from now.' That stuck with me."

FCI El Reno was not De'Juan's first time behind bars. He had been in and out of Kansas boot camps and jails from the time he was a teenager. He could easily endure a month or two in the local lockup. But this was different. This time De'Juan was facing years in a federal penitentiary. "I got to be here all of next year, and I get out the year after that," he thought to himself. "There's some guys, they don't mind being locked up. It's normal. Me, I'm in fucking depressed mode. I'm sitting there like, 'Fuck.'"

De'Juan was profoundly impacted by his inability to see his children, sons Diabolique and Mehki, and daughter Vasiah. "I had to go three, four years without seeing the kids," he says. "Some guys, they don't talk to their kids on the phone. Baby mom, wife, whatever, they're on bad terms. I called the kids at least once a week, staying in contact, just talking. Some days the conversations go well, some days they don't. When I left, my daughter wasn't even talking; she was one. Before I come home, I'm on the phone with her having full conversations and shit. She was like 'Dad I can't remember where you're at.' That fucked me up. That was huge, man. I still carry that."

Trying to keep his darkest thoughts at bay, De'Juan immersed himself in a daily routine. The county jail in Topeka was highly regulated, with inmates being directed in and out of their cells for hours at a time. At FCI El Reno, prisoners were not normally confined to their cells and were free to move about all day if they chose. The prison barber shop was a popular hangout, and many inmates took advantage of GED and college courses that were offered. Others studied welding and electrical. De'Juan took classes in plumbing, eventually earning a trade certificate. There was even a band room filled with instruments.

FCI El Reno also featured facilities for basketball, softball, volleyball, and tennis. De'Juan spent most of his time in the weight room. "That's where the motherfuckers go to let out the tension and aggression. The pressure of them thoughts just keep you sitting and thinking all day. Go out there and push that iron."

If this was a Hollywood movie, De'Juan would use his prison time to pen a masterpiece. In reality, he lost all interest in writing lyrics or rapping. His identity as a musician vanished in prison. De'Juan says he only wrote two verses the entire time. "There wasn't an artistic bone in my body. There was no sit-down-and-write bug that got me. Every time I sat down to write, everything comes out the same. It's about prison. 'I know some niggas that ain't never going home again.' I can't write thirty songs about that."

De'Juan had spent nearly six months in jail during his trial and sentencing. He also earned a month of credit for staying out of trouble. The final six months of his sentence were to be served in a halfway house. In total, De'Juan spent nearly three years at FCI El Reno before being discharged to a Topeka halfway house on January 16, 2012.

Residents of the halfway house were expected to work full-time before returning at night to sleep. De'Juan had studied plumbing for two years in El Reno, but his attempts to find work were hamstrung by his federal felony conviction. "I needed a job," he recalls. "I got child support and things going on that aren't going to go away. I needed to get out of the halfway house. I needed to get on my feet." De'Juan tapped his local networks and found a position at Southwest Publishing, a direct-mail manufacturing company where he had worked more than a decade prior.

De'Juan was sober and had a steady job. He wanted nothing more than to finish his time at the halfway house and move on. But life at the house was a grind, awash in regulation and control. Smartphones were prohibited, and residents were subjected to frequent drug and alcohol screens. "They breathalyze you every time you leave," De'Juan says. "If you fucking walk to the end of the block to go to the Dollar Store, get some deodorant—breathalyzer. Every time you leave and shit. You do what you got to do. I was trying."

Inmates are not released from prison without postrelease supervision. De'Juan was saddled with twenty-four months of parole, meeting weekly with an officer who gave him a hard time. At the time of our interview in 2014, De'Juan was still on parole.

LEGENDARY STATUS

Former athletes sometimes retain residual elements of their previous identities by taking on the role of "legend," preserving status long after their prominence has faded.[3] These athletes "continue to command high social standing and prestige . . . in their local community . . . regardless of their present professional or financial circumstances."[4] Although De'Juan never made it, his standing as a former member of DVS Mindz remains a mark of distinction in Topeka. "We got the kind of history that still allows me to be able to do it. There's still people that ask about it. I'm fortunate enough."

DVS Mindz's dream of making it did not pan out, but that did not necessarily negate the members' involvement in music. Now almost thirty-seven years old and newly out of prison, De'Juan continues to write and perform. Although he is no longer trying to make it, his ongoing involvement in music means not having to completely give up the musician identity.

Rap is a youth-dominated genre, and people are sometimes surprised that De'Juan is still involved in music. "You get to the age where a lot of people are like, 'Really? Are you still rapping?' I still do this. I still got love for this music shit. It's not for the money, it's not for the fame. It's not about getting rich and trying to get signed and blowing up. That's not even a focus. At this point, it's just because this is still my outlet. It became the outlet so many years ago that you don't realize what it does for you personally. I still write. I'm a thinker. It's my therapy. It's about me releasing it or me putting in down. This is just what I do. I've done it so long that this is part of who I am."

What De'Juan misses most about DVS Mindz is the writing sessions with the guys. The hardest part about songwriting now, he says, is having to write all the lyrics instead of one killer verse. "For close to ten years, I never had to write a whole song," he says. "You cram everything into one verse. I'm like, 'What the fuck is the second verse? The first verse is hot but I don't have anything else to say. I put it all in there.'"

De'Juan does not hear from the guys in DVS much these days, but he still feels a connection to everyone in the band. "The one thing that was ever present was the music," he says. "Even once it stopped and everybody went their separate ways, still we connect on music. Even when I wasn't really talking to none of them, one thing that was always constant was the music."

De'Juan still performs live from time to time, generally stepping onstage for a song or two as a guest for an up-and-coming Topeka rap act. His standing as a member of DVS Mindz means that the invitations keep coming. "I still perform," he says. "I still got guys I fuck with that still do it. They pull me into it, more than I'm anxious to get out there and do it. But I get out there, bang out, and release. Leave it right there. That's really what it is, almost that kind of intensity and shit, that kind of passion to get out there and rock the mic and hoot and holler." This provokes the ire of De'Juan's parole officer, who monitors his social media accounts. "You're fucking stupid man! Why you posting all that shit? We look at that shit," the parole officer says anytime De'Juan posts a photo taken at a nightclub.

For De'Juan, the performance is the only part of the club scene he still enjoys. "I don't just be in the clubs trying to kick it and hang out. I get to the club now, and I'm the old guy. I can't talk to her, she just turned nineteen. My oldest son is eighteen; I got graduation pictures. It's not my atmosphere, but I still perform. Life's gonna happen. Kids grow up. There's people that was calling me last night to come to a show that were in diapers back in the day when we were doing this shit. That's crazy. To recognize the time that we've spent doing music, writing music, performing music. Just that whole process, man that's crazy. I don't feel *that* old."

Still, at De'Juan's age, late nights and partying no longer suit his lifestyle. "The mind matures so much," he says. "Inside, I still feel the same. I can still rock the show down but afterwards I'm like, 'Fuck I am so tired.' I usually get up by five o'clock [a.m.] for work. I've done shows and had to be at work the next day. We're in the city. Of course, we got to have a couple drinks and shit. By the time the show goes on, we get to talking, I get back here at three o'clock. I got to be at work about five-forty-five; I'm supposed to be there, in the door at a machine. But even on the days I get home at three, I still go to work."

THE CYCLE

Not long after I interviewed De'Juan in 2014, he had an altercation outside a Topeka nightclub called the Catch. The Catch was located just down the street from Aunt Tang's townhome, where De'Juan's cousin Kevin was staying at the time. De'Juan, Kevin, and two women were leaving the venue, making their way over to Tang's place. Parked outside was an elaborately painted Buick with twenty-two-inch rims, which everyone stopped to admire. Appearing out of nowhere, the car's owner suddenly rushed over.

"Ain't nobody going to do nothin'," he shouted at the group, suspicious that they might try to break into the car or steal it.

"Bro," De'Juan fired back, "if you don't want us to look at the car don't put twenty-four-inch rims and orange paint on the motherfucker."

The argument quickly escalated.

"He pulled his gun out on us," De'Juan recalls, recounting the story years later. "We're standing in a dark alley with no street-lights outside a club. And he's dead ass-serious."

One of the women from the group ran over to Aunt Tang's house. "You know Tang and you know how Tang's spirit is," De'Juan says. "She's the neighborhood mom, Big Momma shit. She knows everybody in the hood. So she comes right across the parking lot and starts calling people out by their names."

"Boy, shut up!" hollered Tang, dressed in a nightgown a slip-pers. She snapped her fingers. "Henry, come here! Yeah. I see you. Move."

The car owner backed down, but De'Juan was shaken by the incident and vowed to buy a gun for protection. "That is the last time I let a motherfucker weigh up my life while I stand here and wait to see what he's thinking," he told himself.

The next day, De'Juan purchased a P89, a 9mm pistol manu-factured by Ruger. At first, he carried it in the trunk of his car, but realized he might need it if he ran into a problem while driv-ing. "What are you going to do, pull over and get out? 'Wait just a minute, there's an exit up here.'"

Not long after buying the gun, De'Juan was pulled over for a traffic violation while driving with his sister. There were two ounces of marijuana under the seat, right next to his loaded 9mm. De'Juan had never had a legitimate driver's license in his life, but he was carrying a Kansas state ID. He gave it to the police officer, being polite and courteous. "Listen man, I don't have my license on me but here's my ID. The girl in the passen-ger seat is my sister."

"Give me a second, not a problem," the officer replied and returned to his car.

De'Juan knew that he would be flagged in the system for prior gun charges and searched for weapons. He had to get rid of the pistol. He pulled it out from under the seat, removed the clip, and wrapped it in an old Arby's bag. "I got to go. I'm out," he told his sister, before dashing out the door and down an alley. He threw the clip in one direction and the Ruger in another.

The police found the gun, the clip, and caught De'Juan, too. He did not resist arrest, which he says is why he is still alive when I interview him in 2020. "If I can get away, I'm getting away. If I get caught, I'm like, 'Where's the car?'" De'Juan throws up his arms, feigning surrender. "I was in the wrong when I took off. I had to take off and throw my gun for a reason. But some of these guys they are killing aren't in the wrong."

From De'Juan's perspective, when there are, for example, white mass shooters, it gets chalked up to mental health issues. The shooters often make it to jail. Meanwhile, Blacks are labeled criminals and treated as such. According to De'Juan, mental health issues are widespread in the Black community. "Everybody's not processing and thinking correctly," he says, shaking his head. "There's schizophrenia, substance abuse, the way it's going on in the world right now. The big picture. It's still like that."

De'Juan connects cases where Blacks are killed by police while legally carrying a firearm to larger forms of systematic racial injustice. He mentions crack cocaine being brought into impoverished neighborhoods. He talks about assistance programs that reduce a child's benefits if two parents reside in the same household, creating a financial incentive for low-income fathers like him to live separately from their children. "They put motherfuckers on the street and put these divides into the families for generations. We're still trying to break the cycle."

It is a cycle De'Juan knows personally. He was poor as a child and continues to struggle financially as an adult. Poverty, he says, creates a never-ending sense of pressure. "Yes, I ended up selling drugs. We used to eat a loaf of bread for fucking dinner. We were in this situation. Yes, mama was addicted to drugs. We've acknowledged as a people that these things have been put into play by the powers-that-be. We've acknowledged that this wasn't just happenstance. It's been set up for these things to happen, the impoverished [communities] that these guys are coming up in. Either I'm robbing someone, or I've got nothing. When you're in that situation, I got to go take it. I don't have it. Have I been able to break the cycle completely? No, because I've been in prison, so I wasn't where my kids were. So I participated." De'Juan makes a circling motion with his hand, like a globe spinning around. "It started before I knew the cycle that was to come."

Upon being convicted for the gun charge, De'Juan served more than a year at El Dorado Correctional Facility, a maximum-security prison that "houses the most dangerous and recalcitrant inmates assigned to long-term involuntary segregation."[5] The conditions at El Dorado were harsh, De'Juan says, worsened by the abusive treatment of inmates.

"You think these people are going to do their job but that's not necessarily the case. You can't get your one hour out a day of leaving your room for two weeks. That's not right. Nobody gives a fuck. We're supposed to have one hot meal a day. Nobody gives a fuck. You start going down the list of things. Hey, you got to give us at least one shower a week. Nobody gives a fuck. Ain't nobody listening. You just stand there and shake your head. You can't even argue with anybody because they can make it longer. They can make it worse, so you just swallow it."

De'Juan was on parole for another year before being completely discharged in late 2017. At the time of his release, De'Juan was the only member of DVS Mindz still living in Topeka.

14

DALLAS

The first and only time I interviewed Daymond one-on-one was in March 2000, when I pulled him aside during a party for a quick interview in my kitchen. I also interviewed Daymond as part of the group in 1999 and 2000. He took the lead in those conversations, which centered around music and the band. At the time, I knew little of Daymond's story, other than that he had served time in prison and had a professional, white-collar job. Daymond was nicknamed the Invisible Man for good reason—he was a mystery.

I am not sure what to expect when we finally have a chance to talk in July 2018. But any reservations I have are immediately cast aside. Daymond is engaging and thoughtful, providing perspectives on DVS Mindz I never heard before. I brought plenty of questions. Daymond has strong opinions and gripping stories and over the course of a six-and-a-half-hour interview that takes place over two days, he happily shares both.

When Daymond departed DVS Mindz in 2002, he said little about it publicly. Asked in 2018 why he left, Daymond offers a laundry list of frustrations, the foremost of which was money. "We got an album out. We're doing all these shows, and we're selling all these tickets. At the album release party, nobody else could get in the door. They had to stop letting people in. It was that packed. We're the ones in the studio. We're the ones doing all the work, and we ain't get nothing out of it. Ain't nobody ever gave me a check on behalf of DVS Mindz. DVS Mindz ain't bought me a pair of socks."

The positive critical response to DVS Mindz's debut CD, *Million Dolla Broke Niggaz*, did not translate into dollars, but its success went to the group's head, according to Daymond. "When the album came out and how successful that was and all the attention that it got, it was almost like everybody had the attitude that we had made it. But it should have been the complete opposite. This is the beginning of the rest of our career. For these last six years, we've been practicing for this moment. But we was stubborn. Everybody wanted to do it their way. We was too caught up in our own egos. Our egos wouldn't let us listen. It was everybody's ego, including mine."

Daymond says he was never happy with the album, that he thought calling it *Million Dolla Broke Niggaz* was unoriginal, and the cover photos, which resembled mug shots, were untrue to the group's hip-hop origins. "It just really wasn't going in the direction I felt like it should be going," he says. "I didn't like the album. I liked what it took to *make* the album, but I don't think it's a very good album at all. I thought it was rushed, it was put together poorly. We didn't seize the moment like I felt like we should. Around that time in 2000, after the album came out, I was always one foot out. I would miss studio sessions. I seen the future. I knew it. We about to self-destruct. I'm not going to be on the boat when it goes down. I left."

Daymond's reasons for leaving were also related to his responsibilities outside the band. He continued to work on the phone as a sales rep for TeleTech during the day and remained a single father to his son, now ten years old. "There was a lot of stuff that

I was dealing with personally that had nothing to do with DVS Mindz," Daymond says. "Just becoming a man, with family. My son. I didn't really know how to balance that."

Thirty years old at the time he left DVS, Daymond's priorities began to shift away from his youthful ambitions of making it as a rapper and towards the responsibilities of parenthood. "I was missing a lot of precious times when I was chasing that dream," he says. "That helped me decide to get out of the group, or at least get away from self-destructive behavior. I don't have time for that, I wanted to be home with my son, teaching him how to ride a bike and how to tie his shoe."

D DOT

Leaving DVS Mindz, however, did not mean that Daymond was finished with music. After departing, he continued to write and record, working closely with his cousin, a producer named Reggie B. He also purchased enough equipment to build a nice home studio and began producing tracks in his apartment. "In my mind, I'm about to show everybody who the truth is," he recalls. "I was mad. Let's see you motherfuckers make it without me. I'm doing my solo shit."

One of Daymond's girlfriends passed his demo to Brad Sparks, an aggressive, fast-talking music manager from New York City. Sparks was searching for an artist along the lines of Fabolous—a good-looking male rapper with catchy songs and a hint of street edge. Daymond had the look, but most of his songs were lyrical screeds that railed against the evils of the music industry. Sparks was blunt: "No, man. I need some shit I can *market*." Daymond was willing to give it a try. He started writing and recording commercial rap songs.

Sparks would call every couple of weeks to check on Daymond's progress. "Put the phone up to the speaker in the studio," Sparks would order. "If that shit ain't hot, do *not* play that shit." Sparks generally hated what he heard and would either offer suggestions for improvement or tell Daymond to throw the song away and write something else. "It was like boot camp for me," Daymond recalls. "I was developing a whole new sound. Trying to tone that lyrical shit down and actually make songs was challenging. It showed me what type of artist I was, 'cause I had to reach into a different bag."

One day, Sparks called and Daymond played him a newly recorded track, an R&B/rap hybrid with a female vocalist singing the hook. "That's what I'm talking about!" Sparks enthused. "Keep making me shit like that." Daymond set to work on scores of new songs, including a romantic love ballad, "Someone for Me," and a couple of dancefloor bangers, "Move Your Body" and "Where My Mommies At?" He even came up with a new, more marketable stage name, doing away with his old DVS moniker D.O.P.E and replacing it with D Dot.

Late one night, while working in his home studio, Daymond got a call from Sparks. "We did it," Sparks told him. "I got you a deal with Arista Records." According to Daymond, it was a development deal with a $100,000 budget attached. "I got my ASCAP, and I set up a publishing company for myself. I was like, 'Man, I finally did it.'"

Daymond continued to write and record songs, preparing for a trip to New York City to sign contracts. One morning the phone rang. It was Sparks, and he sounded panicked. "I don't know what's going on, but they just fired Jermaine Dupri and his whole staff," Sparks reported. Dupri was the senior vice president at Arista. An hour later, there was more bad news: Arista president L.A. Reid had just been let go. Arista was being shut down and folded into Clive Davis's new J Records imprint. Daymond's deal fell through. Having spent months writing and recording material and developing a new sound, he was back to square one. Things were such a mess at Arista, Daymond had to hire a lawyer to get his demo tapes back. Sparks stopped calling.

Daymond shopped his demo to all the major labels, receiving a few nibbles but no bites. Eventually, Daymond decided to take matters into his own hands. He formed a production company, Etc. Entertainment, and, under the D Dot moniker, self-released solo CDs in 2005 and 2006. Both efforts flopped, and Daymond found that doing everything himself was exhausting. Daymond was ready for a change. He was getting older, and work and family responsibilities were weighing larger in his life.

DALLAS

Daymond's decade-plus in the music industry had gotten him nowhere, but he continued to move up the ladder in his day job. TeleTech, the call center where he worked, had been acquired by Verizon. Daymond eventually moved from the phones to a position where he led training sessions. By 2007, he had amassed eight years of experience working for the same company and was a corporate trainer for Verizon. In 2007, when a similar job with T-Mobile opened in Dallas, Daymond decided to take a chance and relocate. "I always felt like I was different from the friends I was around," he says. "Not that I was better than anybody, I just felt that I was different. That's part of the reason why I left Topeka. I felt like a shark. I couldn't move."

For Daymond, leaving Topeka marked the end of his music career. "It was a transition. I was like, 'I'm done with music.

I'm not fucking with this anymore. I'm going to go live my life.' I neglected a lot of time with my son, chasing a dream that didn't come to life. So now it's his turn. I got to be the dad, raise him, make sure he becomes a good man. I don't want to do that in Topeka. Let me just leave. Texas was an I'm-done-with-rap type of deal."

Relocating to Texas enabled Daymond to reinvent himself away from the Topeka fishbowl, where everyone knew him as an MC. "I wanted to be successful at something else other than rap," he says. "I didn't want to be defined as just a rapper. I always wanted to be defined as a businessperson more than anything. Somebody smart, somebody that can figure it out."

When Daymond moved to Dallas in 2007, he worked as a technical trainer for T-Mobile. He also started a mobile barber business that did well, but required long hours and lots of driving. From 2007 to 2009, he took night classes at ITT Technical Institute in Arlington, hoping to one day earn a degree. Daymond could see a path. "I chose the corporate world to get my grind on, and I chose phones. I remember staying up late night on the internet, looking up shit about phones, technology, and computers. I remember thinking, 'This is the future.'"

DOMESTICITY

Daymond met his future wife, Desirae, at the T-Mobile call center where they both worked. She was a transfer, coming to Dallas from Kansas. Daymond used the Kansas connection to strike up a conversation, and the two began dating soon after. Desirae was in the final stages of a divorce and had three children. She was not looking to get seriously involved with anyone. "We didn't go into it like we were looking for matrimony, but we just connected," Daymond recalls. "We couldn't stop seeing each other. Both of us were at a point in our lives where we were ready to be with somebody who loved us the way that we wanted to be loved."

The two merged households in 2008, renting a large single-family home in Irving, Texas, with Daymond's son, fourteen-year-old Daymond Jr., meeting his two new similar-age siblings as they were all moving in together. "It was literally like, pull shit off the truck, 'Hey my name is Daymond.' 'Hey, my name is Dominic,'" Daymond recalls, laughing. "I was like, 'This is a Lifetime movie.' It was sink or swim. We had our times, but it worked. My wife is my soulmate. If you think about it like that, then it was supposed to work. And it did." Daymond and Desirae married in 2010.

The two continued to build successful careers as well. Desirae landed a position in the corporate offices at Toyota, and, in 2015, Daymond took a job as a senior technical trainer for Samsung, where he has worked ever since. "I manage the technical relationships between Samsung and AT&T," Daymond explains. "I'm essentially a trainer-slash-account manager. We train the carriers, the call centers. I manage AT&T and Cricket. We manage the technical side of the house. A lot of data analytics. Looking at the data at their call centers, seeing which one of our devices is causing issues. I work a lot with the quality managers. I work a lot with the product managers. Sometimes I got to create a technical document."

Despite only having a GED, having amassed years in the telecommunications industry, Daymond is an experienced and highly compensated worker. "For me to grind all the way and show my work ethic and my ability to organize things and look at trends, for me to have a job at Samsung. I make damn near $100,000 a year. And I don't have a degree. That's *huge*."

In 2019, Daymond and Desirae purchased a $400,000 four-bedroom home in the tony Winn Ridge neighborhood in Aubrey, located in the far northern suburbs of the Dallas/Fort Worth area. Daymond's house is filled with lots of grownup toys: a pool table, a forty-gallon saltwater fish tank, and in the driveway, a Lexus SUV and a BMW 330e, an electric car that retails for about $50,000.

This is not just mindless consumerism. These purchases have enabled Daymond to reclaim parts of his childhood that were lost when his parents divorced, and he went from video game systems and pool tables to poverty. Surrounding himself with luxury goods has also helped Daymond find peace with his disappointments in the music business. If anything, all these goodies were a repudiation of his teenage ambition to make it through rap instead of climbing the corporate ladder.

"I can't believe it," Daymond marvels, surveying the scene. "I'm accomplishing all this stuff and doing all this shit that I rapped about, thinking that rap was going to get it for me. I couldn't see past that. You know what? My real life is getting this shit for me. I didn't have to rap to do it."

Daymond has spent more than twenty years working in a corporate setting, far removed from his days with DVS, let alone his time as a teenage prisoner. Still, Daymond claims that he has not entirely left that world behind. "I can move between being on the block and going and sitting in the boardroom and speaking professional. Because that's what I seen my whole life."

Exconvicts tend to be "marked" by their criminal records, which reduces their chances of employment.[1] De'Juan believed that his felony convictions hurt his work-related prospects, but Daymond says that his early experiences with incarceration did not slow him down: "I don't feel sorry for people that make excuses for themselves—'I was in prison, I was raised this way, I don't have a way out.' I know everybody's not the same, but I'm an example of success. If I can do it, you can do it. Even if you do two years, five years, ten years, you can get out of jail and change your life. It's never too late."

Daymond's perspective has also been broadened and transformed through travel. His job at Samsung requires significant travel within the United States, but Daymond sometimes leads teams of ten, managing projects abroad. This has included training exercises in Jamaica and El Salvador. Daymond was particularly surprised at how he is perceived by others when traveling abroad. "Black people are treated completely different. They look at us like, 'How do you live in the United States the way it is?' They see the media like we see the media: 'Black men are getting killed, y'all are victimized.' They are really empathetic: 'Why do you keep going back to the United States? Why do you live there?' You don't really think about that as an American until you leave. It makes you kind of look at yourself from a different perspective."

Daymond adds that being a Black man in America is "not as bad as the media depicts it to be. The media will spin the story and make it look a certain way." Daymond repeats many of the tropes of the American Dream, believing that hard work and personal effort were the keys to his success. "My mom always told me growing up that you can be whoever you want to be, whoever you decide to be, but be the best that you can at it. I don't care if you a lawyer or if you are ant farmer, just be the best damn ant farmer in the whole land. You can do whatever you want to do. You can't let your past define how your future is going to turn out. You always are the person in the driver's seat."

Daymond believes that Black men in America are pressured to behave in ways that recreate racial stereotypes. He describes being "groomed" not only by family and friends but also by the entertainment industry. "You're groomed to act like this, say this, walk this way. 'You got to put on those gold chains, you got to buy that Benz.' But in your mind, I don't want no fuckin' Benz; I want to drive a fuckin' Prius. As Black men, we're taught to not show emotion. 'That's gay.' We're taught to not be humble; you got to be tough. Because of the circumstances, just from what happened with our race, certain things are groomed into us. I got to put up this facade. I got to put this mask on so people accept me."

Daymond looks back on his earlier experiences as part of a larger process of personal growth and self-actualization. "When you go from adolescent to a young man to a grown man, you go through these phases," he says. "I went through a lot of stages of just trying to figure out what type of man I wanted to be, what type of person I wanted to be, what type of friend I wanted to be, what type of father I wanted to be."

Daymond even reconciled with his father, who is still alive and living downstate in San Antonio. "Our relationship is a lot better than it was in the past," he says. "In my adult life I really see a lot of stuff that I adopted from my dad. I want to go down there and spend some time and talk to him about all those pieces that are missing."

15

A PIRATE LOOKS AT 40

I t is January 2002, and Barry's girlfriend Stacy has spent the better part of two weeks driving around Topeka, collecting video testimonies from Barry's friends and family. She shot the footage with one of my video cameras, which she asked to borrow, swearing to guard it with her life. She returns the camera, unharmed, fifteen days later, along with a tape full of testimonies that she wants me to edit and compile for Barry's upcoming thirty-second birthday.

I attach the camcorder to my computer and take a look at the footage. Members of Barry's family and various Crew members appear on camera to wish him a happy birthday. Shot over the holidays in Topeka living rooms and kitchens, there are Christmas trees and snow-covered windows in the background. Cute kids and couchbound grandparents crop up saying funny things. "What are you, forty-one?" teases a woman Barry used to work with. Some Crew members wish Barry a happy "C-day," an alternative to "b-day" sometimes used by Crips.[1] Randy, Stu, De'Juan, and Daymond all make brief appearances.

Randy: Happy big three-two, 40 Killa. You been through a lot of shit. I'm glad to see you made it thirty-two years. Hopefully, you'll make it a lot more, and it'll be all good from there. Much love. Happy birthday, nigga. Peace.

Stu: Happy birthday, nigga. You made it to thirty-two, let's see thirty-two more.

De'Juan: Well, shit. I was gonna say a couple of stories, a couple of funny shits, but you're a dirty old man, I can't say those out loud. Thirty-second birthday. Let's get fucked up one time. That's real. Happy birthday. Peace.

Daymond: What's up, B? I can't never remember nobody's birthday but my niggas. For real. I know your birthday is always around the Super Bowl. I don't know who the fuck's playing, but I know it's around the Super Bowl. I just want to say happy birthday, nigga, and I love you for life, nigga. Peace."

Stacy's video testimonies are lighthearted and warm, with everyone saying nice things, lightly ribbing Barry's "old age," and joining in the celebration. So it's startling when one Crew member appears, holding the camera and pointing it at himself, adopting a derisive tone. "I'm gonna tell you like this, nigga. It's 2002, nigga, and ain't a damn thing changed, huh? Still chasin' them broke-ass motherfuckin' dreams. Get off your ass and make that paper, nigga. And *that's* on a C-day. Any day. All day, every day."

SLEDGEHAMMER

Topeka, Kansas, June 22, 2014

The last time I saw Barry was at a Topeka strip club in 2002. Eleven years later, he looks a bit older. Barry is skinnier than I have ever seen him, he has a couple of gray hairs, and his trademark raspy voice is more nicotine stained and smoky than ever.

All of this makes Barry appear a bit more weathered than he did a decade ago, but he seems largely the same.

Barry listed himself as living in Denver on social media but he had cropped up in a few pictures with De'Juan recently, leading me to think he might be in Topeka. As luck would have it, Barry is in town visiting friends and family. I am in town for the weekend to conduct interviews for this book. I interviewed De'Juan earlier that afternoon. While in town, Barry is crashing on the couch of his former girlfriend, Lisa, mother to his son, Marcus. Lisa's pristinely decorated house isn't far from De'Juan's place, but the neighborhood is a hundred and eighty degrees nicer.

In my interviews with DVS Mindz from 1999 to 2003, we talked mostly about music and the band; this weekend I want to know more about the people. I ask about their personal lives, their upbringings, and their experiences with school. We talk about their parents, children, wives, and girlfriends. They tell me their goals, ambitions, and feelings. Stu and De'Juan are open books, but Barry's tough exterior is harder to cut through. I don't want to push him too much, figuring he'll open up eventually. Midway through our three-hour conversation, he does.

Barry tells me that DVS Mindz broke up because success went to everyone's heads. "We were performing three or four times a week. Not even getting paid for it. Didn't have no CD out. No merchandise. No nothing. Kicking ass. That's when the pin came out the ego bomb. Motherfuckers start feeling they are bigger than the group. It got so crazy. It got to the point where there was jealousy among ourselves."

As DVS Mindz became more prominent, everything began to speed up. There was more of everything. More liquor, more blunts, more pressure, more women, more strangers hanging around backstage. DVS would have a concert in two hours, and one of the guys would call, needing a ride from some one-night stand fifty miles away. Everyone bickered constantly. Barry says the infighting spilled over to the band's wives and girlfriends. "They're smiling in each other's face and then over in the corner talking shit on the other two. The other one's over there with the other two talking shit on this one."

After Stu made a drunken pass at one of Barry's girlfriends, tensions within the group reached an all-time high. Barry tried to stay focused, telling himself that the band's career was bigger than the interpersonal problems. "Niggas had to bite a lot of bullets and a lot of bullshit to make DVS as successful as it got—before it got to that breaking point," he says. "It worked great and then it was total fuckery. You can only take so much shit."

Like Stu and De'Juan, Barry also points to the Wu-Tang Clan show as the highlight of the entire experience. "That made me feel like, 'My niggas, we can do whatever the fuck we want. Do you see who the fuck we're opening for?' They don't have a gang of people doing that. And they went out of their way, after canceling that show, to make sure we opened. Didn't pay us for shit. We're like, 'Oh you don't have to. We're about to kick ass.' That's why it was so much of a high point to me."

The changes that occurred in the wake of DVS's demise hit Barry like a sledgehammer. "I never really told anyone. I was going through depression. I mean, close-to-suicidal depression. What brought it all on is a bunch of stuff at once. Lost my job. Then I lost my apartment. I lost my car. And then the chick I was dating, me and her broke up. Then I ended up moving back in with my mom. It seemed like everything that happened was something bad—or that's how I perceived it. And it just depressed the shit out of me even more. How do you lose everything you got in one week? So I was really feeling terrible, like no motivation for anything. I would just sit in my mom's den, not do shit. It was bad."

Barry estimates that he spent three months lying around his mother's house. He didn't go anywhere, didn't talk to anyone, and felt utterly hopeless. "I knew that I was having some serious problems, but I didn't know how to express them, who to talk to about it, or if I even wanted to talk to anybody about it."

Barry's mother, Barbara, recommended that he seek counseling, but Barry was resistant to traditional treatments, such as talk therapy or medication. "What good is that going to do, me telling some stranger that I feel like shit? I've been telling myself that all day for the last couple of weeks, and it didn't make me feel any better. I don't want to take no medications. I don't need any of them side effects. Suicidal thoughts? I'm already feeling that. I don't need them amped up and just decide to blow my damn brains out for no reason."

To make matters worse, Barry started having medical ailments that he believes were a manifestation of his psychological state. He began fainting at random times, blackouts caused by stress. "One time it happened to me when I was at my mom's and I was in the bathroom. I just passed the fuck out. Fell dead on the floor, cut my eye open on this vent. Had to go to the hospital and get it stitched. The doctor be like, 'We don't see anything wrong with you.' It was nuts."

DENVER

One day in 2005, out of the blue, Barry's phone rang. It was Randy, DVS's former manager, calling from Colorado. Three years earlier, not long after Randy stopped managing the group, he moved from Topeka to Aurora, a suburb of Denver. In Topeka, Randy had spent more than a dozen years working in the payroll office at Blue Cross Blue Shield. Randy used that experience and some family connections to land a job with the Department of Veteran's Affairs in Denver. Randy loved everything about Colorado—the cultural diversity, the plethora of activities, and even the mountain views that reminded him he was far from Kansas. Randy and his three teenage sons were living in a large comfortable house in the suburbs.

Randy and Barry had been friends since high school. When Barry confessed how he was feeling, Randy immediately offered to put him up at his place in Colorado for free. Barry had already lived with Randy on three different occasions over the years. "Come out here," Randy said. "I got you. You can stay with me. Anything I can do to make it easier until you get your feet on the ground. Get out here now, and you can just owe me the rent money later."

Barry, a devoted Topeka resident, was initially appalled at the thought of relocating to another state. "Hell no, I ain't leaving Topeka. Fuck all that," he told Randy. But after thinking things over for a few days, the idea of a fresh start in Colorado started to sound pretty good. "I have to get the hell out of here," Barry thought to himself. "Because whatever it is that's stressing me, I need a whole different change of pace or I'm going to fucking kill myself. I just can't take it. It's like nothing's going right. I've got to do something different." Barry tells me, "So I just upped—got all my shit and left."

In Colorado, Barry crashed in one half of Randy's unfinished basement and got a job delivering high-end appliances to the superrich. After that, he did a bit of construction. On June 20, 2007, Barry's mother, Barbara, passed away at sixty-two. Barry was stricken with grief. "She was like my best fucking friend," he says. "I know for sure it affected me later on, like in the last couple of years, just not being able to talk to her. I took that for granted to a certain extent. That was my go-to person with anything. She'd give it to me straight. I really miss the shit out of her. That's a lot of reasoning for some things I do, like, 'If my mom was here would she be proud of me doing that?'"

Despite these challenges, over time, the depression that consumed Barry in Topeka began to lift. "I slowly started to come out of it," he says. "I started to let a lot of stuff go and not dwell on stuff so tough. I'm real thankful for that. I was in bad shape, and nobody knew it. Depression is real. I used to think you can snap out of it until it actually happened to me."

One of Randy's cousins got Barry a position in housekeeping at the Denver Loews, a luxury hotel. Barry stayed on the job for eighteen months, and when a supervisor position came available, he applied and got the gig. Barry spent the next two-and-a-half years working as a supervisor, but he was fired after an on-site injury. Barry had pulled a muscle in his back one day while cleaning a bathroom. Because it was a workman's compensation claim, the hotel required a drug test. Barry, who liked to smoke blunts on the roof with his coworkers, knew he would fail. Barry lost the workman's comp claim and was fired for drug use.

AMERIKILLA

Barry's rap career ended at the same time DVS Mindz split. Or so he thought. "When DVS broke up, I was like, ain't no use for me to rap anymore. No one's gonna give a fuck," he recalls. Just like he did in the earliest days of DVS, Stu urged Barry to make music, telling him, "There's shit you say that people want to hear, that only you can give 'em." Barry was unsure. "I'm like, 'I don't know, maybe but I doubt it.' So I wrestled with that for a while."

Barry eventually recorded a solo track, "Allow Me," that got the creative juices flowing. He enjoyed the autonomy of being a solo artist. "With all of us working together [in DVS Mindz], it's a give-and-take. Not everyone's going to like your idea. You have to try to find a way to compromise the good ideas together and make 'em mesh and make everybody happy, which was way harder than people thought."

It wasn't long before Barry started working with Denver-based rapper Bobby Tek, who would become Barry's most significant musical partner outside of Stu. Randy knew Bobby through mutual friends and played him some of DVS's music. Bobby loved what he heard, and Randy later introduced the two at a local bar. Soon after, Barry began recording features with Bobby and his musical partners. Barry and Bobby eventually became roommates, an odd pairing at first glance given that Bobby was a former Norteno gang member and Barry had history with the Crips. "From then on, we was best fucking friends," Barry says. "Me and that dude have been through so much shit: wars, fights, shootouts, all that shit. That's my fucking nigga."

Bobby had his own label, HardHeaded Records, that had released several Bobby Tek solo projects. The label was affiliated with Crooked Nation, an imprint with a roster of underground Colorado-based rappers, including Ryhno Buddz, Nutty Knockz, and Sleepy Hollow. HardHeaded Records and Crooked Nation regularly hosted showcase concerts starring acts from both labels, as well as special guests such as Barry.

Barry recorded more than forty features in his first five years in Denver, many of them alongside one or more HardHeaded Records or Crooked Nation artists. For example, he raps on four songs on Bobby Tek's 2013 album, *If My Rhyme Waz Az Good Az My Hustle*. Several of these songs were accompanied by low-budget music videos where Barry also appeared.

Although he is older, Barry remains trim and dresses in contemporary fashion. He keeps up with present-day rap music through his children, nephews, and other teenagers. "I don't look as old as I am," Barry says. "I don't act as old as I am. I don't dress as old as I am. So people just assume whatever age I am."

Barry continues to record and release solo projects as well, including a self-issued Killa the Hun album, *Amerikilla*, in 2016. There has also been a string of one-off singles with accompanying music videos: "Blow" (2014), "On My Level" (2015), "Don't Cross Me" (2016), and "Listen 2 Me" (2018). Barry has done little to monetize his music, which he mostly distributes online for free. "There's no restrictions now," he says when I interview him in 2020. "As a solo artist, you can take more risks. I'm just going to do what I'm feeling, and people are going to like it or not. I'm not making music for certain genres: this is for the club, this is for the ladies. I'm just writing straight-from-the-heart music."

Barry remains a purist, a craftsman and artist. "No two songs are going to sound the same. When I write, I try to always make sure the rhyme patterns are different: the cadence, delivery. I might speed it up, slow some shit down, make some shit sound extra slow. I want it to always be all over the place. To me, it's just more entertaining than hearing somebody rap where it's just constant and staying on beat. I try to challenge myself musically, always."

Barry is the first to admit that his level of intensity has waned as he has gotten older. "I got the same passion for it," he says of music before admitting, "I don't think I'll ever be as hungry as I was. For the *Million Dolla Broke Niggaz* album, we were just so hungry. I'm constantly trying to tap back into that hungriness, but I don't think I could ever be that hungry again."

Barry does not worry about his age or chances of making it. "I'll always be connected to music, one way or another," he insists. Barry says he'd like to ghostwrite for others and notes that Jay-Z is still making good music in his forties. Still, Barry has no illusions about making it at his age. "I don't want to say it's a hobby, but I'm realistic enough to know that the time is most likely gone to make a career out of it. If I just keep doing music 'cause I love it, just be independent and keep putting shit out, that would make me happy. Until whatever I'm saying ain't worth shit. Then I'll stop fucking around with music."

FUNDAMENTALS

Barry was the hard-partying pirate of DVS Mindz, and his lifestyle did not change after relocating to Denver. If anything, Barry's steady diet of Newports, high-octane liquor, and recreational marijuana only increased after the move. In the video for his 2018 solo song, "Listen 2 Me," Barry is missing several teeth and has taken on a garish appearance. "He let himself go," Randy says. "At that time, he was still performing, and I'm just like, 'Barry you nice but you can't be out there performing looking like that. You're gonna have to clean that up.' He started taking better care of himself and then falling off again and then just back to drinking and smoking. I would always talk to Stuart like, 'I'm just afraid one of these moments, I'm going to go downstairs and he's going to be dead. Because he's not taking care of himself. The drinking and smoking are taking over the priority of his life.'"

Barry eventually got his teeth repaired, but the constant partying continued. Barry found a job in housekeeping at another hotel, Extended Stay America. After that, he spent a couple of years working for a landscaping company before quitting to take a warehouse position at a plumbing firm. Barry worked there for four years but got fired for missing too many days of work. He is currently between jobs, back to living in Randy's basement, and receiving unemployment benefits.

"I've always told B, literally he is a million-dollar broke nigga," Randy tells me. "I say that respectfully. He's very blessed with so many talents that he just never capitalized on. Even drawing. He had the potential to be an architect at one time, he had the potential to be a basketball player. It's just like, 'Dog, you let so many opportunities to make it slide out of your reach.' It's unfortunate because he could be in a way better place than he is. Today, he don't know where he's going, he don't know how he's going to get there, and how he's going to make it."

Barry insists that he has a plan: stay focused and solidify his fundamentals. "I'm going to get me a fucking job. Get the regular basic shit I need. Get me a spot, car, job. That way I can concentrate on straight music and my damn self. And won't have any distractions. I've been seeing a lot of things starting to come together."

As for DVS Mindz, it remains a central part of Barry's identity, his legacy. "Our group disbanded how many years ago, motherfuckers still talk about us. Stuart still gets motherfuckers wanting to battle him. Apparently, we did something right where people are still wanting to reach that bar. Good. At least we set it high."

16

RESPECT

STU

In the summer of 2014, Stu and I sit for our first interview in five years. We talk in the basement of the townhome he rents. We're hiding down here to muffle the calamity of three young children running, shouting, and laughing upstairs. I tell Stu at the onset that I want to talk about his life beyond DVS Mindz. He obliges with a deeply personal interview that lasts four hours.

At the time of DVS's breakup, Stu's life was crumbling. He and his oldest daughter, Britnea, were living in an apartment off 140th street in Grandview, Missouri. Stu was working in the warehouse at Prier, a company that manufactures water faucets and hydrants. Britnea was a student at Grandview High School. Stu recalls, "I was thirty-one, thirty-two years old. And I looked back at this path of destruction. 'What the hell are you doing, Stuart?'"

Stu worked at Prier for three years, but on December 3, 2006, weeks before Christmas, he was fired on suspicions of stealing copper—accusations Stu denies. He and Britnea moved in with Stu's mother, Christine. Despondent, Stu spent seven months drinking heavily and collecting unemployment checks. "I don't know what the hell is wrong with me, but I kicked it something terrible. On unemployment. Drunk. Recording, making music, trying to push my music the best I could."

From 2002 until 2009, Stu avoided serious relationships, which he believes helped him mature. "I really kind of withdrew," he says. "It was therapeutic. It was good for me to spend some time with *me* and reflect on what had happened—where I'm at now and where I want to go. It was good for me to not be in a relationship for a long time. Being a single man, I went without sex for six months, a year, a year and a half. I just didn't. And I felt it was key. I didn't consciously set out to do this, it just happened like that."

Stu wanted more than sex; he wanted stability. Whether it was in the band or at home, the one thing Stu—an adoptee from a broken home—had always craved was a solid family. Stu had three daughters from three different women, which had led to years of complications and drama. "I never wanted it to be like that," he says. "I could have thirty kids. What I wanted was to have them by one woman. That's what I grew up seeing. Even though my parents were divorced, I still saw my dad with Clementine. He was the man of the house; she was the woman of the house. They both worked and worked together to take care of these kids. I had my uncle Earl and his wife, my uncle Joe in California. I had these examples. So that's what I wanted, but it turned into this."

In 2009, after years of avoiding romantic relationships, Stu met a woman named Nicole, who changed everything. They were introduced at a child's birthday party in Topeka by some relatives of De'Juan and Kevin. "Nicole was there. I saw her. All of them know her; I don't know her. So I'm asking questions. She's talking to people. I try to make little small conversation. I'm talking fast now, I'm going to talk my way up on her. And I talked her into a date. Come back and pick her up at seven.

We go over to Kevin's house. And somehow, we end up talking. Mind you, this is a house full of men, dudes running through the house. We end up talking until at least three-thirty or four in the morning. And we end up spending the night together. And she got pregnant."

After years of being on his own, Stu stepped into the relationship without hesitation. "I didn't take my time on any of this at all," he says, snapping his fingers. "Just jumped into it. My son's on the way. And we go through the process again. Gotta get some money together, gotta get a place. We get married on the twelfth of September, and he was born on October fifth. From there to that next year, my daughter's born, Keely. And a year or two years later, Nyko comes in 2012. And here I am, married for five years with three new ones. Got two boys and a beautiful girl. So I'm alright. I'm in a better space than I was."

FAMILY MAN

Stu's family arrangement is structured in a traditional manner. He works, and Nicole stays home, tending to the needs of their three children, all of whom are under the age of five. "She catches kids, she changes diapers. She gets three meals prepared, she vacuums, she does everything at home," Stu says. Stu is the breadwinner. For the last seven years, he has worked as a maintenance man for the townhome complex the family lives in. "I cut the grass, fix the gutters, paint the houses, repair the shingles," he explains. Stu loves his sixty-second walk to work. He typically eats lunch at home with Nicole and the kids, and Stu's mother, Christine, lives in the complex too.

Stu's oldest daughter, Britnea, now twenty-six, is currently living with the family along with her four-year-old son, Xavier.

Britnea earned a bachelor's degree in marketing and works for an advertising firm. Stu points out that he became a first-time grandfather and also fathered a child of his own at age thirty-nine. Stu's third daughter, eighteen-year-old Awtiawna, is also staying with Stu, Nicole, and the kids for the summer. This fall, she is off to college to study photography.

Stu maintains a good relationship with his biological mother, Janice, who gave Stu up for adoption when she was a teenager. Janice still lives in Wichita, and Stu sees her in person from time to time. He first contacted her at age eighteen and reunited with her when he was twenty. "I felt like I was home. I got to meet my sister. So that was an experience. It's like you're related. I have siblings, a brother and two sisters. And cousins and all kinds of people that I had never met before. It was a relief for me."

Stu has never met his biological father. He tried to get in touch with him, but his entreaties went unanswered. "I would be lying if I didn't say that there was some type of . . . a small void. Not knowing who your father is. I know his name. In forty-four years, I've never seen a picture of this guy. And it kind of bothers me a little bit. Honestly, I'd like to see a picture of him, just to see him."

Despite the damage left by not knowing his biological father, the adoptee from the broken home is now a family man with seven children and two grandchildren. But Stu says the biggest change in his life came in 2011 when he stopped drinking. Prior to that, Stu had been on an eighteen-year bender that began in 1993 when his father died. "At the end of the nineties, people would see me performing, laughing and joking, having fun. But I'm really hurting and crying inside. I missed my dad, and I didn't know what to do. It hadn't dawned on me that the last thing that he would want you to do is go into a damn tailspin and just drink yourself into a stupor. But that's what I did."

Stu drank heavily throughout these years, always beer. He might plow through one-and-a-half or two cases a night and then be at the liquor store first thing in the morning. By the time Stu reached his late thirties, he knew he had a problem and wanted to stop. But he couldn't do it. He would cut back or quit for a few days, but by the weekend, he'd be deep into the beer again. It went on like this for years, then one day, he decided he'd had enough.

Stu quit drinking on July 31st, 2011, his forty-first birthday. "I was like, I am tired of feeling like this. I have had it with waking up feeling like this. I'm tired of being so damn dependent on alcohol. I am no longer scared to know what life is like without alcohol. Because that was the fear. It got to a point where I didn't know how the hell I was gonna live without drinking. This doesn't even make sense. How am I gonna live without a drink? I was scared of that. What's that life like? I don't think I can do that. And I got down and prayed. I asked God to take it off of me, man. I said take this off me. I am done. I'm not buying any more beer."

Stu had three cans left in the refrigerator. He poured them all out. Stu's journey to sobriety had begun. "I woke up the next day without beer. It was hard, because after the third or fourth day, you start getting those urges. It starts kicking in really strong. I had to put my mind on something else. For two weeks, it was hard, kicking it. I don't see any other way to live now. I'm coming up on my third year."

Stu still has to be careful in situations where liquor is being served. "I'm a recovering alcoholic," he says. "Every once in a while, I come across a situation where everybody's casually drinking. And I'm like, 'Hey, I can do that.' And then I'm like, 'No you couldn't, Stuart. That one drink would turn into six, and tomorrow that six is going to turn into twenty-four. And you're going to be right back at it.' I get mad at myself. This is what they mean by alcohol abuse. You abuse it to the point where you can't have it at all."

Stu says that quitting drinking has given him insights into his troubled past and how it impacts his present-day behavior. He is not without regrets. "I'm noticing things that were sitting right in front of me. The relationships with my daughters. When you're an imperfect person or you're doing something imperfect, you tend to hurt the people that are closest to you first. I'm seeing that and recognizing a lot of decisions that I made and things that I did could have been done a hell of a lot better."

Clear and sober, Stu sees positive days ahead. "I feel like everything is available to me," he says. "The world's opened my eyes. It's like I can see. This is what the world looks like, wow. And I couldn't feel better."

RESPECT

Once Stu wasn't drinking his days and nights away, he suddenly had more time on his hands than he knew what to do with. He filled it with music. "I was scared that I would lose my potency in writing, but me being without alcohol only enhanced it," Stu says. "I got way better without the liquor. I went ballistic. I don't need liquor to write or create."

When DVS Mindz split in 2003, Stu lacked the home studio setup required to produce large volumes of music. Instead, he booked recording sessions here and there, usually at a friend's house. Stu might perform a feature for an artist's track in exchange for getting to record a solo number of his own, featuring that same artist.

In the decade that followed DVS Mindz's breakup, there was a sea change in the music industry. Technological developments in broadband internet and digital audio, along with the rise in music and video streaming services, helped decentralize the recording and distribution of music. Musicians no longer needed to collaborate in the same physical space or even in the same country. Trading files back and forth online became not only common practice but preferred.

Stu cobbled together the funds to build a small home studio, attaching a microphone to his desktop PC and converting a basement closet into a vocal booth. Instead of scrounging up time in local studios, Stu could record high-quality vocals at home for free. He began recording at a frenetic pace, amassing a large collection of solo tracks and collaborating with musicians from around the globe, including Japan, Australia, Turkey, Austria, England, Holland, and Canada.

In the mid-1990s, DVS Mindz developed their renowned live act at 1137 Washburn Avenue to compensate for their lack of recording equipment and in-house production. When I caught up with Stu in 2020, he had become a fully independent solo artist, able to write, record, and collaborate around the globe at all hours.

"I wouldn't have it any other way," he says. "I have people that actually pay me to feature on their songs. When they pay me, I can't go off of somebody else's schedule. I can't schedule studio time and then wait two or three or four or five days to get into the studio. I have to be ready to go. I have a set up at the house so that I can send it to you within twenty-four hours. And that's my normal turnaround for a feature."

In addition to features, Stu streams and monetizes his music via Spotify, Apple Music, Amazon, and YouTube, and he promotes his latest offerings on social media. Stu's foray into online recording and distribution was abetted by joining forces with Jason Scholla and Jesse Sandoval, two friends who started an independent hip-hop record label, EDP Records. The division of labor at EDP was such that Jason took care of video and web creation while Jesse handled the musical end of things. Together, the pair could produce an album, design its cover art, create publicity photos, shoot and edit music videos, and distribute and promote everything online.

Jesse, who produced music under the name E. Diggz, was trying to launch EDP by signing one or two key artists. He offered to pair with Stu on a collaboration with a Japanese DJ named Jaybizz. The resulting *Monster Mash Mixtape* was issued on EDP Records in 2012, with Jesse producing a number of tracks and Jason shooting a video. Around the same time, a second Str8jakkett project appeared, *The Survivalist*, an EP Stu recorded with a Miami-based DJ.

Stu's newfound productivity, combined with EDP's technical knowledge and distribution savvy, marked an era of intense creative output. Between 2013 and 2019, Stu issued an astonishing ten full-length solo albums: *G.A.M.E. The Grown Ass Man Experience, Popular Nobody: The Collaboration Files, Middle Finger Mentality, Str8Jakkett, The Black List, Blacklist Indigenous, Blackballed, International, Fire Starter,* and *S.T.U.* There were also one-time album-length collaborations under names such as Str8 Roc and Ground Zero, and dozens of one-off collaborations with producers and musicians. The song and album titles begin to blur together after a while, and Stu can't always remember which track appears on what CD or why a particular album was given its name.

"With EDP, I had a way to start doing this, and getting this stuff out, so there was no reason for me to stop," he says. "I'm an artist, I wrote this music, and I didn't write it to sit on a computer or on somebody's shelf. I want to release this. This is for the world to hear, this is for the people. So I don't believe in holding on to it. We're sitting on these songs. Let's get a name for it, let's get a cover, and let's release them."

Stu's urgency partly stems from the six years he spent waiting for DVS Mindz to issue their debut CD, but it also reflects changing expectations and consumption patterns within today's music-streaming landscape. Previously, marquee artists put out new albums in multiyear cycles that included singles released on a schedule, music videos, concert tours, and promotional efforts to "work" the record. At the cycle's end, the artist wrote material for a new album, and the process began anew. Today's audiences have short attention spans and expect a steady flow of fresh material. "You drop an album, six months later, they've moved on to the next thing," Stu says, snapping his fingers. "If you let too much time go past, you will literally be starting all over. To stay relevant and stay in the race, you have to constantly create. You got to drop something consistently, even if it's a single or a feature."

The pressure to produce new material is not bothersome. If anything, this structure is perfect for Stu, who still gets personal satisfaction from the creative process. Stu says that he does not view it as work. For him, composing, recording, and releasing songs provide an escape from the pressures of day-to-day life.

Stu has spent most of his adult life writing within the context of rap music. He describes his thirty-year trajectory as a writer as an evolution in terms of topics and techniques, all filtered through his own personal experiences and shifting worldview. "My writing started out was about a bunch of nothing, a bunch of egotistical raps: 'I'm MC this, and I slay MC that. Can't no rapper touch me.' There's only so many ways you can say it. Eventually you got to grow up and start talking about something. You need to start making songs and coming up with concepts. After mastering a certain flow, you have to master other flows and cadences. As you get older, you get married, you have kids, you end up having grandkids. Now, a whole 'nother world opens up [lyrically]. Your perspective changes. So I'll tap into fatherhood and grandfatherhood. I got too old to be rapping about nothing. I need to be saying something. I'm fifty, so I got to." Rather than running from his age, Stu utilizes it as a resource and call to arms. With age comes new artistic responsibilities and fresh creative possibilities. Age enables Stu to take decades of experience and use it to write lyrics that are more mature than the esteemed works that he penned with DVS Mindz.

Today's music ecosystem is characterized by increased competition, evolving consumer tastes, and shrinking structural resources, including the widespread closing of retail music stores, the collapse of physical CD sales, and streaming royalties that generate fractions of pennies.[1] Stu's inexhaustible productivity has not brought him wealth or fame, but he continues to create original music, and fans all over the world listen to it. Music streaming means that Stu's reach as a musician is greater today than it was during DVS Mindz's heyday. For example, Stu's 2018 song "Flowing Easy," where Stu rapped alongside Africa Baby Bam of the Jungle Brothers over an instrumental produced by Danish hip-hop act Dafuniks, has amassed nearly half a million streams on Spotify.

Stu recognizes that DVS Mindz never reached that many listeners, but he also notes that his online audience is anonymous, globally disseminated, and disconnected—a far cry from a sweaty DVS performance in a tightly packed nightclub. "DVS didn't have an album out, so we performed live and we were physically able to shake hands and meet people directly. The majority of the people that [stream] my music are not in this country. I know the streams are there. I know people are listening, but I've never met any of these people. They've never seen me perform. We've never locked eyes. We've never had any contact. It feels different than it did twenty years ago when there's a supporter right there."

Reaching a global audience, however, does not happen by itself. Successful independent musicians have to be both artists and entrepreneurs. In 2017, Stu and Jesse established EDP as an LLC in the state of Florida. Today, Stu is not only a musician but also a businessman and co-owner of his own record label. "I definitely look at the reports," Stu says. "Everything from ASCAP to streaming reports. I watch the numbers to see where what is doing what. I kind of gauge, okay, they like this, they like that. I try to stay consistent when releasing my solo projects, giving the people what they want."

At fifty years old, Stu has no illusions about making it, no fantasy that he will one day be a famous rapper or sell millions of albums. "I got over that, probably about 2007, 2008," he says flatly. "And really, I've done a lot more than the average guys who make music and then stop. So I make the music, and I perform the music, and I release the music because there's still a couple of people that like to hear it, and I like to make it. So I do it for that."

Stu learned from the mistakes he made with DVS Mindz and used that knowledge to create a solo career that avoided two pitfalls. First, Stu was no longer trying to support himself through music. DVS Mindz's hunger to make it was partly born of an unspoken promise to provide financially for the band, their families, Randy, and certain Crew members. Not having to worry about the dollars coming in took the pressure off and enabled Stu to enjoy the intrinsic rewards of the creative process. The second thing Stu did differently in his solo career was to retain artistic and financial control. He found platforms that enabled him to record and distribute his music by himself, on his schedule, under his label. There was not a lot of revenue, it was more than he ever made with DVS. Ultimately, Stu chose art over commerce and autonomy over servitude. He has no regrets.

I interviewed Stu in 2000, and he told me that an MC could never earn respect by commercializing their music and that respect was more important to him than making money. "If you don't get your respect, it seems like you're doing it for nothing," he said. Twenty years later, I ask Stu why respect has always been so significant to him.

There are unwritten rules in hip-hop that I came up under. I don't know what these kids are coming up under now. But when I wrote my first rhyme, I'm looking up to Rakim, I'm looking at Big Daddy Kane, KRS-One, I'm looking at Run-D.M.C., I'm looking at EPMD, N.W.A. You just didn't burst on the scene. You had to earn your respect. You had to earn your stripes, you had to earn your way by sounding like you and being an original. So respect was the first thing. Once you get that, then everything else falls into place. But if you're just out here to make a dollar, and put on some funny clothes and jump around and clown all day just to gain an audience to sell something, then that's not really earning your respect as an MC or as an artist in hip-hop. So respect is one thing that I've always pushed for. If I don't make a dollar, at least I got respect.

17

MODERN WARFARE

On February 28, 2018, sports talk show host Jim Rome opens his nationally syndicated television program with a surprise. "So here it is, nineteen years after these guys laid this down, huge shout out to my dudes: Str8jakkett, Killa the Hun, Casanova, and Keith the producer, for this amazing tribute that they laid down back in 1999. So now we're all about to hear this together for the first time, nineteen years later."

Jim Rome then plays "Jim Rome"—recorded nearly two decades earlier in Keith Loneker's 5150 studios—in its entirety. Tragically, Keith will never see his song on television. He passed from cancer on June 22, 2017, at age forty-six. As "Jim Rome" blasts across the planet, the song's namesake bobs along, smiling appreciatively at the inside references from the early days of his program. A large video screen behind Rome displays the cover of Stu's recent album, *The Blacklist*.

"These dudes are incredible," Rome enthuses as the track ends.

I cannot believe how many amazing references there are in that song. You have to listen to it over and over and over again. That is incredible to me. That is absolutely amazing. Fellas, I can't tell you how much that means to me. I can't tell you how much I appreciate that. Two decades later! If not for all the references, if you just listen to the beat and the hook, you'd think that thing dropped last week, and not two decades ago. Two decades later and it still holds up! That is incredible. I can't wait to listen to that again and see what I missed the first couple of times I heard it. It's extremely well done. I wish I'd known about that sooner. I wish I'd known about that when Keith was still with us. Come to find out that he played some football at KU. So I'm sure my man heard that one from up above. I mean, goosebumps! Pumps me up. I've got the Jim Rome hype track nineteen years later. Better late than never. I couldn't be more hyped that you guys finally released that and put that out. That is *so* good. If that's fire nineteen years out, can you imagine how fire that would have been if that had dropped when it dropped?

Stu and Barry are as surprised as anyone that Jim Rome found out about "Jim Rome" almost twenty years after it was recorded. "We didn't know what happened," Stu recalls of the original recording session with Loneker. "We went in and did the song, and that was it." Barry adds, "I knew we killed that shit, but after we recorded it, I don't remember ever hearing that song again."

Two decades later, a fan of Rome's found the track online and forwarded it to the radio host. Rome's on-air recognition meant the world to Stu, who immediately posted a clip of Rome playing the track to his various social media accounts.

"It was weird. It was surreal. I've never had anything like that happen before. He's got a million-subscriber fan base, and he loves the song. It's a wonderful thing. It's one of those stories that I can tell along my journey that happened, that's gone on in my career. It literally took nineteen, twenty years for that song to take off. But it's out there now."

Hearing the song for the first time in two decades, Barry is reminded of DVS's work ethic and high standards. "Getting it done and doing it right and killing it. Not just doing a song for the hell of it."

If there it a bittersweet element, it is that Keith is not here to celebrate. Keith had always been a huge DVS Mindz admirer. He had overseen production on "Jim Rome" as well as "Take it There," the vibrant lead single from Stu's debut solo album *Mood Swings*. Keith wanted badly to produce the second DVS Mindz album, but the group had always demurred, wary about being taken advantage of. It is a decision that Stu says he now regrets.

REUNION

The rediscovery of "Jim Rome" inspired Stu to avail *Million Dolla Broke Niggaz* to streaming sites for the first time, but there remained a treasure trove of unreleased DVS Mindz studio recordings. Stu issued new solo material constantly on EDP Records. Compiling and releasing some of the old DVS Mindz tracks would be a piece of cake. "I'm reading my reports and everything. The people that do listen to my music that pay us every thirty days are overseas. And they actually happen to love that nineties feel of music. So that's another reason that prompted me to release [the old DVS Mindz material]. There's an audience for this. Why is it sitting on your computer? Put it out."

Stu contacted everyone in the group, letting them know of his intentions to issue a compilation of unreleased DVS Mindz tracks. There was enthusiasm all around. Daymond even suggested that the band reunite for a new song to be included on the disc. Everyone immediately agreed.

As talks between the group continued, the notion of a DVS Mindz reunion EP or even album was floated. Daymond had been thinking about it for years. "I had this vision, and heard this music," he says. Daymond put his two decades of business training to use. During a group video meeting, he laid out his concept for a DVS Mindz reunion album like it was a corporation's strategic plan. "This is how we're going to do it, this is how we're going to execute it. Everybody's going to have action items. And once we complete those action items for stage one, we're going to move to stage two."

Excited, Daymond pressed ahead, telling the group, "I got the producer. I got all the beats. I got the concept. I got the marketing plan. All y'all got to do is write the lyrics. That's it. Just come in and just play a part. Let me quarterback this shit."

Stu and De'Juan were amenable to Daymond's businesslike approach, but Barry balked at being told what to do. To Barry, it seemed like Daymond was trying to take over the entire reunion project. "The rest of us have been solo artists doing our thing," he says. "That's different from what DVS Mindz shit is. Ain't nobody in this group the fucking quarterback."

There were also disagreements about the best artistic direction to take. It had been almost two decades since DVS Mindz had released an album. Rap music was different now. Should DVS return to their classic formula or try to fit the current musical landscape?

"We cannot come back sounding like we're continuing from where we were back in the early 2000s," Daymond told the group. "The game has changed. Don't nobody want to hear all that lyrical shit. We got to find a way to marry what's happening right now with what we do."

The group traded a series of beats back and forth online, but a consensus was hard to reach. Eventually, frustrated with the arguing, Daymond backed out of the project altogether. Everyone was disappointed. "We knew that having Daymond part of it would be the best look, just fanwise and for those listening," De'Juan says. "We talked on video chat with him, but in between those group meetings and trying to talk to him about his songs, somehow it just didn't come together."

Stu, Barry, and De'Juan pushed forward, determined to produce a work of greatness but disagreeing over what direction to take. Most of the quarrels were about music: which beat to use, what topic to write about. Stu and Barry had spent years working as solo artists with complete autonomy to follow their personal visions, no questions asked. Now there was never-ending discussion and stifling compromise. "It wasn't easy," Stu admits. "We hadn't been around each other in a group capacity for nineteen years. So there were a lot of growing pains for the first six months. We went through it. There were arguments and fights. Fighting like cats and dogs, until we finally got back in the groove in the swing of things."

The trio sent beats and lyrics to each other online, honing their new material and collaborating in ways that differed from the days at 1137, when everyone lived, wrote, and performed together. The objective was to write songs that had the classic DVS Mindz feel, updated for today's contemporary rap landscape. "It was trying to tap into what our real roots are and be relevant to today's rap scene without selling ourself out," Barry says. "How should we do this shit right without losing integrity? And knowing we're older dudes, we have to keep up with the times."

In July 2019, the trio reunited in Stu's basement studio to record five new tracks that would serve as the foundation for a DVS Mindz reunion album. Stu recalls, "The songs, we did them all together. We were literally all together in my basement, huddled up. We're running in and out of the booth and we're recording."

In fall 2019, the band convened in Denver to shoot music videos for two songs that would appear on a new DVS Mindz album to be titled *Modern Warfare*. "Madness 2.0" was shot in a warehouse with Barry appearing with a crooked crown atop his head. "Madness 2.0" fits well with the band's classic material. The song features no hook and serves as a showcase for De'Juan, Barry, and Stu's distinct rhyme styles and lyrical approaches. Behind them, EDP in-house producer E. Diggz paints a dramatic portrait, presenting the MCs like heavyweight prizefighters, entering the arena to swelling crescendos. Stu explains, "The buildup and the energy of it. This 'Madness,' it's a little different, now it's twenty years later. But it kind of has that same feel and that vibe to it."

A video for the song "Bryght Burn" was taped at Red Rocks, the iconic open-air amphitheater outside of Denver. In it, the band is decked out in matching letterman-style sweaters, rhyming as they roam around the picturesque venue. Stu recalls, "De'Juan was adamant on getting a fresh look, a new look for us, instead of doing the same old same, and shooting the video in Topeka or Kansas City. He wanted to get different scenery behind us, and that's what we did." For De'Juan, the impulse for freshness was all part of staging a legitimate comeback. "It feels like we have to re-prove ourselves," he says.

In November 2019, DVS Mindz issued their first new material in nearly twenty years. *Zip Codes* was a forty-five-minute mixtape consisting of previously recorded solo tracks from Stu, Barry, and De'Juan. The vocals from those tracks were mixed over various popular rap instrumentals by longtime DVS associate Troy "Def DJ" Owens. "We just didn't want to drop out of the sky with a new project," Stu explains of *Zip Codes*. "We kind of wanted to give the reunion a buildup, some kind of promotion, some kind of marketing plan to stir the water slowly and then bring it up to the release of the album. And that's where the mixtape came in. We dropped the mixtape to wake people up—to get people aware that they're back at it again, they're working."

DVS Mindz's return continued in February 2020, when EDP issued *The Genesis*, a fifteen-track compilation of unreleased classic material. There were S.G.-produced recordings from the three-headed dragon era ("Central Time Zone," "Check the Kids from Kansas," "Rowdy Hip Hoppers,") as well as classics such as "Headhunters" and the Daymond-produced remake of "No Coast." "Those were songs that we performed in public throughout the nineties. People knew about these songs," Stu says. "When the [first] album dropped, these songs were not on the album, which was kind of strange to a lot of DVS supporters. What happened to those songs? So it's a missing piece of our history."

Genesis concluded with "Just Us," recorded during the sessions for the unreleased sophomore album after Daymond had left the group. The song openly addresses the band's heyday, breakup, and brotherly love that has persisted over the years. Although "Just Us" was taped nearly two decades prior, it sounded like it could have been written that week.

By mid-February 2020, DVS Mindz's resurrection was well underway. After years of false starts, broken agreements, and plans falling through, the band was finally up and running again. DVS had already issued a mixtape and a compilation of classic tracks. Unlike the days when the group had to hand-deliver CDs to local music shops for consignment deals, their new material was now instantly available online. Moreover, there was a full-blown reunion album in the can and two music videos that were shot and edited. For once, everything was going the band's way, and it seemed that nothing could stop their momentum.

ROAD TO RECOVERY

The rumors began, as they now do, on social media. A whisper or two about a car accident, followed by an alarming headline: "Person Critically Injured in Hit and Run, Dragged in Auburn."[1] Further details arrived on February 16, 2020, at 2:53 a.m., and they were not good.

> Shawnee County Sheriff deputies are trying to piece together exactly what happened, after one person was hit by a car in Auburn. The victim was not breathing when emergency crews arrived on scene. They were then taken to a local hospital where they were upgraded to critical, but stable condition.
>
> They determined the person was hit by a car after an altercation. During the altercation, one subject was dragged by a vehicle, causing life-threatening injuries. The vehicle sped away and has not yet been located.[2]

"I saw it on social media first and I thought it was bullshit," Barry remembers. "Then his baby mom called me. And I knew shit was real."

Daymond heard about it from a friend on social media. "He was like, 'Yo, I don't know if you know but De'Juan was in a car wreck.' So I immediately called my brother [Kevin], because I know my brother and De'Juan, they close. He told me what happened."

I called Stu that morning, and he told me the news. It was devastating. De'Juan had been hit by a car and dragged. He was alive but in critical condition.

Barry was already on a Greyhound bus on the way from Denver to Topeka. "I thought he was dead," Barry says, tearing up at the memory. "I always looked at him as my younger brother.

We always been closer than everybody else. I didn't want to risk not being there for him."

At 9:05 p.m., a stunning news update arrived: "The Shawnee County Sheriff office says the man hit and dragged by a car in Auburn has died. They still have not released the man's name."[3]

Hours later, a sliver of hope in the form of a social media post. "I'm here with him now, been here all night."

Later, another headline: "Shawnee County Sheriff's Office Says Person Dragged by Car Not Dead."[4]

It was a roller coaster. I called Stu, hoping to clear up the confusion. De'Juan was alive, getting an MRI to assess the damage. He was in bad shape, but he was not the person who was dragged by a car. That was a separate accident, also in Auburn, involving a twenty-year-old man named Noah Thibodeau, who later died of his injuries. Because both incidents occurred on the same date around the same time, there was confusion in the media and even among friends and family members.

De'Juan does not remember what happened that night. Earlier that evening, he had attended a memorial gathering for Jerome Travis, better known as Rock, who coproduced some of DVS's most iconic tracks. It was a somber affair. There were food and liquor, but De'Juan did not partake. Afterward, feeling sad about the loss of Rock, he stopped by a local bar to see a group of friends who all worked together in the hair styling industry. De'Juan wasn't much of a drinker those days, but they talked him into having a shot. He wasn't drunk when he left the bar, driving alone in his Chevy Impala, just tired and a little sad. De'Juan believes that he fell asleep at the wheel. His car flipped and hit a pole on the side of the road. A good Samaritan phoned it in.

Tears stream down De'Juan's cheeks as he recalls, "I woke up in the hospital. I had three tubes coming out of my right side, draining the fluid out of my lungs. They kept telling me to leave the tubes alone. I was all morphined up and stuff. They didn't want to tell me what happened, originally. I'd try to put it together in my head, but I couldn't remember. I just laid there, trying to figure it out. It was a couple of weeks before I could really say what happened. I still can't talk about it without getting emotional."

Friends, relatives, and coworkers flocked to the hospital, arriving from every part of Topeka. De'Juan's employer, Southwest Publishing, had food delivered to those in the waiting room. Barry finally got to the hospital, having taken the bus all the way from Denver. "I remember when Barry walked in, I was falling asleep mid-sentence from the morphine," De'Juan recalls. "But it meant the world."

Barry couldn't believe how good De'Juan looked. "He just a little banged up. He didn't look as bad as what it was. Until they told me what it was. Then I was scared he'd never walk again."

De'Juan's injuries were severe. His spine was broken in four places. His entire right ribcage was shattered, and one of his lungs had collapsed. The doctors had doubts whether De'Juan would even be able to stand, let alone walk.

In addition to a major outpouring on social media, De'Juan had a constant stream of visitors and well-wishers at the hospital. "It was like half the city," he recalls. "They brought me a card with four-hundred dollars in it, people put money in. There was so many people worried about me. People praying for me, people that have their church praying for me, put my name in prayer boxes and things like that. I hadn't really recognized how much love that people got for you out there. That's the last thing I would have thought, but the numbers showed it. If this doesn't change you, what will? If this doesn't move your spirit, what will?"

In the hospital, De'Juan was heavily sedated on morphine but did his best to stay positive. This was especially important, De'Juan says, because he wanted to reassure his children that he would be okay. "The accident strengthened the relationship of me and my kids. That's one thing that I can be thankful for that's come out of this. There was so much time to sit still. 'Cause I was in the hospital, I couldn't go anywhere. They would just come sit there with me."

Barry was there too. "I went every day until I left," he remembers. "I actually did see him move around a little bit and talk, and I was like, 'He's good.' Shouldn't nobody survive that shit. That nigga is here for a reason."

Four days after the car accident, one of De'Juan's visitors posted a brief video of him upright and taking a few small, tentative steps. De'Juan smiles weakly at the camera. "I just wanted to put the word out there," De'Juan tells me, "Like, [people would think], 'Okay, he's on his road to recovery. He's doing good, he's decent.' But it was real grim."

De'Juan spent the next two months in the hospital, depressed and lying in bed, anesthetized on morphine. "All I could do is just daydream about what the rest of my life was going to be like. And it didn't look good. I spent a lot of time, woe is me, just being human."

De'Juan says he was motivated by his children, including the impending arrival of his fourth child, a boy, Christian Isaiah Knight, born October 28, 2020. The boy's mother told De'Juan, "You got to get up and get it together because you got to teach your son to walk. He's not going to teach you to walk." De'Juan pushed and worked to get back on his feet full time.

At the end of his months-long stay, De'Juan's hospital bill came to nearly $150,000. Although he had health insurance through his job, he still owed more than three thousand dollars out of pocket. He had also totaled his car, and the auto insurance company was giving him the runaround. "I've never broken a bone in my body. I've never had any surgeries. I'm not allergic to anything. I don't have asthma. Not once any problems at all. But this has got me up to my eyebrows in insurance and the hospitals and the healthcare system. I'm literally starting from zero, and it is baffling. I was definitely caught off guard."

De'Juan departed the hospital and was taken in by some distant relatives in south Topeka. Still recovering, he was told not to bend or twist his body. De'Juan was unable to shower or put on socks without assistance, experiences he found humiliating. His insurance only covered ten physical therapy sessions, which he quickly used. When we spoke in April 2020, De'Juan said, "Right now, I don't have any more physical therapy to help me on my road to recover. I have to get up and keep my physical therapy going myself." De'Juan was healing, but his stomach remained distended, and he had to secure his trunk with a large bandage to hold everything in place.

De'Juan's long recovery was complicated by the sudden arrival of the COVID-19 pandemic, which all but ground Topeka's healthcare system to a halt as hospitals scrambled to prepare. Protocols for medical checkups and physical therapy sessions were extremely rigid, but even everyday necessities like public transportation were tedious and difficult. Furthermore, De'Juan's collapsed lung rendered him a high-risk patient, and masks made breathing difficult. "Going in and out, realizing that even the people at the hospital don't have the right shit to wear. They don't have enough. These are big conglomerates, multibillion-dollar corporations, but they're just people in there. And these people, most of the time don't know what the fuck they're doing. They're just like the guy who used to work with you who didn't want to come to work."

MARTIAL LAW

"Lockdown, martial law, quarantine, kill 'em all." The song is called "Martial Law," and it is featured on DVS Mindz's first album of new material in twenty years, *Modern Warfare 2020*. "With the pandemic coming out, quarantines, and all of this stuff, we seen something crazy going on, so 'Martial Law' was the very last song that we put together," Stu explains. "We literally recorded that song and finished it a week before the album dropped." A teaser for *Modern Warfare* premiered on April 11, 2020, on YouTube, followed five days later by the release of the video for the first single, "Madness 2.0."

Modern Warfare features five group songs, a solo a cappella number from the three members, and intro and outro tracks to start and end the album. Clocking in at around thirty minutes, it is great to have DVS reunited again after all these years. "It's something I always wanted to do," Stu says, smiling. "These are my brothers, these are the guys I came up with. If I could turn the hands of time back, I probably wouldn't have so many solo projects. There would probably be more DVS projects. Going back, making music with these guys was one thing that I really enjoyed. It's always been fun."

The video for "Bryght Burn," shot at Red Rocks, debuted July 25, 2020, and it looks terrific. But the *Modern Warfare* project will always have a bittersweet aura because of Daymond's absence. "We *know* that having Daymond on these songs would be the best look, just fanwise and for those listening," De'Juan says. "Some people said that without Daymond, it's wack. And they're just speaking on principle, not even the song. And that's kind of what it feels like. Those that are close to us and know us just feel like it ain't enough because it's missing somebody."

CONCLUSION

5105 Virginia Avenue

DVS Mindz was overlooked when the band was in their prime. Today, as hip-hop is increasingly recognized as one of the most significant forms of culture to develop in the late twentieth century, the contributions of regional acts such as DVS Mindz have become clearer. As teenagers, these pioneers were beatboxing at lunch tables, learning how to mix and scratch vinyl records in living rooms, breakdancing at talent shows, and rhyming on schoolyard playgrounds. As young adults, alongside the Gucci Guys, Evil-Loc, producers such as Steve Garcia, and a handful of others, DVS Mindz helped build the foundation for rap music in eastern Kansas. DVS Mindz amassed a string of achievements that would make any musician proud and did so with an unwavering sense of integrity. Rap's current popularity in the region is due in part to these efforts. Tech N9ne put Kansas City on the national radar, but Topeka rap music simply does not exist without DVS Mindz.

The high-wire volatility that gave DVS their star power also fueled their eventual downfall. DVS was sometimes their own worst enemy, and internal strife hindered the group's ability to function smoothly. As public figures, DVS could be unpredictable and short tempered. The group was renowned for their live act, but they sometimes castigated concertgoers that failed to match their level of enthusiasm. DVS expended considerable energy waging one-sided wars against Shawn Edwards, the *Pitch*, and the Klammy Awards, but these conflicts gained little traction with the public.

I badly wanted DVS to make it, even though I knew their chances were slim. Like other members of the Crew, I did what I could to help. The Crew collectively shared DVS's dream of making it; there was a vicarious victory for us true believers. Most of the Crew did not rap and were not seeking residual fortune or fame. But every one of us had our own aspirations, and we saw part of ourselves in DVS Mindz's bid for success.

We all have goals that fail to materialize and dreams that do not come true. Our career ambitions are beset with challenges, setbacks, and the occasional outright disaster. Even our greatest triumphs may not turn out to be all that we envisioned. Some people fold but most of us pivot and find new paths, rationalizing our defeats and moving forward. DVS Mindz may not have made it, but the group members found meaning and purpose in other facets of their lives. In that regard, DVS's story is everyone's, yours and mine.

As I got to know the band over two decades, their life histories resonated with me for more personal reasons as well. I am about a year younger than Barry and Stu, a couple years older than Daymond. Like some members of DVS Mindz, I grew up in a household that was rife with poverty, paternal uncertainty, abandonment, substance abuse, and violence. We lived at 5105 Virginia Avenue, in Kansas City, a few blocks from where the 57th Street Rogue Dog Villians came to fore.

When I was a teenager, my single mother and I fought constantly. I found escape in music and books, holing up in my room to read and practice my guitar. When I was twelve,

I started taking lessons from renowned KC musician Ed Toler. At thirteen, I began working at the Music Exchange, a legendary Westport record store that had more than one million pieces of vinyl in stock. Around this time, my mother became involved in concert promotion and I spent my early teenage years hanging out backstage or front row at dozens of concerts that came through KC. I also started playing in punk and heavy metal bands around town.

At fifteen, I ran away from home, taking only my guitar. I fled to Lawrence, where I lived with my stepfather and his new family for a few months before moving on my own. My roommate, Kevin, was a talented drummer whose family situation was also turbulent. We became best friends, closer than brothers, and our musical connection was telepathic. Kevin and I recruited a singer and bassist and decided that we would move to Los Angeles to make it, plans that were nearly allayed after I was arrested for shoplifting.

At seventeen, I dropped out of high school and moved to L.A. with the band. We lived in a house and devoted ourselves to songwriting, rehearsing, and recording. We were certain we would achieve success if we worked hard and stuck with it. Like DVS, my bandmates and I were not just friends, we were a surrogate family.

My ambitions of making it in L.A. did not pan out, so after four years I returned to KC, where I was almost immediately arrested for marijuana possession. As a first-time adult offender, I was sentenced to community service and a year of probation. I rented a room at a friend's house and found a job in telemarketing. With few prospects, at the end of my probation, I got a GED and enrolled in a class at the nearby community college.

Like everyone in DVS Mindz, I found ways to stay involved in music, but like Daymond, I discarded any pretenses of making it and focused on my plan B. Daymond walked away from rap and dedicated himself to climbing the corporate ladder. I pursued education. In both cases, hard work yielded tangible results and our paths to advancement were less ambiguous than trying to achieve musical stardom.

My connection to DVS's story took on new layers of meaning over two decades of keeping up with the band, as my life changed alongside theirs. For example, becoming a first-time father in 2013 gave me a new appreciation for the challenges DVS encountered as they helped raise young children while working day jobs and trying to make it. The interviews that took place from 2014 to 2022 were more in-depth and personal than anything we discussed from 1999 to 2003. The group members were older and reflected on their pasts with accumulated wisdom. Similarly, I was a more skilled researcher and my life experiences gave me new insights and topics to explore. The deeper I delved into Stu, Barry, Daymond, and De'Juan's personal and professional experiences, the more I recognized myself.

I still see myself in DVS Mindz today. Most of those guys I lived and played music with back in L.A. remain close friends. Men are sometimes stereotyped as less "connected" to others, but those typecasts overlook the significance of male friendships over the life course. Furthermore, like Stu and Daymond, I found stability when I got married and created a family, a permanent place to call home. Like everyone in the band, I still struggle to balance my responsibilities to work and family with a desire to create.

I learned a lot about DVS Mindz over twenty-two years, but I also learned from them. Around the same time I began my writing career, I met four passionate wordsmiths who spent innumerable hours making sure every syllable was exactly right. My interactions with the band from 1999 to 2003 influenced what followed. In Chicago, I chose rap musicians as the focus of my dissertation. Upon graduation, I pursued work that placed creative autonomy above money.

Therefore, this book represents not only what I learned about DVS Mindz but what they taught me. I did not spend twenty-two years studying an obscure band because it was lucrative, I did it because DVS Mindz taught me that the craft is more important than catchy hooks, that it's okay to go an extra sixteen bars if you're speaking from the heart. In that sense, this book is my version of a DVS Mindz song, with verses that sometimes go on a little longer than they're supposed to and with slim chances of topping the charts. I'm okay with that. As I learned from DVS Mindz, in the end, you might not make a dollar, but at least you get respect.

ACKNOWLEDGMENTS

Daymond Douglas: I would like to thank God, firstly, for giving me the talent that has made people laugh, cry, be amazed, and feel appreciated. Carlos Steele, for always believing in me when I didn't. Stuart "Str8Jakkett," for pushing me and always telling me I'm too good to quit. DJ Kutt, for always giving me the knowledge I needed to continue being great. Greg "G Mill" Miller, for being my #1 supporter and believing in me. My Top 5 for molding me: Big Daddy Kane, Ice Cube, Jay-Z, Royce da 5'9," and Treach! To my wife, who showed me a different side. My brother Kevin "Wolf," for always keeping it real with me. Reggie B, for bringing out the artist in me. DVS Mindz, for letting me display my talents to the world. Devin Teezy, for being my muse and keeping me young. Scorpeez, for supporting me. My lil bro MAXBET and all my siblings and my legacy. I dedicate this one to my mama, for always supporting me and letting me shine at a young age, for exposing me to music, and showing me how it touched people's lives. I love you, and rest well, beautiful.

De'Juan Knight: My thank yous are for God and my children. So many people I'm grateful for, I wouldn't dare name some and not name others. Thank you dearly from all I am, for your presence in my life. You know who you are. And to Geoff Harkness for still rocking with us. I'm thankful for life itself. Be well.

Barry Rice: To God, my family, and everyone that stayed down and never switched up on us from day one! I love you all.

Stu Tidwell: I would like to say thank you and much appreciation to William Roberson, Winfred Tidwell, Janice Hardgraves, Christine Floyd, 4U2NV, T-Tip Rockers, Evil-Loc/E-City, Carla Daniels, Randy Smith, Kim Divers, Jason Sandoval, Jesse Sandoval, Earl Fowler Jr/Sr, Joe Fowler, Benjamin Clarke, Robert Hesse, Daymond Douglas, John Rice, De'Juan Knight, Lashon Holt, Andre Rooney, Calvin Phillips, Early Ray, Brian Green, Ernie Hobbs, Tracy Ross, Carlos Steele, Vandon Rias, Troy Owens, Casey Burnett, Robert Brown, John Lee, Steve Garcia, Jeremy McConnell, Bill Pile, J. J. Hensley, James Wheeler, B Nasty, Kevin Douglas, Marlow Tombs, Elena Ramirez, Bryant Smith, Kevin Jones, Keith Loneker, Will the Weirdo, Tom Woosley, Eric Summers, Mark Luna, Grant Rice, Panic, Nicole Tidwell, Devonna Wilson, Betina Steele, Kelly Kearney, Dalon Hardgraves, Latoya Hardgraves, Bridgette Redman, Dewi Smith, Winston Tidwell, Kari Tidwell, Aundrea Roderson, Paul Roberson, Tamara Jennings, Rohnda Henderson, Derek Bell, Domenick Logan, Xavier Sydney, Tyrone Bundy, Maleek Hughes, Jackie Perez, Samson Cooper, Nathaniel Hall, DJ 2nen, Jaybizz, M.O.D., Joseph Johnson, Britnea, Tahnae, Awtiawna, Tyla, Stuart Jr., Keely, Nyko, Charles Maxwell, AKO Mack, I.C.U., Flavor Pak, Willie Watkins, Brian Williams, Tommy James, Henry Meyers, and Terry Sierra. Without you, I wouldn't be who I am today. You are appreciated.

Geoff Harkness: To Barry, Daymond, De'Juan, Stu, and their many DJs and producers, thank you for the music. It plays in my "mental jukebox" in regular rotation, alongside the greats, as it should.

Thank you to Eric Schwartz at Columbia, who believed in this project 100 percent and encouraged me to write exactly the book I've spent more than two decades wanting to write. Gary Fine, Kwame Harrison, Matthew Oware, and Eliott Reeder offered crucial feedback on my initial book proposal. Three anonymous respondents and my friend Greg Douros read every word of the original manuscript and offered insightful critiques.

I lived, worked, and went to school in Lawrence from 1997 to 2003. The following entities and individuals made my time there better: Teresa Albright, Berry Anderson, Jan Biles, Chris Choun, Andy Gassaway, C. J. Janovy, KB Posse, KJHK, Keith Loneker, Emily Lubliner, Mac Lethal, Andrew Miller, Kepler Miner, Edwin Morales, Joel Morton, and Salt the Earth.

I am grateful for my colleagues at Rhode Island College: Mikaila Mariel Lemonik Arthur, Tanni Chaudhuri, Desirée Ciambrone, Roger Clark, Jill Harrison, Pam Jackson, Darek Niklas, and Carse Ramos. Thanks also to colleagues elsewhere: Bob Antonio, Pat Bass, Michaela DeSoucey, Wendy Griswold, Charis Kubrin, Leslie Killgore, Tim Pippert, and David Smith.

Special thanks to the Amor, Harkness, Maxfield, and Taylor families, and to my friends Kathryn Kollet, Doug Lerner, Paul Marinescu, Jon Niccum, Ken Perreault, Eliott Reeder, Jeff Roos, and Spencer Wright.

I am proud and grateful to be the father of the two best children any dad could ask for. Emma and Ben, you bring joy and wonder to the world, and I love you so much. And to Laura, without whom none of it would be possible. I love you, now and forever.

WHERE ARE THEY NOW?

Tech N9ne went on to become one of the most successful independent musicians of all time. He has released more than twenty albums on his Strange Music label, collaborating with A-listers such as Eminem, Ice Cube, and Kendrick Lamar. Tech's music has appeared in movies, television shows, commercials, and video games. He remains based in Kansas City and continues to tour, both nationally and internationally.

The **57th Street Rogue Dog Villians'** trajectory to fame was curtailed in 2001 by the arrest and conviction of member Short Nitty (Tyrone Kendall), who was sentenced to life in prison for raping a child. The RDVs continued to record and make music but disbanded in the mid-2000s. RDVs member Big Scoob signed a solo deal with Tech N9ne's Strange Music label. Although the group never broke through nationally, the RDVs significantly advanced Kansas City's regional rap scene. "We pioneered a market for this area when there wasn't no market for that shit," Bakarii, one of the RDVs, told me in 2002. "There wasn't nobody buying local [rap]. They didn't feel that they wanted to listen to it until Tech N9ne and the Rogue Dogs started puttin' that shit down."[1]

Shawn Edwards lives in Kansas City, where he remains a fixture in the local media, appearing as film critic on Fox 4 News. Edwards has spent his career championing African-American film. He is co-founder of the African-American Film Critics Association and is working to create a Black Movie Hall of Fame. Edwards did not respond to interview requests for this book.

Troy "Def DJ" Owens DJ'd for DVS when the band was working around the clock at 1137 Washburn Avenue. He quit the group after becoming a father to two girls in the mid-1990s. "I initially was trying to help them, and then life happened," Troy explains. "I decided I needed to be an adult. So I went and got a job and started raising my kids. And I told them that I couldn't really do music anymore, like we were."

Troy landed an entry-level position in the factory at Hill's Pet Nutrition, best known for the Science Diet dog food brand. He started out as an assistant on the line, loading the machines and throwing meat. "It was a good job with benefits, insurance for kids, 401K, things like that," he says. Twenty-eight years later, Troy is still at Hill's, working as a technician in the Research and Development Center. "I'm still there. I'm happy; I'm not going anywhere."

Troy does not think the members of DVS Mindz should have taken solid jobs and walked away from music the way he did. "Honestly, I think they did right by themselves as far as being a group and performing. Because they all loved it. They had a passion for it."

Troy says that DVS Mindz, along with Gucci Guys (who later became 4U2NV) helped build the foundation for hip-hop culture in Kansas. "They're the beginning of a strong hip-hop scene in Topeka. A lot of people that are really into hip-hop, they know who they are. As far as people that are up-and-coming and making groups, they know who DVS is."

Troy, 55, continues to make music for fun, including hosting DVS Mindz's *Zip Codes* in 2019 and a solo mixtape from Stu, *VeStuvious*, in 2022.

Carla Daniels, the working single mother of two who was DVS Mindz's first manager, focused on finishing her degree after parting ways with the band. "Look, I was just glad to be in school because I was a third-generation welfare recipient. When I started school, I was on welfare, and I fought to get what I got. After I graduated, I went on with my career. I left Topeka and didn't really hear too much after that."

Carla applied to graduate programs, eventually moving to Carbondale, Illinois, where she earned a master's degree in instructional multimedia at Southern Illinois University. Carla married, had a son, and later divorced. Now 57, Carla lives in Columbus, Ohio, where she works as an administrator for a nonprofit that services the developmentally disabled.

Carla says that she does not think DVS Mindz should have pursued a college degree the way she did. "You got to get out the way you can get out," she tells me. "Going to school is not everybody's out. Because we knew some folks that went to school, and they are in a worse situation than they were in before they went to school. And we know some folks who didn't go to school, and they make crazy money."

Carla says that poor Blacks are urged to take on large amounts of debt to fund college degrees, while vocational skills such as welding and HVAC are disparaged as low-status. "You can learn some skills if traditional, formalized education is not for you. That wasn't pushed to us. It was, 'Go to school, go to school.' And the kids that got pushed to those kinds of skills was the ones they thought were losers, drop outs, or they had some kind of criminal record. I know some people that got [vocational] degrees and I'm envious. Some of them are doing better than those of us who are out here praying for student loan forgiveness."

Carla says that the band's legacy is cemented by the fact that they were there, in the beginning, helping to pioneer hip-hop culture in Eastern Kansas. "Just the history," she replies when I ask her what people should remember about DVS Mindz. "This was going on at a time when what we see and hear now was just forming. It was really just getting started. It was just coming about, and they were in it in their area."

Carla says that most of the popular local musicians from back then stopped making music. But not Stu. "Stuart is going to be rapping until he dies," she laughs. "And when it happens, the funny thing is they'll be like, 'He just got started.' And then they're going to pull out this long list of all the things that they have done and all the albums and the accomplishments and stuff like that. And it's going to be like, 'No we didn't just get started. We've been here for a while.'"

Randy Smith, who met Barry in high school and served as the band's third and final manager, still lives in suburban Denver and works for the Veterans Affairs Office. Randy also continues to be involved in concert promotion, putting together R&B nostalgia packages featuring acts such as Jodeci and El Debarge. "I'm still the man behind the scenes," he says.

According to Randy, the financial issues that contributed to his departure from the group were rooted in the band's lack of business acumen. DVS Mindz wanted to be artists—to write songs, record tracks, get their pictures taken, sign autographs, and perform. Management could handle the business side of things. This lack of oversight caused numerous problems, which then resulted in arguments and finger-pointing.

Everyone was expected to make financial contributions to DVS Mindz, but that was not possible for some band members. "These guys just didn't have any money," Randy recalls. "Some of these cats weren't even *eating*. 'Let's go out to eat, let's get you guys fed so y'all can move how you need to.' Killa was having seizures and passing out. We can't have that. 'You're drinking, you got to chill out. Let's get some food in you. Let's look into why you're having these seizures.'"

Randy says that he got tired of being blamed for the band's financial problems and quit, relocating to Denver and starting over. "It was just animosity, and you got cats in other people's ear. 'Randy's this, Randy's that.' It was just too much division for me. 'I'm done, you guys can have it.' I moved on to bigger and better things."

Randy went from being a high school graduate who worked in a slaughterhouse to a successful office worker with a good job, benefits, and a nice house in the suburbs. I ask Randy if the guys in DVS should have followed his route to success instead of trying to make it in music. "I always encouraged the guys—hit your goal from many angles. Don't try to just make it off rap. You got to pursue it from this angle, from that angle, and you can make it work. It may not have worked out how we like it to, but still, there's opportunities. Hell, the guy who wrote the cha-cha song didn't have a career, but he's making a lot of money off of just that one hit.[2] I joke with them and tell them, 'Y'all ought to come out with a catchy hook song, like a cha-cha song, and you guys will have something to really fall back on.'"

Moving to a new state did not end Randy's connection with the band. He doesn't hear from Daymond much, but he talks to Stu regularly, and Barry and De'Juan have lived with him on and off over the years. Despite whatever differences have come their way, the friendship endures.

I ask Randy what the high point of the entire DVS Mindz experience was for him. "It may sound crazy but just the togetherness that we shared at the time. Of any moment, whether it was doing a show with Wu-Tang, we had so many moments where we were all on the same level. Just a feeling of togetherness, of brotherhood. That was my highlight. Man, we had a *great* time."

De'Juan

De'Juan spent the spring of 2020 recovering from his car accident, navigating the complexities of the medical system at the height of the COVID pandemic. He moved into his cousin Kevin's apartment temporarily. "I was trying to get back into the workforce, trying to figure out life after death. Getting out of the hospital, then going back to work and COVID still being so big. I let work go because I'm high risk, with a collapsed lung." De'Juan takes a long drag from a cigarette. "Fucking cigarette," he says.

Despite his frail medical condition, De'Juan participated in some of the Black Lives Matter rallies that swept the nation in the summer of 2020. "I had to be there in person," he says. "Downtown, people were gathering with protesters. I went and saw some speakers at the Capitol." De'Juan says that the police's negative treatment of Blacks caused him to join the summer protests. "That's why I show up," he explains.

Around this time, De'Juan stopped by an old friend's studio to record vocals for a new solo track. The friend, an artist who rapped under the name Scrybetruth Eternal, was putting together a song that addressed police brutality and racism in the criminal justice system. De'Juan liked what he heard, and the pair began collaborating on a number they would call "How

Amerikann." Scrybe had already written some lyrics; De'Juan penned his own verse on the spot. "That song, the whole idea behind it, just wrote itself instantly," De'Juan recalls. "It happened quick; it was one of them joints."

The following weekend, De'Juan returned to record his verse, with Scrybe adding audio clips from a speech at one of the protests De'Juan had attended. The pair also shot footage for a music video at the Brown v Board of Education National Historic Site, located near Monroe Elementary, one of four Topeka schools that were designated for Black children only during segregation. Scrybe added clips of civil rights marches, BLM protests, and police shootings. "It gives that song a certain light," De'Juan says. "There's a certain intelligence to it. It's not a knucklehead version of any part of the movement."

As COVID and the summer protests dominated the headlines, De'Juan looked for work, finding that his criminal record made it difficult to land a job, even as a manual laborer. He also needed to secure a new apartment and had little money for a deposit. There was another option: Colorado. De'Juan had flown to Denver to shoot the videos for *Modern Warfare* and was impressed with everything he saw. In Topeka, De'Juan had relied on friends or low-budget producers to record vocal tracks for the *Modern Warfare* project. In Denver, he could record at EDP's state-of-the-art studio. "I don't have anything like that in Topeka, I don't have the money. I don't have that caliber of anything. I can't reach that level with shit." Moreover, Barry and Randy were in Colorado, and Randy offered De'Juan a place to stay until he got established.

De'Juan pulled Randy aside. "Man, I don't have no money saved up. I ain't got no problem going to work. If I come out this way, am I cool for a minute?"

"Just get here," Randy nodded.

"I could just go to Randy's house, and chill for a minute," De'Juan says. "I could literally move into somebody's house and start looking for work—just get that fresh start." De'Juan was collecting unemployment checks in Topeka at the time and believed he should make the move while he still had a few dollars in his pocket. In December 2020, he relocated from Topeka to Denver.

A year after the car accident that nearly paralyzed him, De'Juan is walking without issue. His spine had been broken in four places but healed as intended. At his eight-month checkup, De'Juan told the doctor he was not experiencing any pain or mobility issues at all. "You're healed," the doctor replied. "You can walk around and do stuff. We'll do a year checkup to see if any of the hardware has moved."

De'Juan asked the doctor to repeat himself. He wanted to hear that word again, *healed*.

When De'Juan arrived in Denver, he took a job unloading trucks in a warehouse. The boxes were not supposed to exceed forty pounds, but De'Juan estimated they were closer to seventy. "They get heavy after six or seven hours," he recalls. "I was tired but I didn't hurt. So I went back the next day. And I went back the day after that, just to feel my limitations."

The car accident had broken every rib on De'Juan's right side. A year later, it is still giving him trouble. "My side is a constant thing," he says. "It's a discomfort, it's irritating, but it's not pain. If you touch the top two ribs, it kind of feels weird. I had to wear the back brace at first. It was wrapped around me when I wasn't laying down. You can still feel where I was wearing my brace because the ribs healed out of line. You can physically feel it."

Fortunately, De'Juan found work as a flagger on a construction crew, a job that required no heavy lifting. "I do the traffic control shit. I just stand out with the construction crews and stop and release traffic when the trucks come in and out. There's minimum wear and tear on the body," he says, gesturing up and down to his torso.

I ask De'Juan where he sees himself in five years. "I'm trying to get situated, settle down," he replies. "I just want to have my own shit and be comfortable, man. With the amount of money it takes, I can't afford my own shit. That's just how it is. That's that one-person income thing. It's built for a two-person income. So I'm investing, I'm looking around. I'm forty-three. Even in five years, I still won't be fifty yet. I'll still be recording. I don't know if we'll be releasing music. But if I can put out a single every now and then and play my character, I don't mind it. I still enjoy it a little bit."

Daymond

Daymond continues to live in the Dallas/Fort Worth area and work for Samsung. In 2019, he became a grandfather for the first time when Daymond Jr. had a child. "Just to be a grandfather is a whole different perspective," he says. "You get another chance. I missed a lot of time with my son, just doing shows and chasing rap and doing the shit that I was doing. There's a lot of shit that I want to do, but when we have him, nah. All that shit goes away."

The COVID pandemic did not disrupt Daymond's day-to-day existence very much. His house was full of life. Desirae's sixteen-year-old son spent his junior year of high school doing remote learning. Daymond's second-oldest son, Brandon, also moved back in, along with his wife and new baby, Daymond and Desirae's second grandson.

Daymond and Desirae were directed to work from home, beginning in March 2020. Fifteen months later, Daymond was perfectly content to remain ensconced with Desirae in their comfortable suburban abode. "I met my wife at work," he says. "There was a time that we worked on the same team together. So it's normal for me and my wife. I like being around my wife. I'm saving money on gas. I'm not putting as many miles on my car. Creatively, it's opened some doors."

Daymond has continued to write over the years, reciting new rhymes into his phone's voice recorder. But recently, he's been recording in his home studio, slowly amassing tracks such as "Misunderstood" that discuss what Daymond believes are serious issues. "My work ethic is a lot different now," he says. "Back when I was really doing it, I was relentless about it. Now I find myself not as relentless about my music as I used to be. And right now, to be honest with you, I'm trying to figure out why. Part of me feels like I have something to prove to myself. Daymond, can you still rap? Can you still put together a song? Can you still put together something and people like it?"

Daymond says that a hurdle he struggled to overcome was his age. Hip-hop is a youth-centric culture, and the popular music industry focuses primarily on teenagers and young adults. "Am I too old?" Daymond asks rhetorically. "I fought that demon for so long. I had to get past that. Ain't nobody in the history of rap ever said, 'That shit's dope! How old is he? Fifty? I ain't listen to that shit.'"

Daymond says the biggest impediment to his making music these days is being so far removed from the people and lifestyle that informed DVS Mindz's lyrics. When he departed DVS, his interactions with the Crew evaporated too. "I don't have my DVS brothers with me, I don't have my fan base with me, I don't have my muse with me, I don't have all that shit I had before," Daymond says. "I had [Crew member] Scorpeez as a muse. I had Stu that I could bounce shit off of. I was going to shows where I could just soak up the culture and just get ideas. It's different when you ain't got none of that shit and you live where you live. I don't see poverty; I don't see a lot of the shit that I want to talk about. It's a little different when you on the grind and you only got a few dollars in your pocket and you get in a beat-up Oldsmobile. That grind is different from walking out of a $400,000 house and getting into a BMW in this beautiful-ass neighborhood. My perspective is a little different."

So Daymond keeps recording, honing, refining, and perfecting tracks for two planned releases, a mixtape and a full-length album. His inner Stu urges him to release it all today: "You keep making all this music, but you ain't putting it out. You got to release this shit to the world. Put this shit out. Stop holding on to it. You're overthinking it. Just do it."

Daymond could not hold back when he saw the video of George Floyd's murder on May 25, 2020. "I see the video of the incident, and I just started crying. I'm like, this is fucked up. I got to say something. If I'm calling myself an artist, it's my responsibility to say something." In a single day, Daymond wrote and recorded a new song, "Never Loved Us," created an accompanying video, and posted it online. In the song, Daymond describes his anger and frustration over the continual killing of Black males by police officers, from those slain during in the Watts rebellion of 1965 to Floyd's murder in 2020.

Daymond says that he was moved to release the song, in part, because of the extended history of police brutality in the United States. "This isn't new. This happened in the early nineties with Rodney King. All those cops were beating his ass on video, and they still got acquitted. Why? How? Now we're being killed on camera. It's really a symptom of something way bigger that's going on. It shed a light on racism and how fucked up our justice system is."

Daymond is a successful member of the upper-middle class. He lives in an expensive house, earns a six-figure salary, and drives a BMW. Yet, he feels as if any encounter with the police can result in his demise. Daymond sees white criminals taken into custody while Blacks who do nothing are killed by the police. "He should have complied? We're *scared*. Y'all don't understand what it's like to be a Black man driving around and the police getting behind you, or the police getting beside you, or they actually pull you over. '*Fuck*. This is the day that I'm going to die.' You could be swimming and get a cramp, and you're going to drown, and you think to yourself, 'This is the day that I'm going to die.' Just imagine you have that feeling every day you get in your car. And you haven't did nothing but be Black. That's *huge*. That's traumatic. That can fuck up somebody's psyche."

Despite Daymond's strong sense of injustice, he did not participate in the protests that made headlines in the summer of 2020. "I'm not marching. Because the change is not going to be me sitting down here in this march holding up a sign. We got to start holding people accountable, not only the people that actually did it but all the people that is sweeping that shit under the rug."

Daymond said that he had two bad choices at the voting booth in 2020. In the end, he voted Republican. "I voted for Trump. I don't care who knows. Joe Biden put so many Black people in jail, I lost count. He signed the bill with Bill Clinton that put a whole bunch of Black men that ain't done shit in jail. And now it's years later, and everybody's changed, but we want to make his ass the *president*? Get the fuck out of here. I ain't trying to hear that shit. Y'all can stay asleep if you want to."

Five years from now, Daymond sees himself still working for Samsung. He intends to go back to college to earn a degree in business, specializing in project management. "I don't see really that much different than what I'm doing now. There's some things that I want to accomplish. One is an actual degree. I know that there's a ceiling. I can only climb up this ladder so far before they'll be like, you have to have a degree to do this job. That's why I'm going back to school. I just got to take it one day at a time. Set some small goals, identify and acknowledge those goals, and try to take it to the next step. So probably moving up a little bit further at Samsung and really embodying that and making sure that I stay successful. The number one thing that made me successful in my life is my job."

As for DVS Mindz, Daymond bears no ill will. "I don't want to be in an accident or on my deathbed and my home-boys are still mad at each other. I'm not going to hold no grudges. You never know when you going to see this person again. Do you want this dude to be six feet and you weren't able to say, 'Bro, I was tripping, I'm sorry?' Life is too short for that type of shit."

Barry

Barry spent most of 2020 laying low, living at Randy's and filling orders and loading trucks in the warehouse of a heating and plumbing supply company. "It got to the point where it was just us in the warehouse there," he recalls. "Nobody from the front office would come in. I was going to work from two until midnight or three, four in the morning. That's what I did five days a week. I really didn't go nowhere. I wasn't out much. Just work, home, that's all there was."

When he wasn't working, Barry spent his free time honing a batch of new songs. "I'd be at home chilling: smoking and drinking, listening to music, writing shit. I didn't have no pressure on when to put them out or anything. It gave me the freedom to experiment on a lot of shit and listen to another lot of other music."

Barry's Denver location has enabled him to remain creatively active. EDP is partly headquartered there, and so are Bobby Tek and his many musical affiliates. Between these two resources, Barry has continued to write and record songs on a regular basis. In 2020, he featured on three tracks on rapper Sleepy Hollow's album *Tied 2 the Streets*. Barry also appeared on a song and music video called "Late Nights," by an artist named Sleep. And he triumphed on "I'm It," a 2020 collaboration with rapper ATF Mischief. Barry continues to perform live, and after De'Juan moved to Denver in December 2020, the two did several shows together.

In 2020, EDP re-released Killa The Hun's solo debut under the title *Amerikilla Re-Kill*, availing it to streaming outlets. In spring 2021, he issued videos for two songs—"Who," and "N.i.k.e.," both of which were produced by EDP. "I don't do shit just because it's popular," Barry says. "I don't make music to please people. My music ain't for everybody. But for the motherfuckers who it's for, they love that shit. And I love that they love it."

In today's segmented media landscape, niche is the new mainstream. Artists like Barry have an outlet for their wares, which are consumed by small groups of listeners with highly specific preferences. "My fan base, my audience, they know what to expect from me," Barry says. "Core fans, whether it's five or fifty, that's how they want me to get down."

Barry does not look back on DVS as a failure. "Me, myself, I feel like we succeeded and we made it. On our own terms. I still do fire-ass fucking music, so that shit doesn't matter to me. If we had made it, I would be financially secure to take care of all of my people. That's cliché also. I don't need that shit or the bullshit that comes with it."

When Barry looks back, he thinks more about family than the music he made with DVS Mindz. Barry's second child, Marcus, is now nineteen years old, and his third son, Devon, is sixteen. Barry has still never heard from Jeffrey, his oldest son who he has not seen for more than twenty years. Losing Jeffrey is Barry's biggest disappointment. "That's one thing that really fucked me up when I was younger," he says. "I think about what my life would have been if I was married and all that shit. Would I have the other two great sons I got? It's kind of a blessing in disguise, I guess, but I really wish I could have all three of them. I really do. I'm thinking, 'Okay, if I track him down, what if that fucks *him* up? 'Cause I *know* it's rough on me, so it's got to be killing him. Maybe I should just leave well enough alone.'"

Barry insists, however, that he has no regrets. "I wouldn't be the dude I am if things wouldn't have worked out the way they did. If I could do things over again, I'd do them smarter. But do I regret anything that's happened to me in my life? No, because it's made me the person that I am."

It is May 2021 and Barry's journey is now taking him elsewhere. He has packed up all of his belongings and is relocating to Saginaw, Texas, a suburb of Fort Worth. The move was inspired by Barry's reunion with a longtime girlfriend.

"You know what, I'm getting the fuck out of here," he says, looking around Randy's garage. Barry's long-term plans include culinary school, but more immediately, he will seek work at the airport. "They are hiring out there," he says. "Fuck yeah. I'll drive forty minutes for working for the airline. That ain't nothing. I'm not scared to work. Work is my hobby. Rapping is my job."

Stu

In February 2020, Stu launched his own lawn care company, purchasing tools and equipment and soliciting nearby neighbors for spring work. A month later, the COVID pandemic hit, and the entire enterprise went belly up before it could get off the ground. "Everything closed down," Stu recalls. "It messed up my whole business and what I was trying to accomplish for myself. As time has gone on and things have opened up and masks and we have the social distancing, I've been able to procure some clients that I'm cutting grass for. By the grace of god, we've been able to pay the bills, keep a roof, and keep food in the refrigerator."

When I interviewed Stu in 2014, he had never met his biological father. "I always felt abandoned," he tells me in 2022. "I always felt like, 'What the fuck is wrong with me? I had an older sister that was kept. What was wrong with me, that I couldn't be kept? I need answers.' I found my mom in 1990, but I had been searching for my dad since then. In 2014, I told myself, 'Look, maybe he don't want to know who I am, but I forgive him.' Literally, when I said I forgave him, a month and a half later, I get hit with, 'Your dad is on the line.' I had carried a lot of shit for a long time. But when I let that hate go, that's when he found me."

Stu's biological father, William Roberson, tracked Stu through Facebook and reached out by phone. The decades-long mystery was solved. Stu and his father talked that day and it wasn't long before the two were reunited in person. "That meeting with him answered a whole lot of shit," Stu recalls. "My temperament. The way that I move and I think. I've never even been around the man and we move the same. This nigga is me." Stu and his dad have remained close ever since.

When I interviewed Stu in 2014, he called himself a recovering alcoholic and had been sober for three years. I ask Stu how that's going today. "I'm an alcoholic and I drink," he says. "I'm not going to sugarcoat it. I'm not going to lie. At that time I talked to you, I had been sober for three years. I fell off the wagon in '16 or '17. I've slowed up considerably, but I still drink."

Beer continues to be Stu's drink of choice. Stu says he drinks because of stress. "The weight of paying the bills and having to fend for everybody in the house. Is this going to work? Is that going to work? Running this business, running the other business. Things just kind of piling up on my shoulders, the stresses of being an everyday man. I need it to calm my nerves."

Stu wants to quit. "I need to stop for health reasons. I'm fifty. I'm too old to be out here. I don't get smashed and tore up sideways, belligerent. Twenty years ago, I was drinking and driving, just doing all kind of wrong. Today it looks different, but drinking is drinking. I shouldn't be drinking but I'm an alcoholic. I got a disease. I am what I am."

If there is a silver lining, it is that Stu is a functioning alcoholic. In addition to his day job, Stu's daughter Britnea convinced him to go back to school. Stu took online courses for two years. He says that a traditional classroom setting would have been out of the question. "If I had to go to a building, it wouldn't have worked. I think the online thing, the convenience of it, and being able to turn on the computer, learn the curriculum, whatever that week's rubric was for. For me it was just easier. If I had to go and just literally sit in the classroom, I don't know if I would have been able to make it."

Even with the virtual setting, there were times when Stu did not know if he would make it. But he eventually found his stride. The pandemic had little impact on Stu's schooling because he was already taking all of his classes online. In October 2020,

Stu earned an associate degree in Business Management and Marketing Administration. "It's been a journey, completing it and setting this example for my children. I realized that I couldn't quit doing it because I've got three small kids. If I quit school, what kind of example am I setting for them? When it gets rough for them in school, are they going to listen to me? Most likely not. So I got into school and I stayed in school and here we are. It really hasn't sunk in just yet."

Stu was proud that his remaining parents got to see him earn a college degree, but he has no idea how having an associate degree might alter things for him. "It's in the air," Stu says. "I have that piece of paper, but I don't know how I'm going to utilize it. I don't know if this degree is going to change my life in any way, shape, form, or fashion." What seems fairly certain is that Stu is unlikely to use his new degree to find white-collar employment in the business world. "I definitely want to work for myself. I don't want to punch anyone's clock."

Stu continues to make music, of course, issuing a steady stream of songs and music videos throughout 2021 and 2022. Some were solo numbers, and others were collaborations. A 2021 collaboration with De'Juan, "I'm Not the Problem," was among Stu's biggest hits to date, generating more than thirty thousand streams on Spotify in its first month online. The popularity of single songs, rather than full-length albums, already has Stu modifying his strategy. "I'm dropping a few more projects, and then I'm going to be done. I'm just going to be dropping singles after that. Projects are so lengthy sometimes. People enjoy my singles more than they do the projects, to be honest."

Stu also sees himself shifting away from the spotlight and doing more work behind the scenes at EDP. "It's not as important to me to be out here rapping all the time. I've done it for decades. Sometimes, it's time to move on. In the beginning, I felt like I had something to prove. I think I've proved it."

Stu hopes that the skills he learned in business classes will help him run EDP more efficiently. "I want to see this music business really get off the ground with some talented and motivated artists on the label. I want to see the label be a success."

For Stu, achievements are also personal and not related to music. "Success for me is seeing these kids grow up without having to touch the ground. My older daughters are out here on their own, and they are thriving. That's success for me, to see them win."

I ask Stu where he sees himself in five years. "I want to buy a home and have somewhere to sit my ass down," he says. "With the music, I think that's going to keep pushing and pumping along. And with the lawn care business, that's just a matter of me getting the clients and the equipment. The rest is history."

DVS Mindz

Stu, Barry, and De'Juan continued to work together as DVS Mindz, issuing a new mixtape, *O.N.L.Y. F.A.N.S.*, in 2021. Unlike *Modern Warfare*, the group did not record the new tracks together, but laid them down separately and then traded files back and forth online. The trio also included features from a number of compatriots, giving the mixtape a disjointed feel that was hard to overcome. Still, standout tracks such as "Snap Count," buoyed by an irresistible hook from De'Juan, were proof that DVS still had vital music in them.

The trio and Daymond continued to discuss the possibility of a full-blown DVS Mindz reunion, and in May 2022 the four reunited to record tracks in Stu's basement studio. Daymond

314 ℣ WHERE ARE THEY NOW?

drove his recording equipment all the way from Texas, but the group argued over the direction of the new material. The four MCs managed to get a new track, "It's Over" recorded during the session, but Daymond's commitment to the project remained uncertain.

On July 30, 2022, I got together with Stu, Barry, and De'Juan to conduct one last interview for the book. It was the first time I had been in the same room with the three of them since the Snafus strip-club show twenty years earlier. We met at Stu's newly purchased townhome in Grandview, Missouri. He bought the place from his mother, Christine, who kept a bedroom upstairs.

It was great to see the guys in person again, but it did not feel like a reunion. For the past several years, we had been in regular contact. I had interviewed all of the guys via video several times, and I bombarded them with questions and clarifications via text and email all the time. Stu and I called each other at least every couple of weeks. So we did not greet each other as long-lost friends, but it was terrific to have everyone in the same room again. Daymond could not be there and was missed.

I wanted to bring everyone together one more time to see how the guys were holding up, and to ask a few final questions that still lingered as I was finishing the book. The four of us sat at Stu's dining room table for several hours, pausing occasionally to step outside for a smoke. The guys threw back a few Coronas and a vape pen went around at one point but it was mostly the type of staid affair one would expect among a group of forty- and fifty-year olds.

The first time I interviewed DVS Mindz on December 31st, 1999, I did not ask many questions and mostly let them lead the discussion. The guys are still happy to talk, but tonight I am comfortable enough to ask them anything. Below are some highlights from our conversation:

GH: Barry, around the time I met the band, you punched a guy in front of the Granada. What happened?

Barry: We were coming out and there was this dude and he was drunker than fuck. He walks up on me and he's just like, "Hey!" And he's beating the shit out of my arm, chopping like he's trying to get my attention. I said, "What?" He said, "Man, these niggers are in here tripping!" I paused. I was like, "What did you say?" He hits me again and he goes, "I said, these niggers . . . " and right there, I just stole on him as hard as I fuckin' could. He stopped talking and dropped. And I swear when my man hit the ground, he was out cold.

GH: Shawn Edwards was critical of your performance at the MayDay beach concert. Nelly was supposed to headline, but it was shut down. What do you remember about that show?

Stu: When we read the article about the MayDay concert, that hurt niggas' feelings. We always prided ourselves on showing up and performing as professionals. I can't speak for none of them other groups, but when we showed up, we showed up as professionals. We did everything they asked us to do. When we see what they printed up in the article, Shawn Edwards put in there that they showed up speaking unintelligible lyrics.

De'Juan: I still know the quote, Geoff.

Barry: Pulling women onstage. Who was you watching motherfucker? When did we ever do that?

Stu: It was hurtful. Listen, if I slapped a broad, if I kicked somebody, if I spit on 'em, if I talked about they mama and I'm guilty, I gotta stand on that. None of that happened.

GH: So it was an uneventful show, nothing unusual?

Stu: Oh, it was a very eventful motherfucking show. We were literally out there in the desert and it was hot as fuck and they were charging for water. This is when the sun is coming down like the sun's surface. When we performed, there was 3500 people inside the gate and 7,500 people trying to get in to the motherfucker.

De'Juan: It was a dope show, we sold out of shirts. I sold the shirt off of my back. It was subjective. Shawn Edwards was like, "I was trying to show ya'll props. Not even Topeka's mindblowers DVS Mindz could get a spark out of the crowd." He said, "I was showing ya'll love." We took it personally. And then he got into "paced the stage, spewing unintelligible lyrics." He said, "I was talking about all the groups then."

Stu: So when you go back and you read that, okay, so this nigga wasn't throwing shots. When I read it, I was instantly pissed. But it was me not reading it right. I see what he was saying, but he led into that naming our group. He didn't name nobody else.

Barry: Yeah, once you say they paced the stage right after you say our name . . .

GH: De'Juan, we talked a lot about your mother, but less about your father. What was the situation with him?

De'Juan: He was just kind of out there living that same kind of life. He was getting high. He's had addiction in his life. He's had times of sobriety in his life. It's back and forth. He was here, he was there. I'd see him. I used to go to his softball games. But he was just moving. I knew where he was, but I couldn't call him. He was locked up for maybe two years. Me, moving around, I didn't know where my mom was or who she with. I didn't know what the hell was going on with them. I was off and on.

Daymond and Kevin's mother, De'Juan's aunt Lenora, passed away in 2021 and everyone gathered in Topeka for the funeral. Afterwards, De'Juan stopped by his father's place in Central Topeka, a neighborhood he rarely visits because he believes there is a high probability of being pulled over by the police.

De'Juan: They're hunting niggas over there. If they see you drive by and it's just you. [Snaps fingers.] It's just the neighborhood. That's how it is. As you drive towards central Topeka, the poverty gets thicker and thicker and the cops get thicker and thicker.

De'Juan's father, 67-year-old Marcus Knight Sr., was arrested in early 2022 after police raided his house and found heroin, methamphetamine, cocaine, and weapons.

De'Juan: I was at his house a couple of Fridays before he got raided. It was for Aunt Lenora's funeral. We kicked it afterwards. You know if they'd have come in while I was there, I have the same charges. That's the problem. We're felons. And I get found at my dad's house with a whole bunch of guns and dope. I went to federal for a gun case. I've got sales cases and possession cases. Who's to stop them from making the case that Dad's giving it to me? This is a whole conspiracy. This is a RICO, this is a crime family. That's the picture they paint.

Three days before our interview, De'Juan's father was charged with drug distribution causing death when a man died after ingesting fentanyl allegedly sold to him by Knight. De'Juan's father faced fifty-four years in prison for that count alone.

De'Juan: It's gone from a drug case to a murder, but I don't believe he knew anything about it. He ain't no fucking chemist. It's more of a circumstantial case but that's not how they are portraying it in the media. It only works if you have a criminal record, a history, for us to fit you. And Topeka is small. The town's not big enough for them to forget you. The name rings bells because there's three generations of Black men coming from those circumstances and doing those kinds of things.

De'Juan made good on his promise to take advantage of his professional opportunities in Denver. He has appeared frequently with Bobby Tek and his associates, in the studio and on stage. De'Juan has also issued a string of singles, EPs, and three complete mixtapes in 2022 alone.

GH: *Where do you see yourself in five years?*

De'Juan: Working and making sure I got good [health] insurance.

GH: *You look good, how do you feel?*

De'Juan: I have my days. My back itself, which was the most important, doesn't really hurt. But my ribs, I broke 'em all and it's different. I feel it all the time. Like if I eat too much, I feel it. It's weird but I'm up and at 'em. I'm moving. It's not restrained in any way. But just working and having good insurance. I can't ask for too much more than that myself. That's the size of it. But nothing too major, man. I got no big dreams.

GH: *Do you think you'll stay in Colorado?*

De'Juan: Maybe. I don't see going back to Kansas. I'm still doing music. I'll probably still be releasing music in five years. I'll be forty-five in November. My compadres are fifty. So in five years, I'll be their age. People have been asking me how come I'm not getting disability. I've been working. What are you supposed to do for the two years you're waiting, trying to get it? I don't have that kind of life where I can just be there without some income. I don't have no under-the-table shit going on. I really should be getting disability for my injuries.

Barry's plans for Texas did not pan out and he returned north, first to Topeka, and then to Denver, where he was crashing on a friend's couch.

GH: Barry, where do you see yourself in five years?

Barry: I have no clue. I don't know what I'm going to do in five minutes to be totally honest. All I want is just to be happy, healthy, and anybody I got love for is just taken care of. Period. If there's anything I can do to do that, that right there would make me feel like I'm rich. I really don't know. Day-to-day, I put some things ahead of what I'm doing. I don't know, to be totally honest, I don't know. Who knows what tomorrow will bring? I might want to do this, or I might want to do that. I don't know.

GH: You mentioned that you want to be happy and healthy. How do you feel today?

Barry: Um. [long pause] At the moment, today, I feel fuckin' fantastic. This was a great day, being with the three of y'all.

Stu, Barry, and De'Juan, July 30, 2022

Photo by Geoff Harkness

RESEARCH METHODS

My initial contacts with DVS Mindz were through my work as a music journalist. As a Lawrence-based journalist from 1999–2003, I interviewed scores of local musicians, including those working in rap: Tech N9ne, the 57th Street Rogue Dog Villians, Mac Lethal, Ces Cru, Miles Bonny, Approach, Bombsquad, Nezbeat and ID from Archetype, Negro Sco and Brother of Moses of Sevenfold Symphony, and more. As part of this work, I also interviewed DJs, producers, promoters, radio disc jockeys, filmmakers, retailers, and record label owners. I attended hundreds of concerts and saw most of the above acts multiple times. I drew upon some of those interviews and experiences in writing this book.

Unlike most of the groups I wrote about, I almost immediately became a collaborator with DVS Mindz. This began with the "Tired of Talking" music video and moved on to a series of collaborative and creative projects. I loved the band's music and wanted to help. I wrote the copy for the bio page that they used on their website and created a thirty-second advertisement for the CD release party that ran on local TV stations.

While my relationship with DVS Mindz was close, it was not unique. During my time in Lawrence, I shot and edited music videos for local bands working in genres that included alt-rock, reggae, R&B, rap, and ska-punk: Mac Lethal, Brent Berry and the Roots Crew, Salt the Earth, KB Posse, Bombsquad, Sturgeon Mill, X-Dash, and 3 a.m. I also filmed numerous local artists in concert, including acts that shared bills with DVS Mindz. (Tech N9ne and the RDV's management were always adamant that I not record any of their performances.) For every local band I videotaped, I saw another twenty-five in concert as part of my music journalism gig.

I did most of this work for free, although on a few occasions, I asked groups to help cover my expenses. I was a graduate student and did not have much money. Still, any time I asked a friend to help videotape a concert or work on a music video, I paid them $25 (about $45 in 2023 dollars). I wanted to compensate people for their time and also keep them coming back. There was also the cost of videotape, which could run $8–$16, depending on how much was needed. On some occasions, I hired two friends, each operating a video camera, costing me around $70 to record a single performance (about $130 in 2023 dollars). My journalism job paid less than $500 per month, and I covered most of these expenses with student loans.

Looking back at the video footage from 2000 to 2003, it is striking how much has changed in such a short amount of time. The concerts take place in nightclubs filled with young people, many of whom smoke cigarettes indoors without reprobation. There is not a single cell phone in sight. No one is texting or staring at a screen. Groups of friends are not taking selfies or posting to social media—social media did not exist. And the only way to hear DVS's music was to purchase a CD at a local record store or focus on the concert taking place that night. It's easy to romanticize the past, but one senses that some vital aspect of human connection has been handed to technology corporations.

In the summer of 2003, I moved to Chicago to pursue a PhD in sociology. By this point, DVS Mindz had disbanded. I remained a fan of their music and followed everyone in the group via social media. When YouTube came online in the mid-2000s, I uploaded a handful of music videos and live performances. In 2009, I videotaped an interview with Stu during the botched DVS reunion in KC. That footage went into a shoebox with the rest.

My collaborations with DVS Mindz inspired me to make rap music the topic of my dissertation. In Chicago, I immediately picked up where I had left off in Lawrence, videotaping performances and conducting interviews with local underground rap musicians. In 2008, I amassed this footage into a two-hour film, *I Am Hip Hop: The Chicago Hip Hop Documentary.*

Ultimately, I spent six years researching Chicago's underground rap scene. This yielded my first monograph, *Chicago Hustle and Flow: Gangs, Gangsta Rap, and Social Class.* Writing that book inspired me to return to the DVS story, which paralleled my Chicago research but also diverged in substantial ways. In Chicago, I had become friendly with several local MCs, but our interactions lacked the closeness I had with DVS, which was rooted in my being a fan, journalist, documentarian, and creative collaborator. Now that more than a decade had passed, I wanted to know what happened after the group broke up and how things were going for the band members today. In field notes from June 2014, I wrote:

> I keep up with the guys on social media, and we have all kept in touch over the years, to varying degrees. I've always wanted

to revisit DVS Mindz, to go back and have another look at all the work we did fifteen years ago. I was a burgeoning sociologist at the time we met, during my first semester of graduate school. Now I am not only interested personally, I am also interested sociologically. What becomes of all these young, Black aspiring rappers when they turn forty, when they're too old to make it in the youth-obsessed rap music business? Has the dream died? What happens when dreams die? Do people become dispirited? Do people get new dreams?

In June 2014, I contacted Stu, Barry, Daymond, and De'Juan and proposed to write a book about DVS Mindz. They immediately agreed. Stu explained, "If you really get down to the brass tacks of it, the reason we gave the book the green light was because we've been working together for more than twenty years ago and got to know each other really well. You wrote that story of us opening for U-God, and we did the 'Tired of Talking' video, and you shot a documentary on us and gathered a lot of information and did excellent with that. So, it only makes sense for you to write the book."

In the summer of 2014, I conducted a series of in-person interviews with Stu, Barry, and De'Juan. To make it clear that I was not creating another documentary, I audiotaped the interviews but did not videotape them. I wanted to approach these new interviews differently to move away from the performative elements of videotaping and go deeper into the band members' personal histories. These interviews were longer and more in-depth than those conducted earlier. In 2018, I interviewed Daymond online, via video. It was our first in-depth interview, and our two conversations took place over six-and-a-half hours.

My intention was to return to interview the band members in person in 2020, but the COVID-19 pandemic interrupted those plans. Instead, I spoke with Stu, Daymond, Barry, and De'Juan by video in the spring and summer of 2020 and 2021. In 2022, I interviewed Carla Daniels, Troy Owens, and Randy Smith via video and Steve Garcia and Daymond by phone. On July 30, 2022, I interviewed Barry, De'Juan, and Stu at Stu's house in Grandview, Missouri. The formal interviews for the project totaled 53 hours.

I transcribed every word of every formal and informal interview. I also watched every minute of the noninterview video footage: fifteen complete live concerts, hours of outtakes from the music videos, a documentary, and a short movie. Because we were making a documentary, I shot footage all of the time. If the members of the group were around, I usually turned on the camera and started asking questions or just let the camera observe. I drew extensively on this material in writing the book.

Throughout the text, I lightly edited some interview quotes for clarity. On the rare occasion where I replaced a word in a quotation, I noted it with brackets. Luke, a character who appears briefly in chapter 3, is a composite of two people. I incorporated material from more than one informal interview in the gathering at my apartment in chapter 8.

This book represents more than two decades of obsessive fandom with a band that few have ever heard of. What more could a music geek ask for? As a creative endeavor, getting to write this book exactly as I have always wanted to write it is nothing short of a dream come true. I still can't quite believe it exists. I did it because from the first time I saw DVS Mindz at the Bottleneck in 1999, all I wanted to do was tell the world how great they are. It has been my honor to do so, then and now.

TABLE A.1 FORMAL INTERVIEWS (RECORDED)

Group	12-31-1999	1.5 hours
Stu	3-15-2000	1 hour
Daymond	3-25-2000	30 minutes
Barry	5-24-2000	1 hour
De'Juan	5-24-2000	1 hour
Stu	10-2000	30 minutes
Randy	10-2000	1 hour
Group	10-2000	2 hours
Stu	9-5-2009	2 hours
Barry	6-22-2014	3 hours
De'Juan	6-22-2014	3 hours
Stu	6-23-2014	4 hours
Daymond	7-25 and 7-26, 2018	6.5 hours
De'Juan	4-15-2020	3 hours
Stu	9-7-2020	4 hours
Barry	5-7-2021	2 hours
De'Juan	5-7-2021	2 hours
Daymond	5-15-2021	4 hours
Carla Daniels	1-30-2022	1 hour
Randy	2-12-2022	2.5 hours
Troy Owens	3-10-2022	1 hour
Stu	4-10-2022	30 minutes
Steve Garcia	4-27-2022	45 minutes
Barry, De'Juan, and Stu	7-30-2022	4.25 hours
Daymond	8-10-2022	1 hour
		53 hours

A BEGINNER'S GUIDE
TO DVS MINDZ

I wrote this guide for those who are new to DVS Mindz. The recommendations that follow are suggested starting points but certainly not exhaustive. DVS Mindz released just one album during their initial run, 2000's *Million Dolla Broke Niggaz*. It's a great disc but many of the band's most-beloved songs, those they played in concert, were not included. DVS partly rectified this in 2020 with *The Genesis*, a compilation of previously unreleased material recorded from 1994–2003. In 2020, the reunited group issued *Modern Warfare 2020*, followed by a mixtape, *O.N.L.Y.F.A.N.S.*, a year later.

Most of the material described in this guide can be streamed for free and without advertising at: https://www.youtube.com/c/DVSMindz1137.

TWELVE ESSENTIAL TRACKS

"Rowdy Hip Hoppers"—This exuberant early number features the "three-headed dragon" lineup slaying all lyrical contenders.
On *The Genesis*

"DVS Mindbender"—Bar after raw bar, without embellishments. As close as it gets to the type of sessions that took place in the living room of 1137 Washburn Avenue.

On *Million Dolla Broke Niggaz*

"Real MCs"—A high water mark for the original three-MC lineup that features an irresistible refrain: "Any fool can rap, but can you represent?"

On *The Genesis*

"Headhunters"—DVS took things up a level on their first track recorded with De'Juan as an official member of the group. Like many of the band's songs, commercial considerations were rejected in favor of hardcore rhyming.

On *The Genesis*

"No Coast" (remake)—Daymond produced this remake, which topped the original and features a standout performance from De'Juan.

On *The Genesis*

"Tired of Talking" (video version)—This track showcases the four MCs at the height of their powers. The popular video version is substantially different from the earlier, Daymond-produced track included on *Million Dolla Broke Niggaz*.

On YouTube

"Bust Somethin'"—A posse cut pairing DVS Mindz with members of KC rap outfit, the Zou. Grand in scale and polished to a shimmer, "Bust Somethin'" marks a noticeable upgrade in production courtesy the Zou's Boogieman and Rock. DVS delivers mightily here, with Barry turning in one of his most legendary verses.

On *Million Dolla Broke Niggaz*

"Niggaz (1137)"—The closest things DVS Mindz had to a hit single, "Niggaz (1137)" was the band's most popular and well-known song.

On *Million Dolla Broke Niggaz*

"Heat"—"One afternoon, Barry walked in with a brand-new song that blew everyone's minds." This one-listen classic represents an even tighter embrace of hardcore rap set to an unforgettable hook. The original version, issued on the *Scars & Tattoos* compilation, is superior to the remix released on *The Genesis*.

On YouTube

"Flamethrower"—A high-velocity return to the group's early caffeinated tempos, Barry openly threatens to murder members of the Topeka Police Department, some of them by name. Daymond quit the band before recording his verse, but the unfinished gem was a keeper anyway.

On *The Genesis*

"Madness 2.0"—A throwback to the band's classic sound. The song features no hook and serves as a showcase for De'Juan, Barry, and Stu's distinct rhyme styles and lyrical approaches.

On *Modern Warfare 2020*

"Snap Count"—Buoyed by a catchy hook from De'Juan, this banger from the band's 2021 mixtape proves that DVS Mindz continues to make vital music.

On *O.N.L.Y. F.A.N.S.*

MUSIC VIDEOS

"Tired of Talking" (2000)—The video emphasizes the group members' distinct personalities and rhyme styles. The idea came from the heavy metal group Kiss, whose four "characters" are distinguished by costumes, makeup, and signature colors. In the video, each MC is constantly moving toward the camera. For inspiration, we drew from iconic movies such as *The Shining*, where a young boy glides on a tricycle through a hotel's hallways, and the James Bond movie *A View to a Kill*, where the British agent does battle up and down the stairs of the Eiffel Tower.

"Niggaz (1137)" (2000)—The video is a mixture of live recordings, clips from the *Murdarous Verses* eight-minute movie, and footage from the January 17, 2000 photo shoot at the Topeka State Capitol.

"No Coast" (remake) (2000)—The video blends footage taped at KJHK 90.7 FM radio station, the April 9, 2000 performance at Area 51, and DVS Mindz and the Crew just hanging out.

"Flamethrower" (2002)—This high-concept video was shot in my apartment in Lawrence on three different days. Our intention was to record Daymond's verse and then shoot the entire group together doing the hook. Daymond did not record a verse and the video was never completed.

LIVE CONCERTS

Area 51, April 9, 2000. "Area 51 might not be much to look at, but DVS treats it like Madison Square Garden, turning in a committed set that crackles with self-assurance and energy."

The Bottleneck, April 26, 2000. "The Crew has been pumping up DVS all week, telling the band how the audience at this show will consist of true hip-hop heads, aesthetes with sophisticated taste in rap music. DVS will need to bring their lyrical A-game. Barry immediately began concocting a novel way to open the concert."

Liberty Hall, August 7, 2000. "The group launches into their new song, 'Heat' and delivers one of the strongest performances of their career, pummeling the audience with rhymes and energy. On the big stage, with professional sound and lights and a sold-out crowd of hip-hop fanatics, DVS Mindz gives their all."

The Granada, April 23, 2001. "Everyone is in a good mood. The bartenders are serving beers two at a time, and DVS Mindz can seemingly do no wrong. The quartet opens with a pulse-quickening version of 'Madness' that transforms the audience—in a single song—into rabid disciples, with hundreds of attendees windshield-wipering their arms in unison."

DISCOGRAPHY

DVS MINDZ

Million Dolla Broke Niggaz	2000
Paper (unofficial release)	2002
Zip Codes mixtape	2019
The Genesis	2020
Modern Warfare 2020	2020
O.N.L.Y. F.A.N.S. mixtape	2021

Appears on	
ICU: The Revival	1998
Scars & Tattoo's Midwest Compilation	2001
G-Coffee!!!	2001

STR8JAKKETT

Napalm (unreleased)	2004
Mood Swings	2007
G.A.M.E. The Grown Ass Man Experience	2010
Monster Mash Mixtape	2012
Popular Nobody: The Collaboration Files	2013
The Survivalist	2014
Str8Jakkett	2014
Middle Finger Mentality	2014
The Black List	2014
Blacklist Indigenous	2015
International	2015
Indigenous	2015
Fire Starter	2015
Blackballed	2016
S.T.U. (Support The Underground)	2019
A.R.T.	2021
VeStuvious mixtape	2022

Appears on

Def DJ - *DVS Mindz* mixtape	2003
The Grant Rice Empire mixtape	2003
Ground Zero	2011
Str8 Roc	2013
Str8 Urbantech	2014
Westside Alumni (with Stik Figa)	2019

KILLA THE HUN

Amerikilla	2016
Amerikilla Re-Kill	2020

With Bobby Tek

If My Rhyme Waz Az Good Az My Hustle	2011
Teknically Speaking	2013
Robert DeNairo	2015
A Thin Line Between Hood n' Great	2019

With Ryhno Buddz

Out of Time	2016

With Sleepy Hollow

Tied 2 the Streets	2020

With Scorpeez

Venomous	2020

With Lil Jgo

Str1ve Through Wh4tever	2021

Appears on

Def DJ - *DVS Mindz* mixtape	2003
The Grant Rice Empire mixtape	2003

D.O.P.E

Dangerous On Paper & Etc. The D.O.P.E LP (as D Dot)	2005
No Coast (as D Dot)	2006

Appears on

The Grant Rice Empire mixtape	2003
Reggie B—*The Traveler*	2010

DL (AS DL DE'JUAN)

The Official JHawk Mixtape	2022
Willt Chamberlainn'	2022
Welcome to Kansas State	2022

Appears on

Phat Albert—*Phat Albert*	2001
KB Posse—*KB Posse*	2002
Easy Button mixtape	2006
Young Pain—*Propane Mixtape, Vol. 1*	2012

NOTES

INTRODUCTION: "U-GOD OUTSHINED BY TOPEKA GROUP"

1. The "L.A." in the L.A. Ramblers moniker stands for "Lawrence Area."
2. Jon Niccum, interview with author, July 12, 2021.
3. In rap-music parlance, what might traditionally be called the chorus is known as the hook. As such, I use the term *hook* to index "chorus" throughout the book.
4. Geoff Harkness, "U-God Outshined by Topeka Group," *Lawrence-Journal World*, December 9, 1999.

1. THE GENESIS

1. *Biography of Winfred Lavern Tidwell* n.d.
2. *Biography of Winfred Lavern Tidwell* n.d.
3. Fifty thousand dollars is worth approximately $105,000 in 2023 dollars. Stu says he received a total of about $22,000 in compensation for his work-related injuries. "It wasn't a lot of money. I injured my back at twenty-one. I'm going to have back problems for the rest of my life. For them to throw me that little bit of money, and then I'll never be the same in my elbow again, that's bullshit."

3. DAYMOND PULLING CHAINS

1. "Charles Douglas," Sports Reference College Basketball, n.d., www .sports-reference.com/cbb/players/charles-douglas-1.html.

2. Ross Elementary School: www.greatschools.org.
3. Eisenhower Middle School: www.greatschools.org.
4. The program was discontinued in July 2001. Oklahoma Department of Corrections, n.d., https://digitalprairie.ok.gov/digital/api/collection /stgovpub/id/36780/download.
5. Oklahoma Department of Corrections, n.d.

4. 1137 WASHBURN AVENUE

1. "Check the Kids from Kansas" is alternately titled "Sleepin' on the Midwest."
2. Kansas was formed as part of the Kansas-Nebraska Act of 1854, but whether the state would allow slavery was to be determined by vote. Pro- and antislavery factions poured into eastern Kansas from around the nation, seeking to influence the outcome. The most famous was John Brown, an Ohio abolitionist who led the 1856 Pottawatomie massacre, where five slavery advocates were murdered. The incident was one of many conflicts that took place from 1854–1861, which collectively became known as Bleeding Kansas. In 1861, Kansas became the thirty-fourth state in the Union, admitted as a free state. It is from this early history that Kansas earned its nickname, the Free State (Davis 1984).

5. UNSIGNED HYPE

1. The group described this concert in detail during our first interview in 1999 and provided me with a complete video of the performance in 2019. Barry recalled, "It was last minute, and we're like,

> "We gotta do something different." It was couple of days before Halloween. It was jam packed. Everybody showed up did their little shit, out there trying to be cool. Only one group did something, just grabbed the crowd, where it just fucked them totally up. It's supposed to be a Halloween jam or whatever. People know we're there. We're walking around. And everybody's checking it out. We're standing there peeping everybody out. "Ya'll gonna do something, man?" "Yeah, we're gonna perform tonight." "Man, I know ya'll gonna show out." A couple of months before, we did a show

where we all had on these *Scream* masks. So nobody knew who who was, but you could kind of tell by the voice. It really tripped 'em out. The lights go out, it's glow-in-the-dark. We did some ill shit. People were like, "How are you going to top that?" We thought we couldn't top that.

The group was also convinced that their horror movie idea was stolen. "Symphony 2000" is an EPMD song, released in June 1999, featuring Method Man, Redman, and Lady Luck. In the accompanying music video, the MCs dress as characters from horror films: *Halloween*, *The Texas Chainsaw Massacre*, *The Shining*, *Carrie*, and a mad doctor. "When it came on, it shocked us so bad our mouths dropped," Barry told me. "I was sick. I literally slid off the couch."

2. For more on microscenes, see Harkness 2013.

3. J. J. Hensley, "Mindz Control," *The Pitch*, March 29, 2001.

4. Nick Spacek, "Throwback Thursday: Watch Evil-Loc Bust Out 'My Hood' Back in '98," *The Pitch*, October 8, 2015.

5. The RDVs released "Let's Get Fucked Up" a second time on their 1999 CD, *It's On Now (Summer Edition)*, which produced an even bigger splash. That year, the band also issued a heavily edited version that received considerable airplay on regional radio.

6. "Unsigned Hype" was the name of a column published by the *Source* magazine that featured talented artists who were not signed to major labels. Relative unknowns featured in the column include the Notorious B.I.G., Common, and Eminem.

7. Forman 2000, 69.

8. Qui-Lo signed a deal with No Coast, recording an entire album, *The Enemy*, which was never released. One of the tracks recorded for *The Enemy* was "Seven," a collaboration between Qui-Lo and DVS Mindz that was produced by Joe Good under the name Dr. Who. The song later cropped up on DVS Mindz's debut CD, much to the surprise of Qui-Lo. "We had a whole album done under No Coast that was never released," Good told me in 2003. "We were doing the album, and DVS came over one night and we did this track. It was dope. It was pretty much a posse cut—seven verses. I didn't know they was gonna put it on the album, but I'm not salty about the shit anymore. It was gonna be on our album, too, but our album never came out" (Geoff Harkness, "Good

Times," *The Pitch*, January 16, 2003). In 2009, Qui-Lo issued *The Enemy* as an online release and included "Seven" as a bonus track.

7. REAL MCS

1. Andrew Miller, "State of Shock," *The Pitch*, August 23, 2007.
2. State of Kansas, Appellee, vs. Bryon J. Kirtdoll, Appellant. No. 94,128. Decided: June 09, 2006. https://caselaw.findlaw.com/ks-supreme-court /1193289.html
3. J. J. Hensley, "Around Hear," *The Pitch*, April 20, 2000.
4. J. J. Hensley, "Das EFX/Black Sheep/DVS Mindz/Shadowlink," *The Pitch*, February 27, 2000.
5. Foster 2014.
6. J. J. Hensley, "The Arsonists/DVS Mindz/Seven Fold Symphony/Mac Lethal & Approach," *The Pitch*, April 27, 2000.

8. THE CREW

1. Brandon Lee, the son of martial artist and actor Bruce Lee, was accidently shot and killed while filming a movie in 1993.
2. In 2003, the Klammies were renamed the *Pitch* Music Awards.
3. Shawn Edwards, "Back from Hell," *The Pitch*, August 23, 2001.
4. The title indexes De La Soul's 1989 true-to-self anthem, "Me Myself and I."
5. *Million Dolla Broke Niggaz* included three short "public service announcements," where Stu, Barry, and De'Juan rap a few bars over an identical backing track. Daymond missed the studio session for the PSAs and does not have one on the album. The PSAs were to be cojoined with solo tracks from each member of the group, but only Stu and Barry's songs were included. Between the PSAs and individual tracks, one-third of the debut consisted of solo material.
6. Hess 2007, 13.
7. In the U.S., the "hyper-gangsterization of hip hop . . . reached a peak in the early 2000s with gangsta rap accounting for hip hop's biggest sales" (Reitsamer and Prokop 2017, 204). Rap musicians who avoided the gangsta subgenre found their live-music bookings drying up in the early 2000s after gangsta became the central focus of rap music.

8. Daymond refers to himself as a "million dolla broke nigga" in DVS's song "Niggaz (1137)."

9. Several of these artists are featured in the 2003 documentary, *Looking For Today*, which can be streamed online.

10. Geoff Harkness, "Good Times," *The Pitch*, January 16, 2003.

11. Geoff Harkness, "It's a Rap," *The Pitch*, May 29, 2003.

12. Geoff Harkness, "Type Writers," *The Pitch*, April 18, 2002.

13. Richard Gintowt, "Architects of Amusement," Lawrence.com, November 14, 2003.

9. HEAT

1. "Sound Bwoy Bureill" (pronounced "sound boy burial") is a 1995 song by Brooklyn rap duo Smif-N-Wessun.

2. Geoff Harkness, "Bring the Noize," *Mag*, May 24, 2001. Glen Mason was the head football coach for KU from 1988 to 1996.

3. Geoff Harkness, "Power Trio," *Mag*, January 17, 2002.

4. Andrew Miller, "Str8jakkett Mood Swings," *The Pitch*, February 28, 2008; J. J. Hensley, "Mindz Control," *The Pitch*, March 29, 2001.

10. KILLA BEES

1. Shawn Edwards, "One More Chance," *The Pitch*, July 20, 2000.

2. Andrew Miller, "Wu-Tang Clan/Killarmy/DVS Mindz," *The Pitch*, August 10, 2000.

3. "Best Albums of 2000: Critics' Picks," *The Pitch*, December 14, 2000.

4. Robert Bishop, "The Klammies Go Uptown," *The Pitch*, April 6, 2000.

11. HATERSVILLE

1. All zip codes assigned to Shawnee County begin with the prefix 666.

2. J. J. Hensley, "Mindz Control," *The Pitch*, March 29, 2001.

3. The Hurricane closed in the mid 2000s; a new venue, the Riot Room opened in its place.

4. Andrew Miller, "Around Hear," *The Pitch*, April 12, 2001.

5. Miller, "Around Hear."

6. Andrew Miller, "Around Hear." *The Pitch*, April 19, 2001.

7. Miller, "Around Hear."
8. Geoff Harkness, "The Inferno," *Mag*, November 29, 2001.

12. THE DVS STORY

1. Andrew Miller, "Str8jakkett Mood Swings," *The Pitch*, February 28, 2008.

13. UNITED STATES OF AMERICA VERSUS DE'JUAN KNIGHT

1. Van Cleve 2016.
2. "FCI El Reno," BOP, accessed July 12, 2022, https://www.bop.gov /locations/institutions/ere/. FCI El Reno is also home to a minimum-security camp that houses 189 inmates.
3. Butt and Molnar 2009.
4. Kanemasu and Molnar 2014, 1397.
5. Kansas Department of Corrections 2013, "EDCF Overview," https:// www.doc.ks.gov/facilities/edcf/overview.

14. DALLAS

1. Pager 2003.

15. A PIRATE LOOKS AT 40

1. Crips go out of their way to avoid the letter *B*, which ostensibly stands for "Bloods." In this usage, it is replaced with a *C*, indexing "Crips."

16. RESPECT

1. Thomson 2013.

17. MODERN WARFARE

1. KSNT 27 News, "Person Critically Injured in Hit and Run, Dragged in Auburn." Facebook, February 16, 2020, https://www.facebook.com /227750827236117/posts/hit-and-run-the-shawnee-county-sheriffs -office-is-asking-for-any-information-you/3068709213140250/.

2. Shawn Wheat, "1 in Critical Condition, 2 Injured After Being Hit by Car in Auburn," WIBW, February 20, 2020.

3. Shawn Wheat, "Man Dies After Being Hit and Dragged by Car in Auburn," WIBW, February 20, 2020.

4. KSNT News, "Shawnee County Sheriff's Office Says Person Dragged by Car Not Dead." KSNT, February 16, 2020, https://www.ksnt.com /news/local-news/person-hit-by-car-dragged-in-auburn/?fbclid =IwAR1PJgjujQEMKAvoLKyMauYr2bBenDPf9oP4FcT4S99E _so4kG_SPeiC7Xw.

WHERE ARE THEY NOW?

1. Geoff Harkness, "Three Dog Might," *The Pitch*, July 11, 2002.

2. DJ Casper's 2000 song "Cha Cha Slide" was a worldwide hit.

REFERENCES

Biography of Winfred Lavern Tidwell. n.d. Kenneth Spencer Research Library Archival Collection. Lawrence, KS: University of Kansas. Call number RH MS 1286.

Butt, Joanne, and Gyozo Molnar. 2009. "Involuntary Career Termination in Sport: A Case Study of the Process of Structurally Induced Failure." *Sport in Society* 12, no. 2: 240–257.

Davis, Kenneth S. 1984. *Kansas: A History.* New York: Norton.

Forman, Murray. 2000. "'Represent': Race, Space and Place in Rap Music." *Popular Music* 19, no. 1: 65–90.

Foster, B. Brian. 2014. "'Everybody Gotta Have a Dream': Rap-Centered Aspirations Among Young Black Males Involved in Rap Music Production–A Qualitative Study." *Issues in Race & Society: An Interdisciplinary Global Journal* 2, no. 2: 25–47.

Harkness, Geoff. 2013. "Gangs and Gangsta Rap in Chicago: A Microscenes Perspective." *Poetics* 41, no. 2: 151–176.

Harkness, Geoff. 2014. *Chicago Hustle and Flow: Gangs, Gangsta Rap, and Social Class.* Minneapolis, MN: University of Minnesota Press.

Hess, Mickey. 2007. *Is Hip Hop Dead? The Past, Present, and Future of America's Most Wanted Music.* Westport, CT: Prager.

Kanemasu, Yoko, and Gyozo Molnar. 2014. "Life After Rugby: Issues of Being an 'Ex' in Fiji Rugby." *International Journal of the History of Sport* 31, no. 11: 1389–1405.

Pager, Devah. 2003. "The Mark of a Criminal Record." *American Journal of Sociology* 108, no. 5: 937–975.

Reitsamer, Rosa, and Rainer Prokop. 2017. "Keepin' it Real in Central Europe: The DIY Rap Music Careers of Male Hip Hop Artists in Austria." *Cultural Sociology* 12, no. 2: 193–207.

Thomson, Kristin. 2013. "Roles, Revenue, and Responsibilities: The Changing Nature of Being a Working Musician." *Work and Occupations* 40, no. 4: 514–525.

Van Cleve, Nicole Gonzalez. 2016. *Crook County: Racism and Injustice in America's Largest Criminal Court*. Stanford, CA: Stanford University Press.

INDEX

Page numbers in *italics* indicate photos.

335; Sleepy Hollow collaboration with, 335; Randy Smith and friendship with, 23–25, 63, 86–87, 210, 253–255, 256, 258–259, 298, 299, 307, 309; as "Smokey Rob-him-some," 18–19; on social media, 251; as solo artist, 154, 255–258, 275, 276, 308, 340n5; with standoff skit for show opener, 132–133; tattoos, 134; Tech N9ne and, 55; in "three headed dragon" lineup 1.0, 150, 278, 327, 328; in "three headed dragon" lineup 2.0, 213; Stu Tidwell and friendship with, 3–5, 7, 9, 14–15, 20–21, 27–29, 50, 174–175, 252, 255, 256, *p3*; with Stu Tidwell and De'Juan Knight, 310, 313–314, *319*, *p16*; with "Tired of Talking" music video, 113–114, 115, 117; today, 307–309, *p14*; in Topeka in 2014, *p15*; on trajectory of DVS Mindz, 121; with 2 Def Crew, 9; wardrobe onstage, xviii, 53, 80, 122; with "Who" music video, 308

Riot Room, the, 341n3

rituals, preconcert, 127, 188

Robert DeNairo (2015), 335

Robinson Middle School, 95

"Rock" (Jerome Travis), 150, 151, 188, 280, 328

"Rockit," 37

Rodney-O & Joe Cooley, 21

Rolling Stone magazine, xiv

Rome, Jim, 172, 272–273

Roos, Jeff, xxv, 158

Roots, the, xiii

Ross, Cornell, 38

Ross Elementary, 33

"Rowdy Hip Hoppers": axed from *Million Dolla Broke Niggaz*, 149; Beginner's Guide to DVS Mindz, 327; at The Bottleneck, 129; on *The Genesis* with "three headed dragon" lineup, 327; at The Granada, April 30, 2000, 142; at The Granada Halloween show, 74

royalties: rates, 89; streaming, 269

Run-D.M.C., xxiii, 7, 14, 57, 271

Ryhno Buddz, 256, 335

RZA, 142

Salt-N-Pepa, 39

Salty Iguanas, xiv

Sam Goody, 119

Samsung, 245, 247, 303, 307

"Sandman." *See* Earl

Sandoval, Jesse "E. Diggz," 266–267, 270

Satan (biblical character), 201

Scarface, 54

Scarface (film), 173

Scars & Tattoos Midwest Compilation (2001): DVS Mindz on, 333; "Heat," 329

"Scenario," 53

Scholla, Jason, 266–267

"Scorpeez." *See* Johnson, Joseph II

"Scratch and Sniff," 222

Scrybetruth Eternal, 300–301

Season to Risk, 199

Seminole State College, 31

servitude, autonomy over, 271